D1505545

ALBERT CAMUS

1913-1960

ALBERT CAMUS

1913–1960

BY

PHILIP THODY

*Lecturer in French Language and
Literature at the Queen's University of Belfast*

THE MACMILLAN COMPANY

NEW YORK

TO

JOY AND PETER

CONTENTS

Chapter One

A GROWTH TO MANHOOD

ALBERT CAMUS was born on November 7th, 1913, in the small village of Mondovi, in the Department of Constantine in French North Africa. He was the second son of Lucien Camus, an agricultural worker of Alsatian origin, and of Catherine Sintès, a woman of Majorcan ancestry whose family had been settled in Algeria since before 1870. Camus never knew his father. Although a second-generation Algerian, Lucien Camus had continued to look upon France as his country, and left enthusiastically for the army the moment the First World War broke out. He was killed on October 11th, 1914, at the first Battle of the Marne, and Catherine Camus went back to live with her own widowed mother in the working-class district of Belcourt in the town of Algiers. It was there that Camus lived until, at the age of seventeen, his first attack of tuberculosis forced him to leave home and lead an independent life in places where he could better look after himself. His mother went out to work as a charwoman in order to provide for her two small sons, and Camus and his elder brother Lucien, born in 1909, were brought up largely by their grandmother. In his first book of essays, *L'Envers et L'Endroit*, Camus has left a touching portrait of his mother, a gentle, uncomplaining woman, whom a neglected ear infection had left partially deaf, and who never learned to read or write.

'The child's mother remained as silent as he did. Sometimes, when asked "What are you thinking about?", she would reply "Nothing". And it was true. Everything was there around her, so she thought of nothing. Her life, her interests, her children were simply there, with a presence that was too natural to be consciously felt. She was unwell, and thought with difficulty. She had a harsh and domineering mother

I

who sacrificed everything to an over-sensitive, animal pride, and who for a long time had dominated her daughter's rather feeble mind. Emancipated by marriage, her daughter had come meekly home again when her husband was killed. He "died a hero's death" as they say. And, in a conspicuous place, you can see his medals hanging in a gilded frame. The hospital also sent the widow the small shell splinter found in his body. The widow kept it. She long ago ceased to feel any grief. She has forgotten her husband, but still speaks of the father of her children. In order to bring up her children she goes out to work, and gives the money she earns to her mother. The latter brings up the children with a whip. When she hits them too hard, her daughter says: "Don't hit them on the head." Because they are her children she loves them. She loves them with an equal love which has never been revealed to them. Sometimes, as on the evenings which he now remembers, returning home from her exhausting work, she finds the house empty. The old lady is out shopping, the children still at school. Then she sits huddled on a chair, and, looking at nothing in particular, loses herself following a crack along the floor. Around her, the night in which this silence is an unredeemable desolation, grows thicker. If the child comes in at that time, he can make out the thin shadow of her bony shoulders, and stops in the doorway: he is afraid. He is beginning to feel a great number of things. He is scarcely conscious of his own existence but he suffers to the point of tears in front of this animal silence. He feels sorry for his mother, but is that the same as loving her? She has never kissed or made a fuss of him, for she wouldn't know how to. So he stands and watches her for a long time. When he feels himself cut off from her, he becomes conscious of her unhappiness. She cannot hear him, for she is deaf. Soon, the grandmother will come back, and life will start up again: the round circle of light cast by the oil lamp, the oilcloth, the shouts and coarse expressions. But now, this silence marks a breathing-space, an immeasurably long moment. Because he is somehow vaguely aware of all that, the child thinks he can feel love for his mother in the upsurge of feeling within him. And, after all, so he should do, for she is his mother.'

The absence of a father and the difficulty which Camus found in expressing his intense love for his mother were to have a decisive effect upon his imaginative works. In only one of his novels—*La Peste*—is there a description of a father–son relationship, and even then it is an unhappy one. The mother–son relationship, however, is essential to two of his best-known works—*L'Etranger* and *Le Malentendu*—and recurs again, in a possibly idealised form, in the description of the companionable silences which link Dr. Bernard Rieux to his mother in

La Peste. The influence which each of his parents uncon-
sciously exercised on Camus's social and political opinions is
also shown in two other aspects of his work which made him
an exception among modern French intellectuals: his opposition to the death penalty and his plea for a solution of the
Algerian problem which respected European as well as Moslem
rights. He was quite open about the effect which one of the
few 'memories' he had of his father—an incident told to him
by his mother—had on his views on capital punishment. One
day, he related in his *Réflexions sur la Guillotine* in 1957, his
father decided to go and witness the execution of a man who
had murdered a family of small-holders, and of whom he had
declared, in company with many others, that 'the guillotine
was too good for him.' He never described to his wife what
happened at the execution. Camus's mother simply told her
son how his father tore into the house, his face stricken with
horror, threw himself on his bed, and was violently sick. 'He
had just discovered,' wrote Camus in 1957, 'the reality which
lay behind the high-sounding phrases which disguised it.' It
was a reality to which his son was to refer again and again in
almost everything he wrote.

In 1957, in a speech which followed the presentation of the
Nobel Prize, Camus was interrupted and asked by an Algerian
student why he did not condemn the use of torture in Algeria.
He replied that he loved justice, but that if he had to choose
between justice and his mother, he would choose his mother.
The fact that Catherine Camus was still in Algiers—she lived
there until her death on September 22nd, 1960—was one of
the most powerful factors influencing Camus in the opinions
which he expressed on the Algerian war. It was because of his
mother that he constantly refused to do anything likely to
exacerbate the conflict or expose the European population to
increased terrorism. Yet it was not only of his mother that he
was thinking when he made this remark, but also of his elder
brother Lucien, an inspector for an insurance company in
Algiers, and of all the friends and relations with whom he had
grown up in Belcourt. A photograph, taken in the open yard of
the factory where his uncle Etienne, a cooper by trade, was
employed, gives a very good indication of the kind of background in which he lived. Camus, aged about five, is sitting
with his brother in the front row of a group of be-aproned and

3

moustachioed workmen, who are sufficiently free from racial prejudice to have a Moslem sitting in the picture with them. It was the understanding which his own childhood gave him of the problems faced by the poorer Europeans as well as by the poverty-stricken Arabs which made it impossible for him to be dogmatically 'progressive' on the Algerian problem. And, as will be seen, he was first, and for a long time the only, French writer to show any concern for these problems at a time when most Frenchmen seemed scarcely to realise that Algeria even existed.

The poverty which this picture also reveals did not make Camus's childhood an unhappy one. 'Poverty,' he wrote in 1958, 'was never a source of unhappiness for me, for the sun cast its wealth upon it.' The obstacle to the full expression of the 'infinite strength' which he felt in himself lay not in a lack of money, but rather in the 'prejudices and stupidity' which he found deeply entrenched in Algerian political and social life. Yet even these did not make him bitter or resentful, and it was not until the fierce controversies aroused by his later political activity in Paris had profoundly wounded him that anything like a note of scorn and anger crept into his writing. At a time when, as he said in 1950, he was learning the importance of freedom not in Marx but in poverty, the 'belle chaleur' which reigned over his childhood freed him from all resentment. In spite of the absence of a father and the presence of the selfish and unsympathetic grandmother, Camus's childhood was not only a happy one but one crowned with promise and achievement.

From 1918 to 1923, Camus attended the 'école communale' of Belcourt, where his first teacher, Louis Germain, immediately saw in him an exceptionally intelligent pupil. He gave freely of his own time to prepare Camus for the competitive scholarship examination that would enable him to continue his studies at the Lycée d'Alger, and Camus succeeded in winning a scholarship in 1923. He attended the Lycée without interruption for the next seven years, and then more spasmodically after his first attack of tuberculosis in 1930. Camus remained grateful both to Louis Germain, to whom he dedicated his Nobel Prize speeches in 1957, and to Jean Grenier, who inspired him with his own enthusiasm not only for literature and philosophy but also for association football.

4

From 1928 to 1930, Camus kept goal for the Racing Universitaire d'Alger, and, if his own confession is to be believed, devoted most of his time and energy during these two years to thinking about football. Because of the team spirit which it helped to develop it remained a favourite activity of Camus' throughout the whole of his life. When he lived in Paris he rarely missed going as a spectator to the Sunday afternoon matches at the Parc des Princes, and he wrote to the French critic Pierre de Boisdeffre that it was on the football field that he had taken his only lessons in ethics. In 1930, however, shortly after he had entered Jean Grenier's class and had been told that, as a potential rebel, he had better sit on the front row, he fell ill with tuberculosis. The change which his illness introduced into his personal life was a considerable one, for it compelled him to leave home and, eventually, to give up his original intention of pursuing an academic career.

Camus went first of all to live with one of his uncles, a butcher of extreme republican and Voltairian persuasion, but soon decided to live alone, continuing his studies as best he could and supporting himself by a variety of different jobs. While still at the University, in 1933, he married Simone Hie, the daughter of a doctor in Algiers, but the marriage was not a happy one and was dissolved a year later. Late in 1934, he joined the Communist Party and was given the task of spreading propaganda among the Moslems. Camus began the work enthusiastically, but in 1935 the Franco-Russian alliance and the needs of Russian foreign policy led to a change in the party line towards the Arabs, and he left the party in disgust. In the same year, 1935, he was also employed by the Institute of Meteorology and prepared a report on the barometric pressure in the Southern territories of Algeria. The other jobs which he took before finally becoming a journalist in 1938 included working as a clerk both in the Préfecture in Algiers and in an import-export business, selling spare parts for motor cars and giving private lessons. His main interests, however, were centred on his studies, his first attempts in writing, and on the establishment of a new left-wing and avant-garde theatre in Algiers. After completing his *licence*—roughly the equivalent of a B.A. general degree—Camus wrote a *diplôme* on the influence of Plotinus on Saint

5

Augustine entitled *Métaphysique chrétienne et néoplatonisme*.[1] This was successfully presented in 1936, but Camus was unable to pursue his academic career any further. Candidates for the *agrégation*, the competitive examination which is the only gateway to a permanent teaching post in a *lycée*, must all pass a medical examination, and Camus was disqualified from the very start by the fact that he had had tuberculosis and was not completely cured. In 1937 he was again very ill and had to go and rest in the French Alps in Savoy, returning home by a devious route which took him through Florence, Pisa and Genoa. In October of the following year, he became a journalist, joining what he later called 'the finest profession that I know' as a member of the staff of the newly established left-wing paper *Alger-Républicain*. Before discussing his openly political work as a journalist, however, it would be as well to examine his early experiments in the theatre, in which, in spite of his left-wing sympathies, his aesthetic interests were never subordinated to his political ones.

In 1935, while still a member of the Communist Party, Camus played a leading part in establishing the Théâtre du Travail in Algiers. It was for this theatre that, in collaboration with a number of other young left-wing intellectuals, he wrote his first and most violently revolutionary play, *Révolte dans les Asturies*.[1] Though ostensibly an experiment in 'collective creation' it was in fact written and composed largely by Camus himself. It was inspired by the violent military suppression of the revolt of the Oviedo miners in Northern Spain in October 1934 and, because of the obvious sympathy which it showed for their political ideals, was not allowed to be publicly performed. It was published in book form in 1936, at the expense of the Amis du Théâtre du Travail, at a time when Camus's departure from the Communist Party had already caused the theatre to change its name to the Théâtre de l'Equipe. The new theatre put on plays that were less openly political—the Théâtre du Travail had begun by an adaptation of André Malraux's anti-fascist novel *Le Temps du Mépris*—but still persevered in its attempt to bring the theatre to the people. It produced, among other plays, the stage adaptation of Dostoevski's *The Brothers Karamazov*— appropriately enough, Camus took the part of Ivan—Ben

[1] See notes.

6

Jonson's *The Silent Woman* and in 1939 Synge's *The Playboy of the Western World*. In 1936 and 1937 Camus also played as a professional actor for the Radio Algiers touring company, whose repertory consisted mainly of French classical plays in which he took the juvenile lead. At this stage in his career he had already come a long way from the crowded flat in which he had been brought up, and the working-class environment from which his own intelligence and powers of hard work had enabled him to escape. Any account of his early life must, inevitably, read like an edifying parable of the success which cannot fail to come to anyone who has talents and uses them, and, indeed, *Paris-Match* presented Camus's career in just such a way in January 1960. However, the role which Camus soon began to play as a political journalist in 1938 and 1939 was, like the pagan sensuality of his early lyrical essays, an indication that he was in no way prepared to conform to the parable and use his talents to defend middle-class values. His first political essays already show him as a keen critic of the society in which he lived, and as a rebel without resentment against the injustices and abuses which existed in French Algeria.

Alger-Républicain, whose first number was published on October 6th, 1938, announced itself from the very beginning as the 'Newspaper of the Workers' and the 'Newspaper of the Popular Front.' Edited by Pascal Pia, it gave its principal aim as the creation of equal rights for all Frenchmen living in Algeria, Europeans and Moslems alike, and devoted much of its space to dealing with the relationship between the two communities. Camus actually began work as literary critic and, during 1938 and 1939, reviewed books as varied and interesting as Sartre's *La Nausée* and *Le Mur*, Giono's *Lettre aux Paysans sur la pauvreté et la paix*, Montherlant's *L'Equinoxe de Septembre* and Ignazio Silone's *Bread and Wine*. His comments on Sartre are particularly interesting in that they reveal how differently the two writers envisage the problem of the absurd; at the same time as he admired Sartre's lucidity, Camus doubted the wisdom of basing a general philosophy of gloom on so personal an experience, and already proclaimed the need to go beyond absurdity. 'Without beauty, love or danger, it would indeed be too easy to live,' he wrote of *La Nausée*, and remarked in March of the following year, in

7

his very favourable review of *Le Mur*, that 'to describe the absurdity of life cannot be an end in itself, but only a beginning.' 'One might,' he then remarked in a phrase which showed how far at least one aspect of *L'Etranger* had already developed in his mind, 'show that the most ordinary of beings was already a monster of perversity, and that all of us more or less long for the death of our loved ones,' but this was not Sartre's aim. This was rather to show how his characters, fully conscious both of their freedom and of the absurdity of their lives, 'plunged into an inhuman world where they create their own chains of madness, sexual perversion or crime.'

The general impression given by the reviews is that of a young man who is determined to be objective, and whose naturally pleasant nature will not allow him to make unfavourable comments on any of the books he discusses. He certainly took the trouble, unlike some reviewers, to read the books given to him, and never treated them merely as a peg on which to hang his own ideas. While this is at times rather frustrating to anyone who reads his reviews with the aim of trying to discover something about Camus's early ideas, it nevertheless shows how conscientiously he did any work with which he was entrusted. More important than these literary articles, however, in view of the part he was shortly to play in the Resistance movement, is the evidence of his political interests afforded by the other subjects he dealt with in *L'Alger-Républicain*. That he should choose to write for such a defiantly left-wing paper is an indication of the general tendency of his political opinions. The more precise nature of his political commitment is indicated by the type of problems which aroused his principal concern.

These articles fall into three groups. The first, which shows the extent to which he shared the normal left-wing attitudes of the nineteen-thirties, included a defence of the International Brigade, an attack on the means used by Daladier to whittle down the achievements of the Popular Front and a recognition that the Peace Treaty of Versailles was at least partly responsible for the disastrous political situation in Europe. Although interesting, these articles are less characteristic of both the early and later Camus than those of the second and third groups which deal with the *affaire Hodent* and with the famine in Kabylia. Both in his readiness to go

8

to immense trouble to ensure that justice shall be done in one particular case and in his determination to offer practical solutions to social problems, he is already putting into practice the 'idea of political modesty' which he later appeared to derive from the philosophical concept of revolt.

On January 10th, 1939 there appeared, on the front page of *L'Alger-Républicain*, an open letter to the Governor-General setting out the details of how Michel Hodent, a technical agent employed by a native insurance company, had been arrested and put into prison for supposedly fraudulent dealings in the corn which it was his task to buy from the Moslems. In a series of articles which continued until the final acquittal of Hodent on March 23rd, Camus described the contradictory nature of the accusations levelled against him, the extremely suspect attitude of the legal authorities who had arrested him without proof and held him practically incommunicado for four months, and indicated the true reasons for the imprisonment. On the 19th of March, the day before the trial which ensured Hodent's acquittal began, he wrote: 'On one side there are men who still wish to carry out the duty which they have chosen and accepted, and, on the other, an élite of *colons, caïds*[1] and administrators who decided to prevent this duty from being performed as soon as it began to have an effect upon their profits.' As Camus convincingly showed in his articles, Hodent was in fact put into prison because the conscientious way in which he applied the official regulations laid down by the Office du Blé was annoying the big land-owners, and the charges made against him were inspired by largely political and economic considerations. The acquittal of Hodent and his friends was a triumph both for Camus personally and for the new spirit of political reform represented by *L'Alger-Républicain*.

A particularly interesting feature of the articles which he wrote on Michel Hodent is the readiness shown by Camus in invoking abstract principles of justice, a readiness which is not easy to reconcile with the nihilistic atmosphere of *L'Etranger* and *Le Mythe de Sisyphe*, the two books which he had already begun to write in 1939. Any literary associations which these articles have are rather with the works that he was to write

[1] *Colon:* a Frenchman owning land in Algeria. *Caïd:* a local Arab chieftain.

9

very much later in his career, and particularly with *La Peste* and *La Chute*. The whole intention of *La Chute* is, indeed, most curiously foreshadowed in the phrase that 'however paradoxical it may seem, it can benefit justice itself if judges are sometimes confounded'.

Camus's success in securing the acquittal of Michel Hodent also showed him that although the social system of Algeria stood in need of far-reaching reforms, a remedy to individual acts of injustice could be found in the due process of law. Throughout almost the whole of his career as a writer —the one exception is the period marked by his enthusiasm for revolution in 1944—Camus stands out among other French left-wing intellectuals, and especially when compared to Jean-Paul Sartre, by his belief that it is possible to solve social and political problems by a correct application of the normal democratic process. When he left the Communist Party in disgust with its cynical political opportunism, Camus also abandoned for a long time any sympathy which he may have had with the Marxist idea that the formal liberties of bourgeois society are nothing but an illusion. The eleven articles describing the causes and effects of the famine in Kabylia which *L'Alger-Républicain* published in June 1939 also showed that it was as a practical reformer and not as a doctrinaire revolutionary that he also approached this particular question.

The two most outstanding features of these articles are the style in which they are written and the number of practical considerations which they contain. When Camus began to insist, in the late 1950's, on the fact that he was first and foremost an artist, he gave the impression to some critics that the numerous political articles he had written and the amount of space he had devoted in his books to a discussion of moral and philosophical problems ought perhaps to be considered as lying outside his main preoccupations. His statements are best seen in perspective when compared with a letter which he wrote in August 1956: 'The truth is that I consider myself first and foremost an artist, and that problems of style and composition never cease to preoccupy me, especially when I refuse to cut myself off from the questions of the day.' What he always tried to do was to give his articles on contemporary problems a perfection of form that would lift them above ordinary journalism and give them something of the quality of a work of art. This is visible in the concluding sentence of his first article, *Le Dénuement*, in which he uses the style already developed in his purely literary essays to write a moving passage on the contrast between the beauty of the world and the suffering of man.

'For today, I end this journey through the suffering and hunger of a people. Readers will have felt already that poverty is neither a phrase nor a subject for meditation. It *is*. It cries out and it brings despair. And, once again, I ask this question: "What have we done to relieve this poverty and have we the right to turn our faces from it?" I do not know if I shall be understood. But I know that when I came back from a visit to the "tribe" of Tizi-Ouso, I went up with a Kabylian friend on to the heights which overlook the town. And at that hour when the shadow which comes down from the mountains brings a moment of peace to the hardest heart, I still knew that there was no peace for those who, on the other side of the valley, were grouped around a meal of bad barley. I also knew what pleasure there would be in yielding to so surprising and superb an evening. But the poverty whose fires were glinting on the other side of the valley denied us all right to enjoy the beauty of the world.'

Similar passages of controlled, well-balanced and highly charged emotional prose are frequent in the articles on Kabylia, as when Camus describes how he looked out from a mountain over 'this immense countryside where the morning light leaped forward, above the dizzy holes where the trees looked like blurs of darkness and where the earth lay steaming beneath the sun,' and understood 'what links could unite these men one to another and what understanding joined them to their land.' At this stage in his development, it is this concern to write well which is the only visible feature linking the socially conscious journalist of *L'Alger-Républicain* to the pagan apostle of the absurd who wrote *Noces* and *L'Envers et L'Endroit*. It is one of the paradoxes of Camus's early career that the man who, to judge by his first literary essays, was completely uninterested in social and political matters and apparently unable to believe in moral values, was also intensely preoccupied with justice and capable of devoting immense time and energy to explaining and suggesting remedies for one of the worst famines in the history of French North Africa.

The explanations which Camus gave for the state of affairs in which there were no schools for 90 per cent of the Kabylian children, in which thistle-roots had become the basic diet for almost all Moslem families, in which 96 per cent of the inhabitants of one village were officially classed as beggars, were at once economic, political and cultural in nature. Economically, he pointed out, the Kabylians were suffering from the general effects of the depression of the 'thirties. In normal times Kabylian workmen in France sent home enough money to keep their families from starvation. Since 1935, however, the French government had made the entry of North African labourers into France much more difficult, with the result that only one-tenth of the money previously sent to Kabylia was now coming through. The more general cultural reasons lay in the fact that 'we are in daily contact with a people living three centuries behind us, and we are the only ones not to be conscious of this enormous gulf.' Yet, he pointed out, there were some features of French administration which served only to make the gulf deeper. The practice of building a few enormously expensive schools as political showpieces instead of the numerous, cheap schools that could be had for the same money was aggravating the situation, as was the practice of using widespread unemployment as an excuse to pay wages much lower than the legal minimum.

The solutions which Camus proposed were essentially practical, and are especially interesting as a sign of the continuity of his thought on the Algerian problem. Most of the financial and technical help needed must, he agreed, inevitably come from Metropolitan France, for 'we see that any regime which separates Algeria from France makes for the unhappiness of both countries.' Camus's perpetual refusal to consider the possibility of Algeria ceasing to be part of France was based not upon national pride but upon the realisation that the economic conditions of North Africa could never be improved without the technical help which France alone could give. Yet for this help to be given, he argued in 1939, a fundamental revision not only of the social system in North Africa itself but also of its relationship with France was essential. Entry into France must be made easier for Kabylian workmen, public works programmes must be encouraged, technical education developed, wages brought up to the legal minimum, greater independence given to villages to run their own affairs, subsidies paid to increase the price of the figs and olives which were the main produce of Kabylia, and 200,000 hectares of unused land in Algeria itself made available for cultivation by the Kabylians.

These articles also show another feature of Camus's writing on Algeria which, together with his insistence on the need to maintain strong links with France, was to attract much criticism in later years. It is his refusal to attribute the situation in Kabylia to the evils of the colonial system set up by the French. 'My task is not to seek out those supposedly responsible,' he wrote in his conclusion. 'I have little taste for the role of accuser . . . and I am too aware of the distress which the economic crisis has brought to Kabylia to make absurd charges against a few victims.' The 'conservatism' and 'timidity' of which numerous left-wing critics accused him in the nineteen-fifties are already visible, by the side of his burning awareness of the need for immediate measures of relief, in these early articles. His efforts on behalf of the Kabylians were not, however, greatly appreciated by the Algerian authorities. When, in 1940, the closing down of his newspaper forced him to look for a different kind of work, he found that official hostility had made him unemployable. When he went to Paris in 1940 it was, as his friend Brice Parain later wrote, as 'the first journalist expelled from Algeria'.

In September 1939, Camus was entrusted by Pascal Pia with the editorship of the evening version of *L'Alger-Républicain*, *Le Soir Républicain*. It soon became the only left-wing paper in Algeria, for *L'Alger-Républicain* ceased publication on October 27th, 1939, and Camus had to carry on the struggle with the French military censorship authorities alone. Two articles in particular, the first published on the day Russia attacked Poland and the second on January 1st, 1940, show the extreme depression which Camus felt at the beginning of the war and give an indication of certain moral and philosophical ideas which would soon be developed in more detail. 'Never, perhaps,' he wrote on September 17th,

1939, 'have left-wing militants had so many reasons to despair. Many hopes and many beliefs have collapsed with the outbreak of this war. And, in the midst of all the contradictions by which this world is shaken, one is compelled to be lucid and to deny everything. . . . We know that when despair reaches a certain extreme point, indifference arises and with it the feeling and taste of fatality.' The men of 1939 had none of the hopes which inspired the soldiers of 1914: 'And if,' he continued, 'we turn towards anything in this mortal hour, it is not to the future but to the fragile and precious images of a past where life still kept its meaning: joy of the body, of sun and of water, late spring bursting into flower, brotherhood of men in the madness of hope. That alone still keeps its value but is no longer possible. It is perhaps the last extremity of revolt to lose faith in the humanity of men. Perhaps after this war trees will flower again, since the world always finally conquers history. But I cannot say how many men will be alive to look at them. And, in any case, they will have the certainty that another day will come in which they will have to sacrifice their life.'

On January 1st, 1940 a more stoical attitude towards the war was visible when Camus wrote that 'the true greatness of man is to fight against that which is greater than he. It is not happiness that we must wish for today, but rather a certain grandeur in despair.' By the side of an attack on the forces of history for the barriers which they set up between man and the enjoyment of the world, there were already, in the Camus of 1940, the first signs of the philosophical justification which he was later to give for his activity in the Resistance movement. Rejected for military service because of ill health and forced to go and work in Paris after the death of *Le Soir Républicain*, Camus had come to the end of his North African apprenticeship in journalism and political action. His task of editing *Le Soir Républicain* was made extremely difficult by the arbitrary censorship imposed on all newspapers in wartime by the French military authorities. Two cavalry officers were given the duty of censoring Camus's newspaper, which on one occasion appeared with its motto, '*Le Soir Républicain* is not like other newspapers. It always offers something to read,' in the middle of a front page containing nothing but censored blanks. Camus's strong sense of humour sustained him for some time in this unequal struggle, and he attributed subversive remarks to historical characters or respectable authors in order to baffle and confuse his censors. On January 8th, for example, the statement that 'When a man is on a horse, the horse is always the more intelligent of the two' appeared under the signature of André Maurois. 'Caligula' also remarked, on January 3rd, that 'Men can be judged by the use which they make of their power. It is noteworthy that inferior minds always misuse the scraps of authority which chance or folly have given them.' One of the main ambitions which Camus acquired in his early career, and which grew more important during his activity in the Resistance movement, was that of creating a newspaper which would be free to print the truth and to comment intelligently upon it. During the first months of 1940, until the German invasion of France, he worked for *Soir à Paris* and wrote literary articles for the extreme left-wing weekly review *La Lumière*. His determination to create a new kind of newspaper can only have been strengthened by the atmosphere of the 'phoney war' and the task of setting up headlines which made the German advance of May 1940 seem like a series of resounding French victories until the exodus from Paris suddenly began. When *Combat* emerged from clandestinity in August 1944 with Camus as its editor, it seemed that his ambition had at last been realised. The war which he had rightly greeted as so great a tragedy was, ironically enough, both to give him the chance to run his own newspaper and to create a climate of opinion in which the literary works born of another aspect of his early life in North Africa would be immediately appreciated and admired.

Chapter Two

THE MAKING OF A WRITER

CAMUS himself assigned the beginning of his career as a writer to a specifically literary experience. He was twenty, he wrote in 1959, when he was first introduced into the world of art by Jean Grenier's book of essays, *Les Iles*. It was Grenier who called him away from the 'happy barbarianism' of the life of swimming and sunbathing which he led on the beaches of Algeria, and showed him, 'in an inimitable language, that the light and the splendour of bodies were beautiful, but that they would perish and that we must therefore love them with the urgency of despair'. 'Perhaps,' he continued, 'this was the only way of guiding a young man brought up outside traditional religions towards a deeper way of thinking. Personally, I had no shortage of gods: the sun, the sea, the night. . . . But they are gods of enjoyment. They fill, but they also empty. With them alone for company, I should have forgotten them in preference for enjoyment itself. I needed to be reminded of mysterious and sacred things, of the finite nature of man, of a love that was impossible, in order that I might one day return to my natural gods with less arrogance. Thus I owe Grenier not certainties which he neither wanted nor was able to give. On the contrary, I owe him a doubt that will never end, and which has prevented me, for example, from being a humanist in the sense which the world has today, that is to say a man blinded by narrow certainties.'

This whole-hearted attribution of the beginning of his literary career to the reading of a particular book—'At the time when I discovered *Les Iles* I think that I wanted to write. But I did not really decide to do so until after I had read these essays'—is especially interesting in the case of a

16

writer as intensely personal as the early Camus. Surely, it might be argued, his experience as he lay ill with tuberculosis and was told: 'You are young and strong and I must be sincere with you: I can tell you that you are going to die' must have been a profound emotional shock. Here, surely, was a personal experience sufficiently intense to show him that the pleasures of the body were fleeting and vulnerable and that man needed to seek out some more permanently satisfactory basis to his life. Most critics have unhesitatingly stated that Camus's first attack of tuberculosis at the age of seventeen was both the first 'revelation of the absurd' and the crucial experience which turned him from an unreflective enjoyment of life to the long and sometimes anguished meditation on existence which informs his whole work. In view of the frequency with which images of breath and breathing recur in much of his prose, it would be unwise to deny that tuberculosis had an influence on his writing. What this preface to Grenier's book does suggest is that it is misleading to look upon the ideas in Camus's first collection of essays as inspired mainly by his own personal experience. On Camus's own admission, the theme of death and of the fleetingness of the world is as much literary as personal in origin. Even if one says that Grenier's book merely acted as a catalyst and an example, it does nevertheless seem—on Camus's own admission—to have determined not only the form of his first published work but also the main theme of its contents.

This is not to say either that Camus is not sincere in these two early books of essays, *L'Envers et L'Endroit* and *Noces*, first published in 1937 and 1939 respectively, or that he is not talking for most of the time about his own personal experience and attitudes. He obviously is, and these two books are the most clearly autobiographical of all his work. What is important to note is that he was inspired to write by the example of another author, and that from the very beginning of his career he was acutely conscious of the problems of style and composition. The first essays, *L'Envers et l'Endroit*, were originally published in a very limited edition, and it was only with the greatest reluctance that Camus agreed to their being reprinted and made generally available in 1958. Their form, he wrote in the long preface which then introduced them, had always seemed clumsy to him, and it was their lack of literary quality rather than any desire to deny the 'world of poverty and light' of his childhood which had made him hesitate before authorizing a re-edition. Some of the clumsiness of *L'Envers et l'Endroit* may be due to Camus's attempt to imitate Grenier's 'prudent and allusive approach' and write in a style for which he was not naturally fitted. Certainly his second book of essays, *Noces*, is more aesthetically satisfying because he does allow himself to write in a more directly sensuous style than the imitation of Grenier's laconic approach would be likely to inspire. A comparison between the text of *L'Envers et l'Endroit* and that of *Les Iles* shows fewer resemblances than Camus's preface might lead one to expect, but there is a similarity in the refusal of both authors to involve themselves emotionally with what they describe. It is perhaps this stilted tone which creates the feeling of slight dissatisfaction to which most of Camus's critics have confessed when discussing *L'Envers et l'Endroit*.

The essays contain much personal material, and the second one in particular, *Entre Oui et Non*, is as detailed an account as Camus ever allowed himself to publish of his relationship with his mother. They show Camus in his early twenties as a young man who finds great difficulty in entering into contact with people and in expressing the sympathy which he feels for their suffering and unhappiness. The first essay, for example, contains a description of three failures to communicate which announces the theme of separation in his mature work. The people described are all old, and are forced by their age into an awareness of the futility and meaninglessness of life from which the young are protected by the variety of interests open to them. An old woman who is left alone while the young people go off to the cinema turns, in the absence of other interests, to religion, and is 'finally plunged, with no hope of return, into the misery of man with God'. An old man learns the supreme misfortune of old age, that of no longer being listened to, and discovers that he is alone, lost and already dead as he stands in the growing silence of the evening and looks at 'the foolish and indifferent smile of the heavens'. A grandmother who has brought up her daughter's children with a whip dies alone and unloved and her death 'redeems nothing'. In the first and third case, one feels that it is his own failure to communicate that Camus is describing, while the example of the old man seems a more general one deliberately chosen to show the shortsightedness of the 'wisdom of the body' philosophy which had been Camus's own before reading Grenier.

Man's loneliness is particularly tragic in *L'Envers et l'Endroit* because all possibility of a religious solution is denied, and because man is shown as unable to find any kind of happiness in his own thoughts. This is emphasised in the third of the essays, *La Mort dans l'Ame*, in which Camus describes his own experiences when travelling in Czecho- slovakia and spending a week alone in Prague. There, in a city where he knew no one and could not speak the language, he was, as he says, 'reduced to despair by this disappointing *tête-à-tête* with myself and with my own poverty stricken thoughts'. Yet this essentially Pascalian view of man—Camus repeated with approval, in 1944, Brice Parain's remark that 'Any philosophy which does not refute Pascal is useless'—is nowhere presented as leading to an acceptance of religion. As the ironic misquotation of Pascal in the first essay showed, Camus considered that, as he said, 'it is sufficient for the hope of life to return again for God to be powerless against the interests of man'. Religion, like man's other activities, offers only fleeting and illusory benefits. In many ways *L'Envers et l'Endroit* is the most depressing of Camus's early works, for it holds out no possibility of escaping from loneliness and frustration. The world is beautiful, but contains no comfort or consolation for man. If his youth fades, or if he moves to a sunless country, the happy barbarian of the Algerian beaches cannot avoid the encounter with unhappiness.

This is brought out in a passage where Camus explains the meaning of the title which the essays have and the image it suggests of the right and wrong sides of a piece of cloth. 'I am linked to the world,' he writes, 'by all my acts, to men by all my pity and gratitude. Between these two sides ('*cet envers et cet endroit*') I do not wish to choose, I do not wish a choice to be made.' The correct attitude, he maintains, is to remain aware of the contradiction between the beauty of the world and the sufferings of man, to allow neither to be overwhelmed by the other, but to cultivate the tension which the conflict between them brings into being. There is here an important link with *Le Mythe de Sisyphe*, for Camus will develop this idea in the later essay by suggesting that tension similar to this is psychologically healthy and morally noble. The only virtue which he is prepared to recognise, in both *L'Envers et l'Endroit* and *Le Mythe de Sisyphe*, is that of lucidity: one should remain aware of the 'absurd simplicity of the world,' while at the same time living 'as if' values existed. 'Don't let them tell you any stories,' he writes. 'Don't let them say of the man condemned to death that: "He's going to pay his debt to society," but; "They're going to chop his head off." It doesn't seem much. But it makes a little difference all the same. And then, there are people who prefer to look their fate straight in the eye.'

L'Envers et l'Endroit does indeed show a swing away from what Camus referred to in 1952 as '*le total abrutissement du soleil*' and towards a more reflective and critical attitude to experience. Basing oneself on the remarks which Camus made in his preface to Grenier's essays, it is possible to distinguish three stages in his early intellectual development. The first, which goes up to the age of twenty and rather curiously includes both his first attack of tuberculosis and his recovery from it, is one of instinctive, animal enjoyment of the life of the senses. It was perhaps to this period that he referred when he made Jean Tarrou, in *La Peste*, say that 'When I was young, I lived with the idea of my innocence, that is to say, with no ideas at all.' Then comes the shock of discovery when he read Grenier's *Les Iles*, understood the reason for his 'sudden melancholies' and ceased to live 'in sensations, on the surface of the world, among colours, waves and the fine scent of the earth'. This awakening produced *L'Envers et l'Endroit*, with its reaction in favour of an insistence upon the darker side of experience and on the value of intellectual awareness. Then, this time in a movement away from the atmosphere of *L'Envers et l'Endroit*, comes the triumphant reaffirmation of the life of the body in *Noces*, the song of the nuptials between man and the earth which contrasts so sharply with the detached irony of the mood of the first essays.

Clearly, such an imaginary biography leaves much to be desired. When a photograph exists of Camus in the dark suit and white armband of the little boy taking his First Communion, it is hard to see how he was 'brought up outside traditional religions'.[1] It leaves on one side the question of how he combined the ironic nihilism of *L'Envers et l'Endroit* with his membership and rejection of the Communist Party in 1934, or how he was later to be at one and the same time the happy pagan of *Noces* and the socially conscious journalist of *L'Alger-Républicain*. Nevertheless, it does explain the difference of atmosphere between *L'Envers et l'Endroit* and *Noces*, as well as foreshadowing the movement from the revelation of the absurd to the discovery of joy in *Le Mythe de Sisyphe*. For *Noces* continues many of the themes of *L'Envers et l'Endroit* but looks at them, as it were, from the more flattering side of the cloth. As Camus wrote in *Le Mythe de Sisyphe* in 1943, 'One does not discover the absurd without being tempted to write a manual of happiness.' *Noces* was such a manual, and the concept of 'the absurd' which Camus was to make so popular in 1943 stems from his insistence in *L'Envers et l'Endroit* that there is no ultimate consolation for human loneliness and the completeness of death. Yet what was a pretext for sombre meditation in *L'Envers et l'Endroit* leads to intense and satisfying happiness in *Noces*.

The idea of happiness is indeed not absent from *L'Envers et l'Endroit*, and it inspires one of the best essays in the book, *L'Amour de vivre*. But it is linked in the first essays with two feelings which appear only intermittently in *Noces*: those of despair and of an indefinable aspiration towards some unknown and unattainable ideal. 'There is no love of living without despair of life,' he wrote in *L'Envers et l'Endroit*, when describing his contemplation of the sun-drenched countryside of the Mediterranean countries, and added to this epigram a definition of 'love of living' as 'a silent passion which was perhaps going to escape me, a bitterness beneath the flame'. It is this awareness which Camus said he owed to Grenier, and which becomes less perceptible as he draws away from the influence of *Les Iles* and writes with less irony and more enthusiasm of the full satisfaction to be gained in the physical joys of life. When Pascal is quoted, in *Noces*, it is no longer with an ironic recognition of the partial validity of his attitude, but in a spirit of self-assertive, confident humanism. 'It is not that one should behave as a beast,' writes Camus in the essay *L'Été à Alger*, 'but I can see no

[1] See notes.

point in the happiness of angels.' It is because Camus feels so completely at home in the physical world that he does not, in *Noces*, stress the world's basic indifference which obsesses him in *L'Envers et l'Endroit*, and that the whole tone of the book, with the picture which it gives of the young Camus, is unlike that suggested by the first essays. The Camus described by Emmanuel Roblès as 'essentially a creature of the sun, made for the simple and intense life of the Mediterranean shores' was also the Camus who wrote this profession of confidence in the world in the first essay in the book, *Noces à Tipasa*: 'I must be naked and then dive into the sea, the scents of the earth still about me, wash off these scents in the sea and consummate on my own flesh the embrace for which, lips to lips, earth and sea have for so long been sighing.' The whole of this essay is the description of the completely satisfying experience which Camus has when he enters into communion with nature, and it introduces a hymn to joy which is taken up in different ways throughout the book. At Tipasa, the sea 'sucking at the rocks with the sound of kisses,' the mountains 'moving with confident and certain rhythm to crouch down in the sea,' the 'melody of the world' which comes through the gaps in the wall of the Christian basilica at Sainte-Sala, all strengthen Camus in his realisation that here man is offered a happiness which is made for him and which is always within his reach. At the end of a day spent swimming, and walking through the flower-strewn ruins of Tipasa, Camus sits on a park bench and meditates on the fullness of the happiness he has found.

'I watched the shapes of the countryside merge in the growing twilight. My cup was brimming over. Above my head hung the buds of a pomegranate tree, closed and ribbed like little fists which held all the promise of spring. There was rosemary behind me, and I could smell the alcoholic tang of its leaves. I could see hills through the gaps of the trees, and, further in the distance, a strip of sea above which the sky, like the sail of a boat motionless for lack of wind, rested with all its tenderness. I felt a strange joy in my heart, the very joy which is born of a clear conscience. There is a feeling which actors have when they know they have played their part well, that is to say when they have made their own gestures coincide with those of the ideal character they have been representing, taken up a position in a picture made for them in advance and suddenly brought it to life with the beating of their own heart. This was exactly my feeling: I had played my part well. I had done the task which awaited me as a man, and the fact that I had known joy all one livelong day seemed to me not an exceptional success but the whole-hearted fulfilment of a condition which, in certain circumstances, makes it our duty to be happy.'

Even when, as on a windy day at Djémila, Camus feels not the 'inner quietness of love satisfied' but rather a full awareness of his coming death, this sense of communion with the world is not destroyed. Indeed, throughout *Noces* the idea that death is inevitable merely adds to Camus's determination to enjoy fully and completely the pleasures vouchsafed to him. It is when the wind has almost destroyed his feeling of his own individuality, when he has been 'polished by the wind, worn through to the very soul . . . mingling the beating of [his] heart with the great, sonorous heart-beats of the ever present heart of nature' that he realises the full extent of the satisfaction which his complete identification with the world and his refusal to seek out any other values can give him.

'Few people understand that there is a refusal which has nothing to do with renunciation. What meaning can words like "future", "improvement", "position" have here? What can be meant by "the heart's progress"? If I obstinately refuse all the "later on" of the world, it is because I do not want to give up my present riches. I do not want to believe that death opens out on to another life. For me it is a closed door. I don't say that it is "a step that we must all take": but that it is a horrible and dirty adventure. All the solutions which are offered to me try to take away from man the weight of his own life. And, watching the heavy flight of the great birds in the sky at Djémila, it is exactly a certain weight that I ask for and receive. I have too much youth in me to speak of death. But if I were to speak of it it is here that I should find the precise word which would, midway between horror and silence, express the conscious certainty of a death without hope.'

This communion with nature, this instinctive wisdom of the body, and this rejection of all attempts to clothe the

23

thought of final annihilation in comforting myths are also qualities which Camus finds and appreciates in the essentially pagan civilisation of North Africa. The essay *L'Eté à Alger* is a long defence and illustration of the virtues of Camus's own countrymen who come of a race which 'born of the sun and of the sea, alive and full of vigour, derives its greatness from its simplicity and, standing upright on its beaches, addresses a smile of complicity to the shining smile of the heavens'. Such a people, Camus writes, have the touch of barbarity typical of all races who have created a new civilisation, and he suggests that they are, perhaps at this very moment, in process of 'modelling the face of a new culture where man's greatness will perhaps find its true likeness'. If they did succeed in doing so, it would apparently be one where man would have to resign himself to the unhappiness of old age, abandon the vague quest for something more permanent described in *L'Envers et l'Endroit*, and accept that the important part of his life is finished when he is over thirty. 'Men find here,' writes Camus, 'throughout the whole of their youth, a life which is made to the measure of their beauty. Then afterwards, their life goes down towards forgetfulness. They have placed their bets upon the body, and they knew that they would lose. In Algiers everything presents a refuge and an occasion for triumphs to those who are young and alive: the bay, the sun, the red and white games of the seaward terraces, the flowers and the sports stadiums, the young girls with smooth legs. But for anyone who has lost his youth, there is nothing to which he can cling and not a single place where melancholy can seek refuge.'

Men must accept that there is no other truth than that of the body, and, for Camus, it is the fact that the Algerians do this which gives them their particular virtue. It is a virtue which Camus took from them and made into one of the important ideas in *Le Mythe de Sisyphe*. The men who were 'gods of the summer at the age of twenty because of their thirst for life, and who are still gods when they live completely without hope', have never committed a sin against life. For, writes Camus, 'if there is a sin against life, it is not so much to fall into despair as to hope for immortality and elude the implacable grandeur of the life we have'. The essential virtue is to recognise that there is no solution to the problem of human mortality, that no consolation of another life can be offered to man, and that he must be satisfied with 'stones, stars, and flesh, and those truths which the hand itself can touch'. Camus's rejection of religion is more absolute in *Noces* than it was in *L'Envers et l'Endroit* because the emotional grounds for it have changed. In *L'Envers et l'Endroit*, religion is presented as an illusory consolation which can never seriously rival the activities of real life. In *Noces*, the suggestion is rather that even if the hope and comfort offered by religion did happen to be true, this would by no means be a good thing: man would thereby lose that intensity of joy which can, in Camus's view, come only from his awareness of the absolute finality of death. In *L'Envers et l'Endroit* there is the suspicion of a nostalgic hankering after an impossible religious belief. In *Noces*, on the other hand, Camus's humanism takes on for the first time something of the defiant quality of *Le Mythe de Sisyphe* and *L'Etranger*.

In *Albert Camus and the Literature of Revolt* John Cruick-shank qualifies Camus's attitude in *Noces* as 'naive atheism' and remarks that 'such direct and unhesitating disbelief . . . is striking and unusual in a writer of Camus's stature and reputation'. Dr. Cruickshank argues that the attitude put forward in *Noces* can be criticised on two main counts. First of all, he points out, it is 'less spontaneous' than it at first appears, since it depends upon a rationalisation of an instinctive sensualism which, left to itself, would never achieve self-consciousness. Secondly, he suggests that there is something in the argument that Camus 'genuinely fails to see what the Christian sees and cannot make any contact with the Christian consciousness'. The first point that Dr. Cruickshank is making is a good one, for there is an essential difference between Camus's own deliberate choice to live without transcendence, and what he considers, rightly or wrongly, to be an instinctive rejection of religious faith by the average Algerian man. This difference does not, of itself, invalidate the view of life set forth in *Noces*, for one may legitimately point out that had Camus not been led by his greater sophistication to recognise this instinctive wisdom for what it is, we should have no work of art. A more justifiable criticism of *Noces*, and particularly of the essay *L'Eté à Alger*, is that Camus is romanticising his compatriots and seeing them as more harmoniously adjusted to the world than they actually are. In spite of the praise which other North African writers have given Camus for the accuracy of his description of Algeria, it is doubtful whether so culturally and politically carefree a race ever really existed. Much of Camus's later pessimism may have sprung from the intense disappointment which he felt when those whom he had seen as creating a new civilisation were engulfed, partly by their own fault, in a murderous civil war. In that case, it was a disappointment which both his early romanticism and the separation between the view of life expressed in these early essays and that implied by his journalism helped to prepare.

The criticism of Camus's 'atheism' in *Noces* is an important one to consider, since the reasons which he gives for rejecting religion remain constant in his early work until the mid-1940's. They are certainly not complicated reasons, though it is perhaps exaggerated to describe them and his attitude as 'naive'. He certainly had both an intellectual knowledge of Christian doctrine and an appreciation of its emotional appeal. His *diplôme* had ended with his remarking of Pascal's *pensée*, 'Since men cannot cure death they have made up their minds not to think about it,' that: 'The whole effort of Christianity lies in opposing this laziness of the heart.' His reasons for rejecting Christianity stem from what any believer must regard as an incomplete view of life, but which is nevertheless both consistent and sincere. If one cannot feel either a sense of sin or the need for an eternal life wholly different from our earthly one, then the essential doctrines of the Redemption and the Resurrection of the Body can have no possible meaning. Camus has recognised this, and has drawn the inevitable conclusion that religious solutions can have no relevance to his own problems and experience of life. His point of view is certainly narrower than that of the Christian, but it is founded on a personal experience which, in its way, is no less sincere than that of Pascal. There is surely no point in pretending to a sense of sin that one does not possess, and the objection that Camus 'really has a sense of sin but refuses to recognise it' is valid only for those who have already accepted the truth of Christian theology.

Camus himself never claimed originality for his views on religion, and was fully aware that his own choice had an unreasoning element in it. In 1943 he published an article in which he remarked that what characterised modern agnosticism was more a 'passionate disbelief' than the rationalist arguments of the nineteenth century. The circumstances under which Camus made this remark are interesting, for they show that he had not lost the intellectual interest in Christianity which he showed in choosing to write his *diplôme* on Saint Augustine. He was reviewing Jean Guitton's biography of a priest, Father Pouget, who had spent his life trying to find a compromise between blind faith and reasonable belief on the problems of the contradictions in the Bible. For Camus, the quarrel between science and religion had no longer any reality, for, as he wrote, 'the problem of faith does not lie in quibbles of this kind'. This peremptory dismissal of the difficulties which drove Renan from the Church is certainly confirmation of Camus's own 'passionate disbelief' and of his desire to avoid sterile disputes on religious matters, but it does not necessarily render his attitude naive. The dividing line in these matters between what is naive and what is penetratingly simple is a difficult one to draw, and each reader will doubtless be influenced by his own faith or disbelief in placing Camus on one side of the line or on the other. Yet as long as Christian apologists defend religion by an insistence on man's sin and on his consequent need for God, the objection of happiness and personal self-sufficiency put forward in *Noces* will remain a valid one.

Another problem raised by both *Noces* and *L'Envers et l'Endroit*, and mentioned already in this chapter, is that of reconciling the two apparently different characters which Camus presented to the world in the 1930's. There was, on the one hand, the young man with a social conscience who wrote for *L'Alger-Républicain* and, on the other, the happy pagan of *Noces* or the ironic observer of *L'Envers et l'Endroit*. His play *Caligula*, first written in 1938 but not produced until 1945, is the only real indication that we have that it was a difference which Camus himself found disturbing. Neither his own remarks nor the reminiscences of his friends present him as a man driven to anguish by a contradiction in his own character. He wrote in 1944 that 'social justice needs no complicated philosophy', and remarked in 1952 that, 'In the days of innocence, I did not know that morality existed.' Without

27

the experience of the Occupation and Resistance movement, Camus might never have felt the need to bring the two sides of his personality together and try to create a philosophy that would both exult the life of the senses and justify political action. His complimentary description of the general morality which prevailed among the working classes of Algiers gives the impression that he himself found it sufficient to most of the problems which confronted him in ordinary life. Like the ethics which he said that he learned on the football field, it satisfied the needs of anyone living in a society where social problems presented themselves in an obvious and accessible form. When what had to be proclaimed was the innocence of a man falsely accused or the need to prevent children from dying of hunger, the simple rules described in *L'Eté à Alger* seemed to provide an adequate general guide. 'You don't let your mother down. You see that nobody insults your wife in the street. You show consideration for pregnant women. You don't attack an enemy two to one because "that's a dirty trick". If anyone fails to keep these elementary rules, we say "He's not a man," and that's an end to it.'

Yet the war came, the Algerian summer ended, and Camus was swept up, against his will, into the tumultuous and disorderly movement of history. The trip which he had planned to take to Greece in September 1939 had to be postponed. He was taken from the world in which social justice could very well find its place by the side of pagan hedonism, and plunged into one where philosophers created injustice and abstract ideologies justified mass-murders and deportations. 'Brought up in the sight of beauty, which was my only wealth, I began by plenteousness. Then came the time of the barbed-wire fences, of tyranny, war, and police forces, the time of revolt. We had to come to terms with the night. The beauty of the day was now only a memory.' In spite of the fame which surrounded Camus from 1944 onwards, his great success as a writer, his reputation as a thinker and moralist, and his triumphs as a theatrical producer, it is clear from the books which he wrote after he had left North Africa behind him that he never again knew the complete happiness and perfect harmony with the world which he had expressed in *Noces*. The success which his gifts as an artist and thinker secured for him when *L'Etranger* and *Le Mythe de Sisyphe* were published placed him in a position where he could not avoid taking on the rôle of prophet and director of conscience to a whole new generation of young Frenchmen. In the Paris of the 1940's the time of the irresponsible writer was over. Sartre's insistence that the writer could no longer avoid the moral responsibility for the acts and attitudes inspired by his books reflected the general climate of the time. An intellectual atmosphere was created which no one, and certainly not a person of such high moral sensitivity as Camus, could possibly hope to escape. At the very moment when he had transformed the experiences described in the essays of *L'Envers et l'Endroit* and *Noces* into a perfectly finished novel and a compact philosophical essay, his triumph as an artist forced him to leave the original source of his inspiration behind him. André Malraux, it is said, 'imposed' *L'Etranger* and *Le Mythe de Sisyphe* on Gallimard, and Camus's career as a public writer began. Yet no sooner had the North African summer given its literary fruits than Camus was forced to move on and explore a different emotional climate from which works of equal value would eventually be born.

Chapter Three

THE OUTSIDER

THE immediate success of *L'Etranger*, published in Paris late in 1942, and of *Le Mythe de Sisyphe*, published early in the following year, was based to some extent upon a misunderstanding. Camus's automatic assumption that life had no meaning, his denunciation of hope, his determined refusal of any comforting transcendence, exactly fitted the mood of the time. Cataclysmic defeat had drifted into the monotony of occupation, the prospect of liberation seemed almost infinitely distant, and a philosophical view of the universe in which all paths to the future were rigorously closed and all naive optimism suppressed, corresponded exactly to the historical situation of the French people. In such an atmosphere it was perhaps inevitable that the positive side of Camus's work—the call to happiness, the creation of an 'outsider' who was completely satisfied with his lot—should have passed relatively unnoticed. Camus himself remarked in 1946 that most critics had failed to see '*la présence physique et l'expérience charnelle*' which for him were the essence of Meursault's character. 'The men in Algeria,' he told Gaëton Picon, 'live like my hero, in an absolutely simple manner. Naturally, you can understand Meursault, but an Algerian will understand him more easily and more deeply.' What Camus meant by this was that Meursault had the same concern for the physical side of life and the same indifference towards both Christianity and bourgeois morality which characterised the Algerians described in *Noces*. The story of *L'Etranger* is that of a man who, having decided to base his life upon the pagan values described in *L'Eté à Alger*, discovers that official bourgeois and Christian society will not tolerate such a defiance of its favourite myths.

What characterises Meursault, the hero of *L'Etranger*, is a complete indifference to anything except immediate physical sensations, together with an absolute refusal to lie about his own emotions. He receives the news of his mother's death merely with faint annoyance at having to ask for two days' leave of absence from the office where he works. At her funeral he has no sadness or regret, and feels only the physical inconveniences of watching over her body and following the hearse to the cemetery under the burning sun. He notes automatically and objectively everything which strikes his eye: the bright new screws in the walnut-stained coffin, the colours of the nurse's clothes, the large stomachs of the old ladies who had been his mother's closest friends, the whiteness of the roots in her grave. The day after the funeral he goes swimming, meets a girl whom he knows vaguely, takes her to see a Fernandel film and goes to bed with her that night. He shows no more affection or feeling for her than he had shown for his mother. When she asks him to marry her, he accepts with the calm remark that it is all the same to him. At his work, he is more interested in a detail like the pleasant dryness of a hand-towel at midday and its clamminess in the evening than in a possible promotion and transfer to Paris. He becomes involved in a rather sordid affair with his next-door neighbour, in which he shows himself as indifferent to friendship and to the purely social convention of truthfulness as he was to love, and as a result of a series of accidents finds himself one day with a revolver in his hand, standing on a beach facing an Arab who is threatening him with a knife. Almost unconscious, under the blinding sun, of what he is doing, he shoots the Arab and then fires four more shots into his inert body. 'And it was like four sharp raps which I gave on the door of unhappiness.'

In the second part of the book, until the very last page, Meursault remains as detached and indifferent as he was in the first, equally preoccupied by his own sensations and equally reluctant to pretend to feelings which he does not have. He never thinks of pleading self-defence when accused of the murder of the Arab, and expresses no remorse or feeling of guilt about his victim. His lawyer warns him that the reports of his apparent indifference at his mother's funeral might prejudice the jury against him, but Meursault refuses to allow lies to be told on his behalf. 'I explained to him,' he says of his lawyer, 'that my nature is such that my physical needs often interfered with my feelings. On the day I buried mother, I was very tired and felt sleepy. So I didn't fully realise what was happening. What I could certainly say was that I would have preferred mother not to have died. But my lawyer didn't seem satisfied with this. He said: "It's not enough." He thought for a moment. He asked me if he could say that I had dominated my natural feelings. I replied. "No. Because that would not be true." '

Meursault maintains the same attitude throughout his trial, refusing all opportunities to weep over his mother and express histrionic remorse for the man he has killed, and is consequently sentenced to death. The only explanation which he is prepared to give of his act is that he killed the Arab 'because of the sun'. As Camus shows, he did fire the revolver in a desperate, absurd attempt to escape from the heat which was pouring down on him from the sky, and his explanation represents, for him, the absolute truth of why he acted as he did. Yet at no time is he sufficiently interested in the proceedings in the court-room to make more than a very perfunctory attempt at self-justification. What holds his attention are the different colours of the fans used by the jurors to keep themselves cool, the sunlight and sounds coming in from the street, and the subtle changes which reflect the progress of the day outside. It is not until the evening before his execution that Meursault brings out the reasons that have governed his attitude and, at the very moment when he is going to lose his life, openly expresses an attitude which has been conscious and implicit all along.

During the year which he spends in prison between his arrest and his execution, Meursault adapts himself to his new life and recovers from the initial unhappiness caused by his loss of liberty. He learns how to remember, and becomes capable of spending hours simply making a mental list of all the objects in the room where he used to live. He comes to realise that were a man to have lived for only a day, the memories he acquired would be sufficient to enable him to live a hundred years in prison without ever being bored. He also realises that if he had been made to live imprisoned in a tree-trunk, the sight of the sky above him would have been

32

sufficient reason for remaining alive. 'I should have waited for the passage of the birds or the strange forms taken by the clouds in the same way as I now waited for the curious ties worn by my lawyer and, in another world, I waited until Saturday to take Marie in my arms.' Such reflections prepare the reader for Meursault's final outburst to the chaplain, in which the latter's prayers, and the consolation which he offers of another life, sting Meursault into a violent affirmation that this life alone is certain and that in it the inevitability of death obliterates all significance. The chaplain goes, and Meursault is filled for the first time with 'the tender indifference of the world'. He realises that he has been happy in his life, that he would like to live it all over again, and hopes, 'in order that all may be fulfilled', that there will be many people at his funeral and that they will greet him with cries of hatred.

The importance of physical sensation in Meursault not only accounts for his final revolt against death, his affirmation that this life alone can offer certainty, and his rejection of the hopes of immortality held out by the priest: it is also used by Camus to offer, by a sudden change of style, an explanation for Meursault's killing of the Arab which both his hero's taciturnity and the narrowmindedness of the legal authorities prevent them from discovering. When Meursault told the judge that he killed the Arab 'because of the sun', he was telling the truth and giving the only true explanation which there is for his act. This is well brought out by Camus in the way in which the events are presented to the reader, for the story of *L'Etranger* is told in two different styles. The one which predominates consists of short, precise sentences, totally lacking in images and metaphors, and doing little more than reproduce exactly everything which Meursault sees, hears, and feels. This style, which Camus made no secret of having borrowed from Hemingway because it suited his purpose of 'describing a man with no apparent consciousness', also has another feature in common with that of Hemingway. It shows how important each individual physical event is in Meursault's life, in the same way as the notation of colours and sensations in *The Sun Also Rises* is used to explain Jake's liking for life in Spain. Meursault's awareness of the colours, lights and sensations of the external world is so acute as to recall at times a mystical experience. Objects exist for him in their absolute newness as they exist for the illuminate. Camus's precise, accurate descriptive style enables him to show, by implication rather than by explanation, how Meursault delights in existence as he finds it, how each detail is for him infinitely valuable, and why his revolt against death is so absolute. Meursault is also, however, someone who is essentially passive in his attitude towards the world, and it is his passivity towards physical sensation which leads to his crime.

Camus indicates this—as W. H. Frohock pointed out in one of the most perceptive articles so far published on Camus's fiction—by suddenly changing his mode of narration in the description which he gives of Meursault's killing of the Arab. He replaces the laconic style of the opening sections, in which images personalising the world or explaining natural phenomena in human terms are studiously avoided, by a style which is its exact opposite. When Meursault's act comes upon him—he does not say that he pulled the trigger, only that 'the trigger gave way'—sun and sea are strongly personified as living creatures exercising an overwhelming influence upon him. The sun strikes as with cymbals on his forehead and the sea engulfs him in its hot thick breath. He is entirely possessed by the forces of nature and is passive under their influence. In an absurd world, where sensations and objects are all-important, they are also ambivalent. The sea and the sun, the objects of his only enthusiasm, impel Meursault to commit the crime for which he will be executed.

This explanation by change of style is very skilfully done by Camus, but it has led to an interpretation of Meursault's passivity towards the forces of nature which contradicts most of the remarks which Camus himself made about the meaning of *L'Etranger*. In her *Camus*, Mme Germaine Brée argues that Meursault's story is an attempt to point out the dangers involved in accepting too uncritically the view of life set forth in *Noces* and *Le Mythe de Sisyphe*. Correctly identifying Meursault's attitude with that of the 'absurd man' described in *Le Mythe de Sisyphe*, Mme Brée writes that 'in *L'Etranger* Camus thus suggests that in face of the absurd no man can afford just passively to exist', and argues that Meursault is condemned, like Parsifal in the Graal legend, because of his refusal to ask any questions. This can be accepted as a correct explanation only if one neglects almost all the statements which Camus made about *L'Etranger*. Prefacing a schools' edition in 1955, Camus made the ideas he had already suggested to Gaëton Picon more explicit when he wrote: 'For me, Meursault is not a piece of human wreckage, but a man who is poor, naked and in love with the sun which leaves no shadows. Far from being lacking in all feeling, he is inspired by a passion which is profound because unspoken, the passion for the absolute and for truth. It is still a negative truth, that of being alive and experiencing life, but without it no conquest of oneself or of the world will ever be possible.' Meursault can surely not be at one and the same time both an exemplary figure—Camus also refers to him in the same preface as 'the only kind of Christ whom we deserve'—and the subject matter of a cautionary tale. Both the remarks which Camus made about *L'Etranger* and the way in which he incorporated into Meursault's character all the features which he most appreciated in his fellow-Algerians indicate that he strongly sympathised with him. Critics who state, as Robert de Luppé did, that *L'Etranger* shows us our own miserable life, 'eaten up with sleep', or argue, like Wyndham Lewis, that Meursault 'represents an important fact of contemporary demoralisation' are on Camus's own showing completely misinterpreting his work. The many reminiscences of *Noces* in *L'Etranger* show that the later comments were in no way an attempt to project on to the book a meaning which it had not originally had.

The witnesses for the defence at Meursault's trial include Céleste, the proprietor of the small restaurant where Meursault took most of his meals. In an interview in 1959, Camus said that Céleste was one of the three characters he most preferred in his own work, and it was Camus's own view of Meursault that Céleste was repeating when he said of him in court that 'he was a man'. To the reader of *Noces*, the reference to the elementary moral rules which Camus described as being automatically observed by the Algerians is obvious, but Céleste is too inarticulate to make the lawyers see his point. Meursault, it must be remarked, had not 'let down' his mother. He had placed her in an officially instituted home because he had not enough money to look after her properly and because she was unhappy living alone with him in their small flat. In his honest recognition that his mother would be happier away from him, his refusal to play the game of romantic love with Marie, his refusal to join in the fight between Raymond and the Arab because this would make it two to one, his sympathy for the old man Salamano, his dislike of the police, his boredom on Sundays—'Sundays in Algiers are amongst the gloomiest I know,' wrote Camus in *Noces*—his worship of the sun and his love of swimming, in all these Meursault incarnates everything that Camus admired in the people of Algeria.

There is also a strong autobiographical element in Meursault's character which is reflected not only in his one memory of his father returning home to be violently sick after seeing a man guillotined, but also in less important features like his job in an important export office and his dislike of Paris. Although Camus always denied that he had depicted himself in any of the characters of his novels, and objected to the romantic habit of identifying an author with his creations, it does seem that he put much of himself into the person of Meursault. Further examples of this are the way both Meursault in *L'Etranger* and Camus in *Noces* feel the blood pulsating through their temples when they are hot or excited, and the love which they both have for the brief twilight of Algiers. When Meursault's attention wanders from the long speeches which both defence and prosecution counsel make about his soul, he hears the sound of the little trumpet of an ice-cream merchant in the street outside. Then, he says, 'a rush of memories came into my mind, memories of a life which was no longer mine, but in which I had found the surest and humblest of my pleasures: smells of summer, my favourite streets, the laughter and dresses of Marie'. Here again he is speaking of the pleasures which Camus described in *Noces*, and echoing Camus's own idea that such pleasures are enough to fill a man's life with happiness. In 1947, Camus remarked, speaking of his meeting with René Leynaud in the Resistance movement, that 'then as now I had no imagination', and Meursault is made to say exactly the same thing when he is thinking of his own death.

The most important feature of this resemblance between Meursault and his creator lies, however, in the reasons which they both give for refusing the idea of a life beyond the grave. When Meursault shouts out to the priest that the only future life which might perhaps interest him is one in which he could remember his earthly one, he is voicing the same ideas which Camus put forward in *L'Envers et l'Endroit* to explain his own lack of interest in the immortality of the soul. 'What use had I for a life relived in the soul, if it meant no eyes with which to see Vicenza, no hands with which to feel the caress of night on the road from Monte Berico to the villa Valmanara?' In almost every respect, Meursault is the fictional embodiment of the strongly personal attitude towards life which Camus had expressed in his early lyrical essays. He is also, if Camus himself is to be believed, a character who is fully conscious throughout the whole of the novel of the value of the attitude he represents.

The most frequent interpretation offered of Meursault's character by critics writing both under the Occupation and immediately after the war, can fairly accurately be summed up as follows: Meursault is a poor fool who, living a dull and uninteresting life, is caught up in a network of circumstances over which he has no control and killed by an incomprehending society at the very moment when he has begun to understand how infinitely valuable existence can be. Camus's published remarks have shown how incorrect it is to see Meursault as a character whose life had no interest or importance in his own eyes. In private conversation in 1956, he also remarked that the correct interpretation of *L'Etranger* was the one which insisted upon the fact that Meursault was conscious, from the very beginning of the book, of the nature and value of the attitude he represented. Meursault was not, in his view, to be seen solely as the ideal Algerian hero, but also as one of the 'absurd men' whose fuller description is to be found in *Le Mythe de Sisyphe*. He confirmed that the phrase in *Le Mythe de Sisyphe* stating that 'a temporary employee at the Post Office is the equal of a conqueror if they both have the same consciousness of their fate' applied exactly to Meursault, and remarked that he had intended Meursault to be seen as having gone through the experience of discovering and reacting to the problem of the absurdity of life before the story began. From the ideas expressed in *Le Mythe de Sisyphe* and from the incidental remarks which Meursault makes about himself in *L'Etranger*, some kind of tentative reconstruction of the experience which led him to be an 'outsider' and an 'absurd man' is possible.

When his employer offers Meursault the chance of being promoted and of taking charge of a new office to be set up in Paris, Meursault refuses this opportunity to 'improve himself'. Afterwards he thinks to himself that he is not unhappy as he is, and that he has no desire to change. 'When I was a student,' he remembers, 'I had lots of ambitions like that. But when I had to give up my studies, I very soon realised that all that had no real importance.' To the critic who might, very understandably, not wholly accept Camus's remarks about his own discovery of the fleetingness of youth in the essays of Jean Grenier, Meursault's comment reads like yet another indication of the strongly autobiographical nature of the book. Here, it could be argued, is the young Camus who had to give up his own studies because of ill-health, who had at the same time an overwhelming experience of his inevitable death in his first attack of tuberculosis, and who is now translating his own discovery of the absurd from real life into fiction. Meursault, it seems, had originally had ambitions to rise in the world of business as Camus himself had had ambitions to become a teacher of philosophy, but both these sets of ambitions had had to be given up because of an interruption of studies. That Meursault had discovered the absurd in one of the ways with which Camus was very familiar is evident when his outburst to the chaplain is read carefully and compared to Camus's description of the revelation of the absurd in the first pages of *Le Mythe de Sisyphe*.

'I was sure of myself, sure of everything, surer than he was, sure of my life and of the death which was coming to me. Yes, that was the only thing I had, but at least I held that truth as much as it dominated me. I had been right, I was still right, I had always been right. I had lived my life in such and such a way and I could have lived in another. I had done this and I had not done that. So what? It was as if I had been waiting all this time for this moment, for this early dawn where I should find my justification. Nothing, nothing at all had any meaning and I knew why. He knew why as well. From the far-off depths of my future, during the whole of this absurd life that I had led, a dark breath rose towards me, blowing through the years which had not yet come, bringing with it an equal insignifi-cance to the no more real years that I was living through. What did other people's death matter, what did love for my mother matter, what did his god matter, what did the choice between different lives matter, since one fate would single me out and together with me the thousand million others who, as he did, said they were my brothers?'

For Meursault the absurd is essentially the result of his awareness of his own mortality, of what Camus calls, in *Le Mythe de Sisyphe*, the 'bloodstained mathematics which dominate the human lot'. He is the 'everyday man' described in the essay who, before his discovery of the absurd, had projects, hopes, ambitions, the belief that he was free to order his life, but who has realised that 'all that is disproved in one breath-taking sweep by the absurdity of a possible death'.

Even if one does discount the arguments in favour of an autobiographical interpretation of at least this aspect of Meursault's character, the tenses which Camus makes him use in his final outburst are as clear an indication as it was possible to give that Meursault was not just discovering his values for the first time. He was affirming them in response to the challenge represented by the priest's offer of religious consolation, in the same way as Camus was moved to reaffirm his own rejection of religious consolation when he read the inscriptions on the tombstones at Florence. 'Alone, with my back against the pillar,' he wrote in *Noces*, 'I was like someone seized by the throat, who shouts out his faith as if it were his dying words. Everything in me protested against such a resignation. "You must accept," said the tombstones. No, and I was right to rebel. I must follow this joy that goes (as one of the tombstones said), "indifferent and absorbed as a pilgrim upon the earth", must follow it step by step.'

That Meursault was conscious of his attitude all along, but proclaimed it only when the priest had provoked him into doing so, is well brought out in Robert Champigny's admir-able essay *Sur un héros païen*. M. Champigny also shows how Meursault's condemnation to death is a necessary part of his exemplary quality as a pagan hero, and explains why he should want crowds to greet him on the morning of his execution with cries of hatred. When society condemns

Meursault to death, argues M. Champigny, it also challenges the validity of the attitude on which he had based his life. Left to himself, Meursault would never have openly challenged society in any way, for he was of a naturally tolerant and agreeable nature, eminently prepared to live and let live. After he has been condemned to death, however, and after the priest has put forward a philosophy of life which challenges and contradicts Meursault's own, Meursault no longer has this easy-going approach. He wants the crowds to be there because he wants society to give some sign that it realises how much he defies it, and because he knows that he is right and the others wrong. There is, certainly, an evolution in Meursault's character at the end of the book, when he makes his attitude explicit and ceases to want people's sympathy. But it is the kind of evolution which leads from a philosophy elaborated in silence and privacy to a philosophy openly proclaimed in public, not the evolution which accompanies the sudden coming to awareness of a previously unreflective attitude to life.

It is Meursault's tolerance and easy-going temperament which make him such an attractive character and which ensure that he enjoys the reader's sympathy in spite of his apparent heartlessness and indifference towards his mother and Marie. He is by far the most attractive of the 'outsiders' which were once said to characterise modern literature. By the side of his very definite reasons for staying alive—the sun, Marie, swimming, the sounds of evening—he also has a tolerance towards those who do not share his views which contrasts most pleasantly with the intolerant sarcasms of Sartre's Roquentin and the hysterical scorn of Anouilh's Antigone. This tolerance, moreover, is not accompanied by any readiness to sacrifice his own ideals to even the most tempting personal advantage. He is prepared to lie to oblige a friend—in fact, his attitude to truth in the whole of the early episode with Raymond is disquietingly cavalier—but he is most careful not to lie about what he himself thinks and feels when he might benefit from it personally. 'One would not be much mistaken,' wrote Camus in 1955, 'in reading L'Etranger as the story of a man who, without any heroics, accepts to die for the truth.'

This is brought out in the story both in the description of

Meursault's behaviour at his mother's funeral and in the presentation of the trial scenes. Meursault at least has the honesty not to pretend to feelings which he does not at that moment have, whereas the Director of the Old People's Home, telling what Meursault knows is a blatant lie about his mother's wish for a religious burial, incarnates the essence of bourgeois hypocrisy. Time and again, in the scenes with the examining magistrate and in the court, Meursault is given the opportunity of regretting his act, making a show of repentance, and preparing the judge and jury to consider him as an honest but weak-willed young man led astray by evil companions. At times, this honesty even worries those who have to deal with him, and the examining magistrate, after having waved a crucifix in Meursault's face in an attempt to bully him into repentance, is clearly thrown off balance by his calm refusal to express belief in God. 'He plumped down in his chair indignantly. He said it was impossible, that all men believed in God, even those who turned their faces from him. That was his own absolute belief, and if he were ever made to call it into doubt, his life would no longer have any meaning. "Do you want my life to lose all meaning?" he shouted at me. In my view, this was none of my business and I told him so.' Meursault's lack of illusions about human nature and the human heart is absolute. When his lawyer asks him if he had suffered at his mother's funeral, he receives the surprising reply that 'Certainly, I was fond of mother, but that didn't mean anything. All normal people had more or less wished for the death of their loved ones.' It is this refusal to disguise what he feels and thinks in hypocritical phrases that leads to Meursault's condemnation, for Camus's account of the trial leaves little doubt that a few well-judged tears about his poor mother would easily have secured a verdict of homicide or self-defence. L'Etranger is, in this respect, almost as much a novel of social criticism as the story of a martyr to the absurd or of the conflict between pagan and Christian values.

Most critics agree that Camus had few powers of invention as far as the plot of his novels was concerned, and he undoubtedly drew heavily on his own experience as a reporter for L'Alger-Républicain in the description of the trial scenes in L'Etranger. According to the authors of the long obituary

41

notice in *Paris-Match*, even the basic plot of *L'Etranger* had been given to him by a *fait-divers* which he had had to describe in his law reports. It is certain from the other articles which he wrote in *L'Alger-Républicain* that he was already concerned as a young man with the problems presented by the legal machinery of his country—it was a problem which he later treated in much greater length in his *Réflexions sur la Guillotine*—and the temptation to bring this concern into *L'Etranger* was clearly a considerable one. As far as the plot of *L'Etranger* is concerned it is a very good thing that he did so, since he thereby forestalled an important minor objection. The description given of Meursault's shooting of the Arab strongly suggests that he fired under the illusion that he was being attacked. He had seen the Arab use a knife on his friend Raymond earlier on the same day, and although he shoots in the haze produced by the sun and heat, it is the flash of the blade in the sun which causes him to screw up his eyes in pain and squeeze the trigger with what is almost a reflex action. Meursault himself, it might be argued, could not base his defence on the idea that he had fired in self-protection, since this would have demanded that he affirm as true events of which he was not absolutely sure. Any competent lawyer would, however, surely have based his whole case on the notion of self-defence, and would have stuck to it in spite of all the arguments about Meursault's character brought forward by the prosecution. Camus's point is, however, that Meursault's lawyer is not a very good one; that he followed the time-honoured but fatuous custom of arguing about the character of the accused rather than about the crime he had committed; and that he thereby missed the vital piece of evidence that was right under his nose. This is well brought out in the two short sentences in which Meursault both resumes the speech for the defence and indicates the real reason why he is condemned. 'My lawyer made a rapid plea of provocation and then, like the Counsel for the Prosecution, he too began to talk about my soul. But he seemed to me to have much less talent than his learnèd friend.' Meursault is condemned not only because he will not play the game and lie about his feelings, but also, like so many other men who have been sentenced to death, because his lawyer was not as clever as he might have been.

42

There are, however, other criticisms which have been made of *L'Etranger* and which are more valid than the objection that Camus weighs the balance too heavily against Meursault in the trial scene. One is that, although Meursault's honesty is admirable when contrasted with the hypocrisy of bourgeois society, he is nothing but a poor fool in his relationship with Raymond. He kills an Arab whom Raymond wanted to get rid of anyway, and does so after he has already given the police a very powerful weapon to use against him by telling lies to help Raymond out of a difficulty. This is a justified criticism and one which shows how Camus fell victim to that Romantic dislike of bourgeois society which leads to preferring pimps to judges. Another and more serious objection is that Camus had tried to do too much in *L'Etranger*. What John Cruickshank refers to as his 'complicated attempt to appear uncomplicated' led him to try to be Hemingway and Heidegger, Kafka and Valéry, all within the space of a fairly short novel. In particular, it might be argued that the frequency with which Meursault's character was misinterpreted by the critics indicates a failure on Camus's part to make his intentions entirely clear rather than a systematic incompetence on theirs.

In *L'Etranger* Camus was trying to illustrate two apparently contradictory ideas. The first, expressed in *Le Mythe de Sisyphe*, is that human life will be even more worth living because it has no meaning. The second is that a person who is apparently lacking in self-awareness can nevertheless be a conscious representative of a valid attitude towards life. It requires a very careful reading and interpretation of the text to see through Meursault's apparently complete indifference to life and unawareness of what is happening and perceive the truly exemplary and conscious character beneath. The first impression that Meursault gives is that of a man who believes in none of the things which normally give significance to life: family affection, love, ambition, friendship, even deliberate pleasure-seeking have no meaning for him. When he has a free Sunday, he spends it wandering aimlessly about in his small flat, eating his meal without bread because he cannot be bothered to go down and buy any, and feeling glad when night comes and he can go to bed again. His failure to show enthusiasm for anything almost loses him the sympathy which so tolerant a person inevitably attracts, and it is not until one reads the book for a second time—guided, perhaps, by the ideas of *Le Mythe de Sisyphe* or Camus's statements in his preface—that the 'real' meaning of Meursault's character becomes apparent. Similarly, Camus takes pains to show, by a prose style that systematically avoids causal expressions like 'because' and 'since', how the world appears to a man who has ceased to regard it as meaningful. Consequently, he can only afford brief indications that Meursault does know what it is all about after all. Camus certainly had every right to present his readers with a book that needs to be looked at more than once if its true meaning is to be understood. Like Gide, he might well say: 'Hard luck on the lazy reader. I want readers of a different sort.' Nevertheless, the reaction of the early critics who saw in *L'Etranger* not an expression of pagan happiness but a reflection of European mid-twentieth-century despair is fully understandable. Altogether, one might doubt whether Camus was wholly successful in presenting his two paradoxes to a mind not prepared for them by a reading of *Noces* or *L'Envers et l'Endroit*.

These objections are less valid, however, if one tries to judge *L'Etranger* as a work of art rather than as a philosophical novel. Like all Camus's novels, it keeps the reader's attention from beginning to end, and any objections which he may feel to the ideas expressed do not destroy his pleasure in a well-told tale. Camus holds the balance very skilfully between the style which he uses to express the disconnected nature of Meursault's experience, and his own, more colourful prose which is introduced to highlight certain passages. He does this again with even greater effect in *La Peste*, and much of the value of both novels comes from the variations of tone and tempo introduced by the contrast between a lyrical and highly coloured style and a mode of writing deliberately adopted because of its suitability to a particular subject. Camus is fully in control of all the material which he uses in *L'Etranger*, and what he called the 'slightly ironical affection which the artist has the right to feel towards the characters he has created' prevents him from spoiling the novel by over-emphasising the exemplary quality of his hero. When Meursault connives in Raymond's brutal treatment of his Arab mistress, we share the temporary revulsion which put Marie off her lunch, and although Camus is certainly on Meursault's side for most of the novel he is sufficiently detached to see the limitations of the attitude Meursault represents.

It is largely because of this detachment that the reader has the illusion of Meursault's existing as a character independent of his creator. In *L'Etranger* Camus took one of his own moods—there are a number of references to them in the early essays—where the blinding light of the sun had shown him the 'absurd simplicity of the world', and developed it to its fullest extent. He did not, however, identify himself wholly with Meursault, and was consequently able to present him with the objectivity necessary to a classical work of art. His own personal experiences are indeed there, but they have been refined and transmuted into a pure essence which they could never have achieved in real life. In his later essay, *L'Homme révolté*, Camus puts forward a theory of art which underlines this aspect of *L'Etranger* and gives the clue to the correct way of looking at his relationship with his characters. He argues that the main value of art, as far as the novel is concerned, lies in its ability to present lives 'with a coherence and unity that they can never have, but which are obvious to the observer'. In real life, where no event is ever final and definitive, Meursault might have kept up his attitude for a day or even a week. Then, as Camus himself undoubtedly did, he would have got bored and read a book. But as an imaginary character he can be given a unity and consistency which he could never have attained in real life. Camus described *L'Etranger* as a *récit* and not as a *roman*, but in this particular respect the ideas on the novel expressed in *L'Homme révolté* do apply to all his fiction. It is thanks to Camus's art that Meursault will always be the young man who buried his mother under the burning sun and who was executed because he did not weep. *L'Etranger*, in particular, has the quality of being able to fix in an unchanging light an attitude which, in reality, can only have been transient and impermanent. Like Camus's other novels it has a contained passion which, breaking through the style chosen for its suitability to the subject matter, gives these finished works of art their living quality.

The sensuality of the relationship between Meursault and Marie is, like the pleasure which Meursault takes in all aspects of physical existence, hinted at rather than analysed.

When he meets her in the swimming-pool, he climbs on to the raft where she is lying and allows his head to lean back on her stomach. 'I had the sun full in my eyes, all blue and gold, and I could feel Marie's stomach rising and falling gently under my head.' It is incidental touches like this which make the novel worth reading again and again, and which make Meursault's attitude and pleasures more understandable at each successive reading. Just before the end, for example, Camus answers the objection that it may after all have been a sign of inhumanity that Meursault did not weep at his mother's funeral. 'Then, just at the edge of daybreak, I heard a steamer's siren. People were starting on a voyage for worlds that had ceased to concern me for ever. Almost for the first time in many months, I thought of mother. I seemed to understand why, towards the end of her life, she had taken on a 'fiancé', and why she had played at starting everything all over again. There too, in that Home where lives were flickering out, evening must have been like a melancholy truce. So near to death, mother must have felt as if she had been freed and was ready to live everything all over again. No one, no one in the world had the right to weep over her.' If Camus had said openly that 'with his approaching death, Meursault accedes to that stage of wisdom where, like Œdipus, he judges that all is well'—and a remark in *Le Mythe de Sisyphe* shows that this was what he thought—the reader would have thrown the book down in irritation against such pomposity. Yet when Meursault thinks this as a result of the 'marvellous peace of this sleepbound night' which 'flooded into him like a tide', it seems so natural and so in keeping with his character that no such objections occur. It is because the limpid prose in *L'Etranger* contains so many hints of this kind while at the same time expressing a controlled and intense passion for life that the book remains fresh and vivid at each re-reading. From this point of view, the objection that Camus tried to do too much in *L'Etranger* ceases to be valid. It is the characteristic of truly classical works of art not to reveal all their secrets at the first reading, and the complexity which the apparently very simple technique of *L'Etranger* disguises is a constant invitation to the intelligent reader to renew and increase the pleasure which the novel first gave him.

The value of *L'Etranger* as an example of the way in which
style can be used to express ideas is not immediately apparent
to English readers. To hear Camus himself reading passages
from it—there is an excellent commercial recording of the
trial scene—is perhaps the best way of realising how successful
he is in reproducing that 'weariness tinged with amazement'
that he gave in *Le Mythe de Sisyphe* as one of the first intui-
tions of the absurd. The style of the opening sections has
been much admired by writers of the 'New Realism' school
of fiction in France, and it is certain that there are few texts
which better bring out the appearance which objects assume
when the mind throws off its habit of seeing them as part of
a coherent pattern. Camus's use of the perfect tense in
L'Etranger in order to convey the arbitrary and disconnected
nature of events has been excellently analysed by John
Cruickshank, and there is little to be added to his discussion.
It should perhaps be noted, however, how Camus's use of the
passé composé indicates the limited nature of the debt which
he owed to Hemingway. He almost certainly read Hemingway
in French—probably M. E. Coindreau's 1933 translation of
The Sun also Rises—and the tense always used to put Hemingway's descriptive prose into French is the past definite. The
decision to use the *passé composé* was certainly his own, and
the limpidity of his prose in *L'Etranger* is more an inheritance
from the French classical tradition—Sartre compared *L'Etranger* to a *conte* by Voltaire—than the result of imitating
American models.

One of the most interesting problems which future critics
who have access to Camus's unpublished notebooks and
manuscripts will be able to consider is this: when and how
did the moment occur when Camus saw how to transform
the early and apparently rather immature novel *La Mort
Heureuse* into the perfectly finished work of art which
became *L'Etranger*? The description which Mme Germaine
Brée gives of this early, unpublished novel in her *Camus* is
that it was almost completely lacking in form and had the
rambling, undecided quality of a novel by a young man who
had not yet learned to discipline his writing. The story of
Mersault, the white-collar worker in Algiers who kills a
certain Zagreus, a figure 'symbolising the forces of the
physical universe', and then discovers how to 'measure fully

the values present at every moment of living', seems to have nothing of the balance and economy of *L'Etranger*. From the very clear description given by Mme Brée, it is obvious that Camus intended the work to be a kind of *summa*, in which the ideas of *Noces*, *L'Envers et l'Endroit*, and *L'Etranger* were all fused together. The question of how and why he decided to present his ideas separately, in the medium of the short novel and the essay, will be a most fascinating one to consider.

Artistically, Camus made a very good decision in breaking up his early work in such a way that he produced shorter, more accessible and admirably controlled books like *L'Etranger*, *Noces*, and *Le Mythe de Sisyphe*. The understanding of his different ideas is in no way made more difficult by the fact that they are expressed in different books. He remarked himself in 1952 that: 'In some writers, it seems to me that their works form a whole in which each of them is to be understood in relation to the others, and in which they are all interdependent.' This is true not only of the work of his early period—that is to say, that written and published before 1945 —but also of that which came later. However different they may appear on first reading, all Camus's works do form a consistent, rational whole. In a world in which no values are given in advance, and where at any moment man may find himself overwhelmed by the absurd, there is no reason for despair and no need to fly from a meaningless universe into the arms of an incomprehensible god. When the chaplain asks Meursault to think of all the criminals who, in the condemned cell, have seen the Divine Face appear on its walls, Meursault replies that, in truth, he had looked for a face in them. 'But this face had the colour of the sun and the flame of desire. It was the face of Marie.' In Camus's early work, it is the 'colour of the sun and the flame of desire' which preserve him from a despair which might find its physical expression in suicide or its intellectual expression in the acceptance of religious faith. In his later work, it is his intense awareness of the importance of every individual life which causes him to reject any argument justifying the sacrifice of men who are alive to-day in order to bring about a possibly perfect society of the future.

Chapter Four

THE THEORY OF THE ABSURD

A READING of *L'Etranger* is the best introduction to *Le Mythe de Sisyphe* for two reasons. The novel communicates the 'feeling of the absurd', and contains the most convincing evidence which Camus presents to support the basic presuppositions of the essay. In his outburst to the chaplain, Meursault speaks of the 'dark wind' which, blowing through the whole of his life, had obliterated all present, past and future significance. The fact that he knew that he was going to die made everything pointless in Meursault's eyes. Similarly, in the opening passages of *Le Mythe de Sisyphe*, it is in the awareness of our own mortality that Camus finds the best proof of the absurd when he writes that 'no morality and no effort can be justified *a priori* in face of the bloodstained mathematical certainties which dominate the human lot'. All that we need to do is count, suggests Camus, and we have the certainty that we shall one day die. Meursault's thoughts as he lies in his prison cell also introduce, in an uncomplicated way which suits his character, the answer which Camus finally offers to the problem of the absurd in the second part of *Le Mythe de Sisyphe*. 'Basically,' thinks Meursault, 'I knew that it didn't matter whether one dies at thirty or at seventy since, naturally, in both cases other men and women will live on for thousands of years. Nothing, in short, was clearer than this. It was still I who was going to die, now or in twenty years' time. At this point I was rather troubled in my reasoning by the terrible leap of joy which I felt at the thought of another twenty years of life.' 'Let me express it even more simply,' writes Camus in *Le Mythe de Sisyphe*. 'The only obstacle, the only deficiency to be made good, is constituted by premature death.' Life is the only value, and Meursault knew it in his instinctive leap of joy.

49

Le Mythe de Sisyphe presents, in a more intellectualised form, the same feelings, arguments and conclusions that Camus had already expressed in *L'Envers et l'Endroit* and *Noces*. In saying that it was 'directed against existentialist thinkers' Camus was drawing attention to the fact that its main purpose was to condemn the way in which these thinkers introduced hope and transcendence—particularly the Christian hope of an eternal life—into a world in which there were no answers and death was final. Camus's first major philosophical essay was an attempt to express, in a discussion of the thinkers whom he had himself found interesting and who were becoming fashionable in French intellectual circles, the fruits of his North African inheritance. It represents, in the development of his thought, the high-water mark of his meditation on man as an individual. After 1942 it was with man as a member of society, faced with moral and social duties and responsibilities, that he was concerned in most of his literary work.

Possibly in order to disguise the fact that he is presenting an intensely personal attitude to a particular experience, Camus puts forward the argument of *Le Mythe de Sisyphe* in a rather formalised way. He begins by enumerating the various ways in which the absurd manifests itself: our train of thought may be broken, our companion may ask us what we are thinking of, and, suddenly conscious that our mind was completely empty, we are aware of 'this singular state of mind where absence becomes eloquent . . .' which may be the first revelation of the absurd. Suddenly, in the midst of the normal monotony of life, we stop to ask why and our existence becomes 'a weariness tinged with amazement'. The world shows itself bleak, hostile and unknowable and we do not recognise ourselves in the looking-glass. Above all, we are suddenly aware of our own mortality and it is this consciousness of inevitable death is the most overpowering emotional evidence of the absurd. An examination of the intellectual manifestations of the absurd, however, reveals more clearly its true nature. We can never satisfy our longing for absolute knowledge, for science can do no more in the way of explaining the world than enumerate phenomena and describe them by images. By way of illustration, Camus quotes the example of the modern physicist who tries to explain matter in terms of

50

the electronic theory, but is finally obliged to admit that no real and rational explanation can be given. It is from the clash between our desire for complete explanation and the essential opacity of the world that the absurd is born. But this is a new piece of evidence, and begins a fresh stage in the analysis of the absurd.

To say that the world itself is absurd is to anticipate and to affirm something which no argument can as yet justify. In itself, the world can be neither absurd nor reasonable, since it is only man's mind which introduces the concept of reason by which, since it does not conform to it, the world can be judged absurd. The absurd can occur only when two elements are present—the desire of the human mind that the world should be explicable in human terms, and the fact that the world is not thus explicable. 'What is absurd,' writes Camus, 'is the clash between its irrationality and the desperate hunger for clarity which cries out in man's deepest soul. The absurd depends as much upon man as upon the world. For the time being, it is their only link.' The absurd, like the Cartesian *cogito*, is the first result of thinking about the world and about ourselves. It results from the conflict between our awareness of death and our desire for life, from the clash between our demand for explanation and the essential mystery of all existence. In the present age, when rationalism has so often been shown to be an inadequate principle of explanation, this experience of the world has been widely shared. What, asks Camus, has been the reaction of thinkers towards it, and how have they replied to the first question which, in his view, it poses: if life has no meaning, ought we to commit suicide? Have Dostoievski, Kierkegaard, Kafka, Chestov, Husserl and Jaspers reached any valid conclusions as to the attitude to be adopted towards the absurd? A review of the solutions which their philosophies offer to the problem is the third stage in the argument which leads Camus towards his answer.

None of them, he immediately perceives, has been faithful to it and maintained it in its true position as the *unique donnée*. If none commits suicide, thus removing its original cause, which was the intrusion of the human mind, all find some other way of destroying it. All become reconciled to the irrationality of the world and consent to see man's demand for the reasonable refused and his intellect humiliated. All take the rationally unjustifiable leap which enables them to transcend the antinomy between man and the world, and destroy the real tension of the absurd. Jaspers and Kierkegaard deify the absurd, Chestov identifies it with God, and all three thinkers, whatever their other differences, unite in worshipping the incomprehensible because of its mystery. Husserl and the phenomenologists illogically find absolute value in individual things, and thus restore the principle of explanation whose absence was at the very origin of the absurd. Camus refuses to follow these thinkers in their unjustifiable leap into reconciliation. It is because the universe is not explicable in human terms that the absurd exists. To offer, as a solution to the problem which it creates, an explanation of the universe which is by definition beyond the reach of human reason is unjustly to dismiss the absurd by altering the nature of the problem. 'For the absurd mind,' writes Camus in one of the phrases whose clarity and intensity mark him out as a writer among philosophers, 'reason is useless and there is nothing beyond reason.' Camus adopts, on the plane of knowledge, the same refusal to accept that which is beyond his understanding as he will assume later towards the problem of suffering. He is already *l'homme révolté*, the rebel who justifies man and refuses an inhuman world.

The same intellectual rigour which caused Camus to criticise irrational evasions of the absurd also brings him to reject physical suicide. Human destiny, with all its contradictions, must be accepted as it is and life must be lived in accordance with this acceptance. 'Now man will not live out his destiny, knowing it to be absurd, unless he does everything to keep present in his mind the absurdity which his consciousness has revealed. To deny one of the terms of this opposition is to escape from it. . . . Living consists of keeping the absurd alive. Keeping it alive is essentially a question of looking at it. Unlike Eurydice, the absurd dies only when one looks away.' In his first important piece of philosophical writing, Camus exalts the value of consciousness which is one of the oldest parts of the humanist tradition. The final conclusions which he reaches also link it with the hedonism of *Noces* and with Meursault's longing for another thirty years of life.

The absurd frees man from all feeling of responsibility, annihilates the future and leaves only one certainty: the sensation of being alive. The question is now not to live well in a moral sense—for the absence of moral values renders this meaningless—but *vivre le plus*, replace the quality of experiences by their quantity. In the second part of *Le Mythe de Sisyphe*, Camus describes four men—the actor, the seducer, the conqueror and the artist—who illustrate by the very nature of their lives the 'passion to exhaust everything which is given'. Each of them, to put it more crudely, tries to get the most out of life while he can. Neither the Don Juan by the women he seduces, the conqueror by the countries he subdues, the actor by the rôles he incarnates, nor the artist by the books he writes is hoping to solve problems or discover the truth. The artist who recognises that 'to create is to live twice', the actor who shares the life of each character he represents, the seducer who finds the same joy in each new woman, the conqueror who knows that action is useless but fascinating, are all laying their bets on the certainty of happiness in this life and nothing afterwards. Yet each of them, Camus insists—and here the essay takes up a theme which was only implicit in the novel—is an absurd hero because he is conscious of the fact that his activity is completely useless. Each of them has rejected the illusion of a future life and has received in exchange the gift of liberty. 'Outside the sole fatality of death, everything, joy or happiness, is liberty. A world remains in which man is the only master. What held him back was the illusion of another world. The destiny of his thought is now no longer to deny itself but to rebound in images.' In the concluding passage, Camus finally abandons the tone of abstract philosophising which has been growing less marked all the way along and gives an essentially lyrical description of Sisyphus, the legendary hero who, for him, incarnates all the virtues of the absurd.

The different versions which exist of the myth of Sisyphus all show him as prepared to rebel against the Gods, cheating them if necessary, if only by so doing he can retain the priceless gift of continued physical life. Each version shows his 'scorn for the Gods, his hatred of death and his passion for life' which he retains and which make him heroic even in his punishment. In Camus's view, Sisyphus is the ideal of the 'absurd man' because he knows his task is futile. If he were comforted by the thought that one day the stone might stay on the top of the hill and that he might thus be freed from his torment, then he would cease to be admirable. As it is, however, he has no hope of any such deliverance, and remains satisfied with the pure physical effort needed to push the stone to the top of the hill. In the same way that every individual object which he saw or felt constituted a wholly satisfying experience for Meursault, so, for Sisyphus, 'each of the specks on the stone, each glint of light on the surface of this mountain shrouded in night, is a universe in itself. The fight towards the summit is itself sufficient to satisfy the heart of man. We must think of Sisyphus as happy.' Far from inviting his readers to a *delectatio morosa* in their own hopeless condition, Camus showed, in 1943, that the absurdity of the world was, paradoxically enough, an invitation to happiness.

It was here that his originality lay. In making the absurd the centre of his preoccupation he was dealing with a problem which had been popularised by thinkers before being made acute by everyday life. As early as 1926 André Malraux had dealt quite fully with it in *La Tentation de l'Occident* and, in 1928, had made of Garine, the hero of *Les Conquérants*, a man who rejected normal society because of its absurdity in his eyes. In 1938 Sartre's *La Nausée* had been almost entirely devoted to the expression of the absurdity of all existence. The thinkers whom Camus discussed in *Le Mythe de Sisyphe* were well-known, at least in philosophical circles, before the war. Camus neither invented the absurd nor introduced it into France. Wishing to express his own views on life in a fashionable manner he chose to write a philosophical novel and an essay on the absurd. By studying the way in which other writers on the absurd abandon their revolt and become reconciled, he confirmed his own instinctive rejection of any value that would deprive his life of its full tragic intensity. He used the example of other thinkers, as he was to do in *L'Homme révolté*, in order to make his own ideas stand out more clearly by contrast. 'One finds one's way,' he writes, describing his own technique, 'by discovering the paths which lead away from it.' The writers examined in *Le Mythe de Sisyphe* are all used to show how difficult it is to maintain the tension of refusal demanded by the absurd. As far as Camus's own thought was concerned there was nothing essentially new in *Le Mythe de Sisyphe*. It was a coincidence between the ideas which Camus had already expressed in his early lyrical essays and the climate of opinion in the early nineteen-forties that made Claude Mauriac describe *Le Mythe de Sisyphe*, in retrospect, as 'a revelation and the putting into order of the spiritual confusion in which, like most young men of my age, I then found myself'. Mauriac was not alone in expressing such a high opinion of *Le Mythe de Sisyphe*. For Daniel-Rops it was 'the profoundest evidence yet offered of the problem of our time', and Roger Stéphane, writing in 1947, compared it, 'with a due sense of proportion', to the *Discours de la Méthode*. The main reason for these inflated judgments undoubtedly lies in the atmosphere in which the book was first published. Then, the collapse of the whole pre-war world had confirmed that 'impossibility of justifying moral values', which, for almost a century, had inspired a certain tradition of European thought. This is well illustrated by a remark which Claude-Edmonde Magny made when discussing Camus's work in 1945. The *'non-garantie des valeurs'* which *Le Mythe de Sisyphe* described was, she wrote, 'a philosophical shock compared to which the discovery in the eighteenth century of the plurality of worlds, in the nineteenth of the evolution of species, are as nothing. The Kantian critique has taken more than a century to attain the final development of its philosophical consequences. One must admit that it has succeeded with remarkable thoroughness.'

It is very salutary to go suddenly from the audience for which Camus wrote and which automatically accepted all his implicit assumptions to the very different atmosphere of contemporary English philosophy. It was in 1946 that Professor Ayer subjected Camus's early work to an analysis which revealed just how much *Le Mythe de Sisyphe* suffered from being the presentation of an emotional experience in supposedly rational and philosophical terms. It is when it is examined from a philosophically critical standpoint that the weaknesses of the 'essay on the absurd' are most apparent. To begin with, as Professor Ayer has pointed out, Camus's 'proof' of the absurdity of the world is most unsatisfying. For example, Camus uses a traditional argument from Aristotle in order to show the world's incomprehensibility. 'No one,' he writes, 'has given a more elegant proof of the mind's incapacity for distinguishing truth from falsehood. If I affirm that everything is true, I affirm the truth of the contradictory statement, and thus the falseness of my own original statement, for its contradiction implies that it cannot be true. If, on the other hand, I say that nothing is true, this also is wrong, for I cannot say that only the statement which contradicts my own is false without being obliged at the same time to admit the possibility that other statements may be true.' Professor Ayer wrote of this argument that, while it was an ingenious piece of philosophical reasoning, it proved nothing at all about the absurdity of the world. 'All that it proves,' he wrote, 'is that the terms of truth and falsehood cannot be significantly applied to the totality of all propositions. . . .' He argued that in order for Camus's requirements for a 'rational' world to be satisfied, matters of fact would have to be logically necessary. Camus, in making this demand, is expressing what modern English philosophers would call 'a pointless lament' and asking for the impossible. Similarly, if one examines the illustration taken from modern physics, it simply reveals that Camus is requiring the world to be intelligible in the terms of the absolute necessities of nineteenth-century mechanistic physics. The more personal example of the man finding his train of thought interrupted proves merely that we are so physiologically and psychologically constituted that our conscious mind is not always working. To require that it should be is once again to put forward a theory of the nature of consciousness which does not correspond to the facts. In *Le Mythe de Sisyphe*, Camus is asking for the philosophically impossible, and ensuring, by the extreme nature of the demands which he makes, that they can never be satisfied.

In the study already mentioned, John Cruickshank enlarged upon Professor Ayer's criticisms and pointed out how Camus loaded the dice against a rational explanation of the world by asking more of science and logic than they can reasonably be expected to provide. He also noted a 'disturbing lack of clarification of terms' in Camus's use of the word 'absurd' and a considerable ambiguity in the use of the word 'freedom' brought to light by a close analysis of the text. While these criticisms are justified, they are seen in better perspective if one remembers Camus's own insistence, throughout his essay, on the limited and provisional nature of the problems he is discussing. This is less the question of suicide, which is used principally to begin the essay in as startling a dramatic a way as possible, than that of the relationship between absurdity and religious faith. The question of physical suicide rapidly gives way, in the course of the essay, to what Camus calls philosophical suicide, the acceptance of the *credo quia absurdum* of Tertullian. In this respect, Camus's insistence that the absurd cannot legitimately be used as a springboard into religion is an extremely salutary one. The fact that reason cannot give a satisfactory reply to all questions is no excuse for abandoning it entirely and plunging into a rationally unjustifiable mystical explanation. Since science—or rather scientific philosophy—lost its nineteenth-century assurance and admitted that in many cases it could not be absolutely certain of the truth, religious thinkers have tended to proclaim that, 'reason being useless', man should therefore return to the true faith, accept authority, and worship God because he cannot understand the infinite mystery of the universe. It is almost the same idea which Camus convincingly refutes in *Le Mythe de Sisyphe*. Even though his premiss of the absurdity of the world may be highly personal and unproven, his attitude towards it is most consistent. Basically, it is the traditional Protestant cry of 'By what judgment can I judge but by mine own?' revived in the context of a new set of thinkers, and linked with a modest realisation that, although reason and individual judgment may be fallible, they are in fact all we have.

This is certainly a feature of Camus's thought most appreciated by those already prejudiced in favour of scepticism, and hostile to the irrational paradoxes of religion. Nevertheless, it is one which he himself emphasised when he remarked that *Le Mythe de Sisyphe* was directed against existentialist philosophers. One of the best ways of looking at this essay is as a critique of certain tendencies in contemporary religious thought, a 'demystification' of the absurd, parallel to the denunciation of false rebels in *L'Homme révolté*. Professor Hanna notes this when he writes in his admirable study of Camus's ideas, *The Thought and Art of Albert Camus*, that: 'This critical attack by Camus is of great interest not only to those interested in existentialist philosophy, but also for the many who have seen in the conclusions of these thinkers the grounds for rejuvenating Christian theology.'[1] Although its

[1] See notes.

immediate popularity owed much to fashion and to a coincidence with the spirit of the times, *Le Mythe de Sisyphe* has a permanent value because the attitude which it criticises has often occurred in the history of Christian apologetics. Camus did not include Pascal among the authors studied in the book, but the criticism applies just as much to him as it does to Kierkegaard. So much is clear from an article which he wrote in 1944 and in which he discussed Pascal's awareness of the difference between a literal and a spiritual use of language. 'It is for this reason,' he wrote, 'that Pascal proposes not a solution but an attitude of submission. Submission to traditional language because it comes to us from God, humility before words as a way of discovering their true inspiration. We must choose between miracles and the absurd, there is no middle way. The choice Pascal made is sufficiently well known.'

Le Mythe de Sisyphe has other qualities which also compensate for the weakness which it reveals when subjected to an examination by precise-minded philosophers. It contains some very interesting literary criticism, particularly of Kafka, and some excellent poetical prose. The essay on Kafka, originally published separately and incorporated only in later editions of *Le Mythe de Sisyphe*, concentrates on *The Trial* and *The Castle*. In Camus's view these contain the same readiness to submit to the absurd and to hope for an incomprehensible salvation which is criticised in the main body of the essay. 'Kafka,' he writes, 'denies his God the qualities of moral greatness, clarity, goodness, consistency, but it is in order to throw himself more readily into his arms.' The whole of this section is the best reply yet written to those critics who, like Ronald Gray, praise Kafka for writing books likely to induce a due spirit of acceptance and humility in man, as well as being, in itself, a brilliant interpretation of Kafka's work.

In spite, however, of the value of its contents, *Le Mythe de Sisyphe* is most admirable for the prose style in which it is written. This varies from the terse, epigrammatic phrasing of 'for the absurd mind, reason is vain and there is nothing beyond reason,' and the 'life will be all the more fully lived in that it has no meaning,' through the occasional brilliant touches like the image of Prince Muichkine living 'in a perpetual present, shaded with smiles and with indifference' to the final lyrical evocation of the values implicit in the 'absurd man's' choice. In the passage on the Conqueror, Camus writes:

> '*Oui, l'homme est sa propre fin. Et il est sa seule fin. S'il veut être quelque chose, c'est dans cette vie. . . . Visages tendus, fraternité menacée, amitié si forte et si pudique des hommes entre eux, ce sont les vraies richesses parce qu'elles sont périssables. C'est au milieu d'elles que l'esprit sent le mieux ses pouvoirs et ses limites.*'

> 'Yes, man is his own end, and he is himself the only end to which he can aspire. If he wants to be something, it is in this life. . . . Tense faces, fraternity in danger, the shy strong friendship of men for men, these are true riches because they are mortal. It is in the midst of them that the mind feels best its limits and its powers.'

In *L'Etranger* and *Le Mythe de Sisyphe*, Camus is most completely and most convincingly the anti-Pascal, the author whose hero finds life so fully satisfying that he would be quite happy to spend the rest of it simply in one room. It is when reading *Le Mythe de Sisyphe* that one understands fully the reasons why Camus has so repeatedly stated that he is *not* an existentialist, since the existentialist attitude, as he describes it, is one which denies the competence of man to decide his own destiny.

If it is true, as Maurice Cranston suggested, that Camus's most consistent success was as a stylist rather than an artist, *Le Mythe de Sisyphe* and *L'Etranger* are the two works which best show this side of his achievement. There are inconsistencies in *L'Etranger* which prevent it from fully satisfying the intellectual as well as the aesthetic demands put upon it, and *Le Mythe de Sisyphe's* weaknesses make it something less than a perfect philosophical essay. Yet in both books Camus achieves triumph in the actual use of the French language by the consistency with which he uses a particular style to express his ideals. This is a fairly obvious feature of *L'Etranger*, but it is almost equally important in *Le Mythe de Sisyphe*. The idea of the absurd, such as Camus expresses it in this essay, is associated with a perpetual cult of tension and contrast, and it is this which is admirably brought out in the style which he uses. He speaks of the effort to '*soutenir le pari merveilleux et déchirant de l'absurde*', of living in '*un univers brûlant et glacé, transparent et limité, où rien n'est possible mais où tout est donné'*. In this world, existence is at one and the same time *'mensongère et éternelle'*, of infinite value precisely because it is finite in time. His style brings out the effort of remaining lucid and the tension of living in this world where consciousness is a perpetual defiance and effort of revolt, and where, paradoxically, happiness springs from despair. It is a world from which God is exiled, and where destiny is a human affair, *'qui doit être réglée entre les hommes'*. Camus's style enables him to express this revolt, and the love of man which results necessarily from it, without falling into any sentimentality. His early humanism, like his style, is virile, intense and proud. The *'univers farouche et limité de l'homme'* is brought unexpectedly to life in this philosophical essay through the creation of an autonomous world by a highly controlled and individual style.

There are few contemporary French writers who can rival Camus in their mastery of lyrical and semi-rhetorical prose. One of these is Henry de Montherlant, whom Camus greatly admired and who was one of the first to recognise his merit. When *Noces* was first published, Montherlant wrote Camus an enthusiastic private letter congratulating him on the excellence of his prose. The early Camus has much in common with Montherlant, both in his style and in his attempt to construct a personal ethic in the midst of a universal nihilism. Where he differs from him, however, is in the attempt which he made to go beyond nihilism and to criticise its effects. If this sometimes led him, as in *L'Homme révolté*, to write prose inferior both to that of *Le Mythe de Sisyphe* and to that of Montherlant's essays, it nevertheless makes him a more interesting and attractive writer. Camus may, as Angus Wilson suggested, have been going against his own natural talent in talking about men rather than about nature, but it was his decision to do so that enabled him to renew himself as an artist after *Le Mythe de Sisyphe*. He always insisted that the essay on the absurd was not to be looked upon as recommending a universal attitude, and that it was simply an objective and provisional statement of what conclusions could be drawn from a particular starting-point. 'What did I do,' he later wrote, 'but reason on an idea which I found in the streets of my time?' *Le Mythe de Sisyphe*, unlike *L'Homme révolté*, is certainly not a didactic essay, but it is not a wholly impersonal one either. It resembles *L'Etranger* in being the result of Camus's ability to stand aside from his own feelings and look at them objectively, but it is nonetheless the expression of a very personal attitude. In spite of its defence of the value of consciousness, *Le Mythe de Sisyphe* is, like *L'Etranger*, a nihilistic book: there is no suggestion that any action can be either praised or blamed on moral grounds, that man can be held responsible for the consequences of his acts, no possibility that words like duty, self-sacrifice, charity or generosity can have any meaning. Camus's achievement is to have held up his nihilism for examination and to have used it to create works of art. His next two works, the plays *Caligula* and *Le Malentendu*, were to show that the need to escape from it was an urgent one.

Chapter Five

TWO PLAYS

ONE of the first results of the success of *Le Mythe de Sisyphe*
and *L'Etranger* was the opportunity which it gave Camus of
satisfying his greatest ambition: that of having his own plays
performed by first-class actors in a Parisian theatre. He had
written *Caligula* as early as 1938, and had originally intended
to play the leading part himself in the Théâtre de l'Equipe.
Both for political and technical reasons, however, this play
was not finally produced until September 1945, after it had
already been made available in book form. Camus's first play
to be performed in Paris was *Le Malentendu*, written in 1942
and 1943 when Camus was living in and around Lyons. It
was his first literary work to be both conceived and written
outside North Africa, and its extreme pessimism can be
partly explained by the circumstances under which it was
written. The deep impression which the gloom and poverty
of a French industrial city made upon Camus can be gathered
from the remarks he made in 1947 when he wrote, in a preface
to the poetry of René Leynaud, that 'if Hell existed, it would
be like these grey, unending streets where everyone was
dressed in black'. He added to the natural gloom of the story
by setting it in Czechoslovakia, a country of which he had
kept unhappy memories after the visit described in *L'Envers
et l'Endroit*, and it is significant that the memory of North
Africa returns only in the form of an impossible dream. Yet
the metaphysical background to *Le Malentendu* is very similar
to that of *L'Etranger*, for its basic plot is referred to in the
second part of the novel. What is different is the geographical
atmosphere which dominates throughout, and which brings out
the extreme pessimism hidden by the sunlight of *L'Etranger*.
    In an old newspaper cutting which had slipped between

the mattress and the wooden bed in his cell, Meursault finds the description of a story which had taken place in Czecho-slovakia. A man had left his native village, made his fortune and married, and returned twenty-five years later to the village where his mother and sister kept an inn. They did not recognise him, and, as a joke, he asked them to give him a room without telling them who he was. That night his mother and sister murdered him in order to rob him—as they did all travellers—and threw his body into the river. His wife came to look for him next morning and revealed who he was, with the result that both his mother and sister killed them-selves. Meursault found the story unbelievable from one point of view but, from another, quite natural. He comments, in his matter-of-fact way, that 'in any case, I thought the traveller rather deserved what had happened, and that one must never fool around'. Something of Meursault's criticism recurs in several of the remarks which Camus made both before and after the first night of his play, in which he also tried to bring its apparent pessimism more into line with his new moral concerns. Nevertheless, his later insistence that the play is best read as a warning against certain romantic illusions in no way alters the extreme pessimism of *Le Malentendu*. At first reading it seems clearly intended as an illustration of that darker side of the absurd at whose existence Camus had hinted in *L'Envers et l'Endroit*.

This is brought out by the principal difference between the story read by Meursault and the actual plot of *Le Malentendu*. The reason why the traveller, Jan, does not reveal his identity is that he wishes to be recognised and find his home. He tells his wife: 'One cannot always remain an outsider; a man needs happiness, it is true, but he also needs to find his place in the world.' Not everyone can adopt the attitude of Meursault and remain an outsider, indifferent to the world. But Jan's desire to be recognised, his search for a universe in which he will be at home, ends as tragically as did Meursault's attempt to remain uncommitted and uninvolved in society. The tea which his sister Martha brings him, and which he takes for the welcome to the prodigal son, has been drugged in order that his mother and sister may more easily murder him and carry his body to the river. Thus a wholly natural desire for a son to be recognised by his mother leads to the tragic ending of *Le Malentendu*. The rather abstract thesis of the general metaphysical absurdity of the world which informs *Le Mythe de Sisyphe* is here replaced by an insistence on the malevolent absurdity of fate.

Camus's treatment of the anecdote seems deliberately aimed at emphasising the impossibility of escaping this malevolence, for he makes the guilty as well as the innocent suffer for the world's absurdity. Martha's ambition in murdering the travellers who came to her inn was to obtain enough money to escape to a country in the South, and live in 'that other country where summer crushes everything, where the winter rains drown the towns and where, at last, things are what they really are'. When Jan's wife Maria reveals to Martha what she has done, Martha cries out in revolt against the cruelty of the universe in which such frustration of love and desire is inevitable, and in the natural order of things. 'We have been robbed and cheated, I tell you. What use is our great cry towards the sea, the awakening of our souls? It is empty mockery. Your husband has his reply now, that dreadful house where we shall be all packed tight one against another.' The reply which Jan has been seeking is that exile and separation are the truth of a world in which no one is ever recognised. 'Understand that your suffering will never equal the injustice done to man,' Martha cries out before going to drown herself, rejoicing that Maria who had been happy should have to choose between 'the unfeeling happiness of the stones and the sticky bed where we are waiting for you'. In *Le Malentendu*, there is no gleam of consolation, and the solution to the absurdity of the world suggested in the praise of the physical life in *Noces*, *Le Mythe de Sisyphe* and *L'Etranger* is deliberately shown to be impossible. Here Camus seems to admit how personal the reply proposed to the absurd in *Le Mythe de Sisyphe* inevitably is. To those who are not born in a country of the sun there is no consolation. Happiness becomes a matter of luck, a question of geography or economic opportunity. In *Le Malentendu* the absurd reveals an aspect absent from *Le Mythe de Sisyphe* and the demand for an escape from it is stronger.

The metaphysical pessimism which had formed the background to happiness in *Le Mythe de Sisyphe* is given a particularly forceful expression in *Le Malentendu* by a crude but striking use of symbolism. Twice in the play characters call out for a reply to their questions. Alone in his room in the inn Jan seeks to escape from the haunting terror of absolute loneliness, 'the fear that there is no reply'. The only answer when he rings a bell is an old servant who appears and remains silent. At the end of the play this servant comes on to the stage again, in answer to Maria's passionate appeal to God to come to her help. 'Oh, my God!' she cries out, 'I cannot live in this desert! It is to You that I shall speak and I shall find my words. . . . For it is unto You that I commit myself. Have pity upon me, O Lord, and turn your face towards me! Hear me O Lord, and stretch out your hand to me! Have pity for those who love and who are separated.' The old servant pronounces one word: 'Non'. In Le Mythe de Sisyphe this silence and indifference—which are the only characteristics of God throughout Camus's work—did not matter. Here, when the world in question is a profoundly unhappy one, they do. The expression which Camus gives to the absurd varies from optimism to pessimism in the degree to which his memory of North Africa is strong or weak. This memory is never absent, but it can never be a constant source of consolation when the problem of evil and suffering dominates. In this respect, Le Malentendu forms an essential part of the expression which Camus gave in his early work to the different aspects of the absurd. Theatrically, however, it is possibly Camus's least successful work, rivalled in this only by L'Etat de Siège, a play of a very different type and a failure for very different reasons.

Le Malentendu was first performed in June 1944 at the Théâtre des Mathurins, and returned to the stage in a more friendly political atmosphere, shortly after the Liberation, in October of the same year. Although the critical notices of the October production were much more favourable than the first ones had been—Camus was now known to have been active in the Resistance movement—it would be wrong to consider the play as having been a theatrical success. Camus himself remarked that he considered it to have been a failure for the simple reason that everybody he met kept asking him what it meant. If they needed to ask, he argued, then the play itself was not clear, and he had not been successful as a playwright. Le Malentendu was taken off after only forty performances, and has not been professionally staged in Paris since 1944. The reasons for its lack of success are not difficult to find. The situation is too static and too obviously designed to illustrate the absurd ever to convince the unconverted spectator. The conversations between Jan and Martha are far too long, and his hesitation in drinking his tea created a destructively comic effect when the play was first produced. The slowness of movement in *Le Malentendu* also gave the more actively minded spectators the time to wonder why nobody had ever noticed the disappearance of former travellers. The play would have been more effective if reduced in length, but even then the basic objection that it presents a highly improbable situation as an illustration for a supposedly general truth would not have been overcome. It must be said in its defence, however, that the text still reads very well and that the purity of Camus's style gives the play considerable literary if not dramatic value. The new version, published in 1958, omits a number of the longer speeches and simplifies some of the more complicated and ambitious ones. The changes do not, however, either affect the basic construction of the play or resolve the contradiction between what *Le Malentendu* seems to mean and what Camus said it meant.

Even before the first performance had taken place, Camus was reported as saying that 'the apparent pessimism of the play hides a deeper optimism by which man, freed from his illusions and his gods, can find in action and revolt the only liberty which he can bear'. Later on in the same year, before the second production of *Le Malentendu* was given in October, Camus enlarged upon these remarks and seemed to offer his play simply as warning against trusting the world too far. Developing the remarks which he put into Meursault's mouth and repeating Maria's warning to her husband that 'When one wants to be recognised, one gives one's name,' he stated: 'Finally, it comes down to saying that everything would have been different if the son had said: "It's me, this is my name." It comes down to saying that in an unjust and indifferent world, man can still achieve his own salvation and that of other people by the use of the simplest sincerity and the most precise language.'

It is noticeable, however, that, apart from the remark which Maria made and which is quoted above, there is little in the text of the play to support this interpretation.

It is impossible to believe that Camus originally meant Martha's last speech to be interpreted as a warning against excessive optimism and over-confidence, or that he originally wrote the play with any idea in mind other than that of expressing a mood of acute pessimism. For the most laudable of motives—by 1944 he was intensely and publicly involved in politics—he asked his readers to interpret a work written and conceived in one mood in terms of new and very different ideas. Like *Caligula*, which Camus also tried to present as a highly 'moral' play, *Le Malentendu* presents an interesting example of the relationship which Camus considered necessary, in 1944 and 1945, between the artist and his time. Later on in his career he was to deal with this problem at some length, and formulate an impassioned defence of the freedom of the artist to deal with any subject that pleased him without considering the moral or political implications of his work. At the end of the second world war, however, he was less inclined to separate art from political morality, and even tried to give his own plays moral connotations quite alien to their original atmosphere.

This appears even more clearly from the remarks which he made about *Caligula* when it was first performed in 1945. Far from being an 'apostle of the absurd', a person horribly right because things were horribly wrong, a Meursault uncharacteristically determined that others should share his lucid awareness of the world's absurdity, Caligula, it seemed, was rather an illustration of the dangers involved in going too far in acting out the consequences of living in a world without values. However, Camus had at least prepared the reader for something like this interpretation by the emphasis which he laid on the character of Cherea, who seems to express more of Camus's ideas than Caligula himself. *Caligula*, the first of Camus's imaginative works to be directly concerned with the problem of the absurd—as Germaine Brée has shown, the play was written, in a fairly complete form, in 1938[1]—is also the first in which the possibility is expressed, within the work itself, of a valid solution to these problems. Whether the play is best understood in the light of the didactic interpretation which Camus tried to give it in 1945 is, however, a question that needs some discussion.

[1] See notes.

Caligula was produced at the Théâtre Hébertot on September 26th, 1945 and ran for over two hundred performances. It was the first play in which the late Gérard Philipe was given the opportunity to show the full range of his talents, and his interpretation of the rôle of Caligula added much to the initial success of the play. At the time of writing, *Caligula* is the only one of Camus's plays to have been given more than one professional production. It was revived at the Théâtre Hébertot in 1950, with Michel Herbault in the part of Caligula, performed again at the Festival d'Angers in 1957 with Michel Auclair, and given a wholly new production, with an amended text and with Jean-Pierre Jorrise in the title rôle, to inaugurate Madame Elvire Popesco's Nouveau Théâtre de Paris in 1958. In spite of the fact that it does not quite maintain the high level of excitement of the first act, *Caligula* is by far the best of Camus's plays and fully deserves the success which it has always had in the theatre. It owes this not to an ingenious plot but to Camus's skilful use of the account given by Suetonius of the crimes committed by the fourth of the Caesars. He kept fairly close to Suetonius's account, particularly in the emphasis which he placed on Caligula's initial virtue and in the details of his crimes and excesses. It was from Suetonius, for example, that he took the scene where Caligula forces the poets to erase their inferior verses from their tablets with their tongues, and the equally effective one in which Caligula, having murdered a patrician whom he suspects of intending to poison him, discovers that what he suspected to be an antidote against poison was in fact an asthma remedy. He explained in an interview given on the radio in 1958 that for him Caligula was the most intelligent of the twelve Caesars, and throughout the play it is the supposedly logical nature of Caligula's actions which is emphasised by those who understand him best. He is shown from the very beginning as a man who becomes cruel through an excess of sensitivity rather than through a lack of it, and whose worst crimes are committed in the cause of truth.

Caligula, the perfect emperor, has disappeared from his palace after the death of his sister—and mistress—Drusilla. On his return he confides to his friend Helicon that he has been searching for the moon, trying to obtain the impossible in order to calm the anguish into which his discovery of the truth about human condition has plunged him. This truth is, he tells Helicon, 'completely simple, completely clear, but difficult to discover and heavy to bear: men die and they are not happy'. Caligula, whose complete political liberty as Roman emperor allows him to pursue the passion for the absolute which now devours him, tries to transcend misery by the creation of 'a kingdom where the impossible is king'. His revolt aims at transforming the very nature of the world, and at destroying everything, even the distinction between good and evil. The discovery of misery has given him an imperious need of the poetically impossible—'of the moon, or of immortality, of something which is perhaps mad, but which is not of this world'. His desire is that the destruction of certainties around him will enable him to achieve this impossible ambition; he hopes that, finally, 'when all is laid flat, the impossible finally realised on this earth, the moon between my two hands, then, perhaps, I shall be transformed and the world with me—then perhaps men will not die and will be happy'.

It is a mad dream and one which the eye of common sense —personified in the play by the cowardly and selfish patricians—cannot either understand or appreciate. It is they, moreover, who suffer most from Caligula's attempt to enforce recognition of this new gospel of the absurd. When Caligula becomes, in the words of an English critic, 'the equivalent for Camus on the plane of metaphysics of what Undershaft is for Shaw on the plane of social ethics', it is the patricians, the representatives of an outworn humanism and of unimaginative middle-class morality, whom he principally attacks. It is Caligula's ambition that all shall be forced to recognise, through him, the absurdity of the world. He arbitrarily decrees famine and execution, rewards a slave guilty of theft with the gift of a fortune because he has remained silent under torture, lays down that the prize for civic virtue shall go to the citizen who has made the largest number of visits to the state brothels, attempts, as he says himself, to equal the gods in the sole medium in which human rivalry is possible, that of cruelty. Camus's task in *Caligula* lies in trying to convince the audience that Caligula is not simply a lunatic monster but a person who deserves sympathy and attention because of his suffering. He sets about this difficult task—and comes very near to success—by making all the likeable characters in the play sympathetic towards Caligula and by emphasising his inescapable unhappiness.

One of the principal changes which Camus made in the 1958 version of his play was to develop the character of Helicon, a slave who had been freed by Caligula and who had become his most loyal friend. He did so in order to bring out the social criticism which the play contains as well as to stress Caligula's ability to inspire confidence and loyalty. It is Helicon who is made to pronounce a violent speech against the patricians, and who does his best to protect Caligula against the conspiracy organised by Cherea. In an outburst which reflects Camus's own hatred for judges and for the self-satisfied bourgeoisie, he declares that Caligula's sufferings make him far worthier of sympathy than all those who are now trembling in their miserable sins and whom Cherea is trying to protect:

'Yes, I am serving a madman. But you, who are you serving? Virtue? I'll tell you what I think of it. I was born a slave. So I'll tell you, you who are an honest man, that I first learned to dance to the tune of virtue under the whip. Caius didn't preach to me. He freed me and took me into his palace. And it was there that I could watch you, all you honest men. And I saw that you had unpleasant faces and the weak, sickly, tasteless smell of people who had never suffered or risked anything. I saw them in their noble attitudes, but with avarice in their hearts, their faces mean and closed, their hands hiding themselves away so as not to give anything. You, judges? You offered virtue for sale, you dream of safety as a young girl dreams of love, you're going to die in terror without even knowing that you have lied all your life, and yet you take it upon yourselves to judge someone who has never counted his own suffering, and who daily bleeds with a thousand new wounds. . . .'

It is not only Helicon, the representative of the poor and the oppressed, whom Camus makes speak in Caligula's favour, but also Scipio, the person who incarnates all the rigour and intransigent honesty of youth. At a poetic contest it is Scipio who wins the prize with a poem about death which comes straight from the atmosphere of *Noces*:

'Quest for happiness which purifies the heart,
Sky where the sun streams down,
Wild irreplaceable rejoicing, ecstasy without hope.'

He is congratulated for knowing the true meaning of death in spite of his extreme youth, and later becomes a kind of 'disciple' of Caligula, giving proof to Cherea's remark that Caligula has at least the virtue of making people think. He leaves Rome to go 'far away to seek out the reasons for all this', and, one feels, possibly to discover some kind of salvation.

The next important character in the play after Caligula himself is, however, the philosopher Cherea, who is forced to abandon his preferred life of contemplation in order to fight against the absurd world which Caligula has brought into being. He, like Helicon and Scipio, understands and sympathises with Caligula but disagrees with his ideas to the extent of accepting to lead the conspiracy which finally kills him. He tells the patricians that Caligula 'transforms his philosophy into corpses, and, for our misfortune, it is a philosophy to which there are no objections'. Both in his reluctance to enter into political action and in the ideas which he expresses in an important scene with Caligula, Cherea reflects very closely the ideas which Camus had expressed in his *Lettres à un ami allemand*, two years before *Caligula* was produced. Like Camus himself, he feels that he must fight against 'this inhuman lyricism by the side of which my life is worth nothing', but admits at the same time that he can find no satisfactory reason why he should do so. This is brought out in the scene in Act III where Cherea confronts Caligula's mad logic with his own normal, instinctive longing for happiness. He admits that Caligula represents an idea by which he is tempted himself, but is nevertheless ready to fight against him. He explains to Caligula: 'I want to live and be happy. I think that neither of these things is possible if one follows out all the consequences of the absurd. I am like everybody else. To feel that I am free, I sometimes wish for the death of those I love, I covet women whom the laws of friendship or of family forbid me to covet. If I were to be logical, I ought to kill my loved ones or possess these women. But I think that these vague ideas have no importance. If everyone acted in accordance with them, we should be able neither to live nor to be happy. And, once again, it is that which matters to me.' The fact that this expression of what was later to become Camus's moral philosophy is still rudimentary supports his own assertion and that of Jules Roy that the play was written in its entirety in

1938.[1] As will be seen in a later chapter, the question of the development of Camus's thought is a difficult one to study in the present state of our knowledge. It is certain, however, that by 1945 he was in full possession of the 'philosophy of revolt' which he was to present as at least a partial solution to the problem of the absurd. It would have been easy for him—and it would certainly have made his 'moralising' statements about *Caligula* more convincing if he had done so —to introduce this philosophy in a far more self-assertive form before the play was first produced in 1945 and reprinted in 1946. His decision not to do so may be explained in three ways. First of all, it would have conflicted with his aim of concentrating the audience's attention on Caligula and of making the play into the study of a single character. Secondly, it would have been irrelevant to his general aim in both *Caligula* and *Le Malentendu*, that of showing that the absurd is as much a source of misery as of happiness. Thirdly, it would have made his task of presenting Caligula and his problems in as sympathetic a light as possible even more difficult than it already is: if Cherea had been allowed to present a strong intellectual case against the absurd, then Camus's insistence on the 'logic' of Caligula's attitude would have been quite unconvincing. Camus would thus have defeated his own aim, and all his careful construction would have been made useless by the creation of a character who would easily win that sympathy which the audience only reluctantly gives to Caligula.

In order to enlist this sympathy for Caligula, Camus makes him into a Romantic hero who suffers because of his greater consciousness of reality, and who—a Romantic touch taken from Suetonius—'sleeps only two hours every night and for the rest of the time, unable to rest, wanders through the galleries of his palace'. Caligula also defends himself against the charge of bloodthirstiness by pointing out to Scipio that his absurd fantasies cause fewer deaths than the smallest of wars undertaken by a 'reasonable tyrant'. His discovery of anguish is described in vivid physical detail: 'My skin is raw, my head is buzzing, I feel like vomiting. But worst of all is this taste which I have in my mouth. Not blood, not death, nor fever, but a mixture of all three.' There is no doubt that

[1] See notes.

Camus does succeed in presenting Caligula as a person who suffers deeply and sincerely. He is, in a way, a tragic counterpart to Meursault, an illustration that the absurd can have other consequences apart from happiness, and he shares Meursault's refusal to flatter other people's illusions. Yet one may doubt whether Camus wholly succeeds in putting the audience or the reader on Caligula's side. The absolute horror of Caligula's crimes is too great an obstacle to be overcome, and the 'logic' of many of Caligula's statements is far from satisfying. It was a mistake on Camus's part to insist on Caligula's logic, since a spectator invited to admire the logic of an argument instinctively looks for holes in it.

An example of how fragile Caligula's 'logic' is can be seen from his argument about the Treasury. 'If the Treasury is important,' he tells one of his administrators, 'then human life has no importance. That is obvious. All those who think as you do must admit the force of this reasoning, and see human life as totally unimportant from the moment that they recognise the importance of money.' Such reasoning may sound convincing if said very quickly in the theatre, but the reader soon notices the deliberate confusion of 'important' and 'all-important', and no longer believes Camus's assurances that Caligula's philosophy is perfectly logical. The fact is that Caligula's discovery that 'men die and are not happy' entails no *logical* conclusions whatsoever. It is a discovery whose violently emotional effect on Caligula is admirably described by Camus, but which could lead, with an equal amount of logic, to the attitude of an Alyosha Karamazov or a St. Vincent de Paul. As long as Camus sticks to his stated intention of studying Caligula as a *character*, as a man obsessed with a desire for the absolute, and of depicting him—as he said his aim was—as objectively as he said Molière drew Alceste, the play is convincing. It is only in the scenes where Caligula is made to preach that the audience's impulse to argue destroys the theatrical illusion.

Such passages are, fortunately, not very numerous, and do not destroy the over-all effect of *Caligula* as a play. Its dramatic value lies principally in the carefully planned correspondence between the sudden violent changes of scene and action and Caligula's unpredictable fits of temper. The rhetoric of certain scenes suits Caligula's own histrionic

73

character, while in others the quiet, subdued, prosaic language —as in the conversations between Caligula and Helicon— expresses the seriousness of his anguish. The first act is excellent, and certain of the later scenes—in particular the poetic contest and the banquet—contain a fascinating mixture of the morbid and the comic. As a study of a man obsessed with the desire for the absolute *Caligula* is extremely moving, and Camus was more successful than in any of his other plays in bringing his characters to life on the stage. Yet, as in Camus's other successful play, *Les Justes*, one very rarely has the excitement of wondering what is going to happen next or how the characters are going to develop. Camus does not write plays which are 'exciting' in the manner of Sartre's *Crime Passionnel*, and, as several critics have noted, one is always trying to look behind and beyond the play itself to find out what Camus 'really thinks'. This is a tribute to the fascination which few people could resist feeling for Camus the man, but it is not wholly a compliment to Camus the dramatist. Nevertheless, it is a tendency which Camus himself encouraged by the statements which he made about the meaning of his plays, and which, particularly in the case of *Caligula* and *Le Malentendu*, are out of keeping with their general atmosphere.

The contradiction between the atmosphere of anarchistic revolt which characterises *Caligula* and the ideas of sanity and moderation which Camus said it expressed is at least partly resolved by the very last scene. When Caligula finally recognises that 'I have chosen the wrong path, my freedom was not of the right kind,' he does lend support to Camus's insistence that the play is to be taken as a warning. Camus made this very clear in the programme note which he wrote for the first production in 1945.

'But if Caligula is right to deny the existence of the gods, he is wrong to deny the importance of men. One cannot destroy everything without destroying oneself. That is why Caligula empties the world around him and, faithful to his logic, does everything necessary to give arms to those who will finally kill him. *Caligula* is the story of a superior form of suicide. It is the story of the most human and most tragic of mistakes. Unfaithful to man through fidelity to himself, Caligula accepts death when he has understood that no man can achieve salvation for himself alone, and that one cannot be free against other people. But he will at least have drawn certain souls, his own and young Scipio's for example, from the dreamless sleep of mediocrity.'

In 1958 Camus brought *Caligula* even more neatly into line with his later moral and political ideas when he said that it should be interpreted, like a Greek tragedy, as a warning against the danger of *hubris*. Like *Le Mythe de Sisyphe* and *L'Homme révolté* it unmasks a leap, and forms part of Camus's denunciation of the dangers of contemporary nihilism. Both in this respect and in its attack on the comfortable assumptions of bourgeois humanism, it is a work of the highest moral intentions. Whether it wholly lives up to them is, however, a different matter.

It must be admitted that, judged on its 'message', *Caligula* is greatly inferior to *Le Mythe de Sisyphe* and to *L'Etranger*. The few who have either the power or the inclination to pursue the absolute with the ruthlessness of a Caligula would not be dissuaded by a work of literature. Those whom a simple-minded rationalism maintains in middle-class intellectual comfort will be too delighted to have understood what Camus is driving at to be greatly disturbed by his play. Yet it would be wrong to take Camus wholly at his word on this question and interpret *Caligula* as a play with a moral message. It differs from most of Camus's other works—and, perhaps, owes something of its relative inferiority to this fact—in appearing in its most favourable aspect when judged purely and simply as a work of art. It is then that its value as a piece of character-drawing is most apparent, and that the audacity and originality of its theatrical technique can be most appreciated. It has all the qualities of a young man's play— exuberance, freshness, vitality and purity. It strangely foreshadowed the Europe of the early nineteen-forties, where mad emperors were apparently devoted to demonstrating the world's absurdity. The fact that this foreshadowing was unconscious[1] adds to, rather than detracts from, the value of the play as a description of the lot of man at a particular moment of history. It is perhaps because *Le Malentendu* was written in the winter of 1943, almost with the deliberate aim of expressing the futile tragedy of modern life, that it is inferior to *Caligula*. Camus's work is often the acutest expression of

[1] See notes.

modern sensibility when it is the result of purely personal feelings and experience.

By 1945, however, the experience which had inspired the four works which made Camus famous already belonged to his past. The moralising interpretations which he gave to his two plays can be explained by his awareness of the difference between the ideas which he was expressing every morning in *Combat* and those which readers and spectators found in his novel, essay and plays. For some people, this contradiction was of itself of great value. In his open letter of 1952, Jean-Paul Sartre wrote: 'You were for us—and tomorrow you could still be it again—the admirable meeting-place of a man, a mode of political action and a literary work. It was in 1945: we discovered Camus, the member of the Resistance, as we had discovered Camus the author of *L'Etranger*. And when we put the editor of the clandestine editions of *Combat* by the side of the Meursault who carried honesty to the point of refusing to say that he loved his mother and his mistress, and whom our society condemned to death, and, above all, when we knew that you had not stopped being either one or the other, this apparent contradiction made us progress in the knowledge which we had of ourselves and of the world. Then you were not far from being an exemplary figure. For you resumed in your own person the conflicts of our time, and went beyond them by your ardour in living them out.' Yet for Camus himself this contradiction was one which had to be resolved. His own personal life, to begin with, was becoming more stable. In 1940 he married Francine Faure, a young woman who had been brought up in Oran, and their twin children, Catherine and Jean, were born in 1945. There was also the influence of the world into which he had been brought by his activity in the Resistance movement, a world in which politics and philosophy were closely connected, and where the effect of philosophical principles on political action seemed very considerable. Camus needed to adapt himself to this new society, and the purely individual morality of *Le Mythe de Sisyphe* was not enough. At a time when critics were incorrectly welcoming him as a disciple of Sartre and as a playwright of the absurd, he had already given the first expression to the ideas which were to lead to the open break with Sartre in 1952 and to the accusations of conservatism and conformity which no one would ever have thought applicable to the author of *Caligula*.

It would be incorrect, however, to maintain that there was anything like a clean break between the Camus whose inspiration came directly from North Africa, and the Camus who had to learn to confront the more gloomy and difficult problems of Europe. It may even be that the ideas which he set out in *La Remarque sur la Révolte* in 1945 had already been put down on paper before 1941, for in an open letter to Francis Ponge in January 1943 he regretted having left behind in Algeria the only piece of political writing he had ever composed, an attempt to define 'a modest political thought'. Certainly, there are many points in common between the Camus of *L'Etranger* and *Le Mythe de Sisyphe* and the author of *La Remarque sur la Révolte* and *La Peste*. There is the automatic dismissal of the normally accepted values of both Christianity and nineteenth-century rationalist humanism, the passionate dislike of the people who fail to recognise the tragic nature of man's fate, the constant rejection of anything but human standards of judgment, and the refusal to accept any value that would be placed higher than the individual. Throughout all his work Camus attacks philosophical ideas which would refuse the individual the final right of judgment, or deny his importance in favour of absolute values based either upon religion or upon a systematic and all-embracing philosophy of history. He never considers any values as given in advance or as existing by virtue of certain eternal truths, but always as based upon a particular attitude and a particular choice which each man must make. The books written after *Le Mythe de Sisyphe* differ from his early work in putting forward values which can justify positive action. The world of Meursault and Caligula is one where all actions—killing, making love, drying your hands on a towel, ruining an empire —are not distinguishable from one another by any ethical code. There is no such thing as crime, guilt, innocence, or action undertaken in common. There are, it is true, the values of truthfulness and manliness represented by Meursault, but, like the lucidity of the heroes of the absurd, they are the virtues of a man who has contracted out of society. For all the happiness which the absurd can offer the individual able to understand its lessons, it does reinforce man's solitude and render all actions equally futile. What Camus expresses in the works which will now be discussed is his own attempt to justify the remark which he put into Cherea's mouth: 'I think that some actions are finer than others.' In doing so he not only gave a new expression to humanism, but also composed a genuine artistic masterpiece in *La Peste*.

Chapter Six

RESISTANCE AND REVOLT

FOR obvious reasons, it is difficult to discover exactly what Camus did in the Resistance movement. It certainly did not occupy him exclusively between 1940 and 1944, since he taught for a time in a private school in Oran in 1941 and devoted his spare time to a production of *Hamlet* in which he was to play the lead, and his wife Francine, Ophelia. He also had to go to the country in 1942, in order to recover from a new attack of tuberculosis brought on by a chill caught when imprudently playing football with his pupils. Discussing the reasons which made him enter the Resistance movement, he remarked in an article published in 1947 that it was on the morning of the execution of Gabriel Péri that 'the wave of revolt' which was in him reached its highest point. Péri was executed on December 19th, 1941, and, according to Roger Quilliot, Camus joined the network 'Combat' in 1942. The allied invasion of North Africa in November 1942 prevented him from returning to Algeria until after the war, and thus separated him from his wife who remained there until the Liberation. This had a very marked effect on the work which Camus composed during the war years, for the theme of separation plays an important part both in *Le Malentendu* and in *La Peste*. Camus had already begun to write *La Peste* in 1941, before he joined the Resistance movement, and a passage entitled *Les Exilés dans la peste*—the beginning of the second main section in the standard edition of the novel—appeared in an anthology of French Resistance writing, *Domaine Français*, published in Geneva in 1943.

According to Germaine Brée, who has had access to much of Camus's unpublished material, he worked mainly on the clandestine newspaper *Combat*, and this would certainly have

79

been where his experience both as a journalist and typographer—he had worked as a type-setter for *Paris-Soir* in 1940—would have been most useful. His writings in *Combat* were naturally anonymous, until on August 21st, 1944, his name appeared on the front of the newspaper as '*rédacteur en chef*'. His two main concerns in the Resistance movement were, to judge from his *Lettres à un ami allemand* and from an article which Jean Sénard published in 1957, the moral problems of political action and the ambition to transform *Combat*, after the war, into a newspaper which combined high principles with a wide circulation. The *Lettres à un ami allemand* were written in 1943 and 1944 and reflect the way Camus identified his own problems with those of the French nation in general. The revolution in journalism represented by *Combat* in the years immediately after the war showed how close he came to realising one of his main ambitions, and for what reasons he finally had to abandon it.

The theme of *Lettres à un ami allemand* can be stated quite simply: is it possible, in a world without God and without ultimate values, to discover an ethical code which will justify political action? Camus's answer is 'Yes', and the reasons which he puts forward to justify his own activity in the Resistance movement provide the first hesitant step forward from the *tabula rasa* of moral values in *Le Mythe de Sisyphe* to the liberal humanism of *L'Homme révolté*. The discussion in these letters, the first two of which appeared anonymously in Resistance periodicals in 1943 and 1944, centres round the different conclusions which Camus and his German friend—who, until further evidence is available, must be looked upon as a fictitious character representing his *alter ego*—had drawn from the idea of the absurd. The German had maintained, when Camus had spoken with him before the war, that 'in a world where nothing has any meaning, those who, like us young Germans, have had the good fortune to discover a reason for living in the destiny of our nation, must be prepared to sacrifice everything to it'. Even before the war Camus himself had felt differently, but had hesitated before coming to an opposite but equally definite conclusion. This had, he maintained, both delayed his ability to fight against his friend and made his own attitude more coherent when it did develop. It was, in fact, by seeing how the Nazis used lies and murder that he had learned to appreciate the importance of the real values that these destroyed. 'What is truth? you used to say. Of course, we still don't know, but we can at least recognise its opposite which is lies: it is you who have taught us to do so. What is intelligence? At least we know its opposite which is murder. What is man? But here I will interrupt you, for we know the answer. He is the power which always finishes by defeating gods and tyrants. He is the force of evidence. It is this human certainty that we must preserve and our own sureness comes from our knowledge that his destiny and the destiny of our country are linked one with the other. If nothing had any meaning, you would be right. But there is something which still has meaning.'

It is in the fourth letter that Camus speaks most openly of his discovery of values, and which is most important in any study of his ideas. While his friend has 'chosen injustice and put himself on the side of the gods', Camus himself has 'chosen justice to remain faithful to the earth'. 'I still think that the world has no final meaning,' he writes, 'but I know that something in it has meaning, and that is man, because he is the only being to demand that he should have one.' Both the scorn which Sisyphus had shown for the gods and Camus's own love for the *univers farouche et limité de l'homme* begin to take on new overtones with the discussion of particular moral values. The actual arguments which Camus puts forward are not particularly impressive, for in the last analysis they come down to saying that because man wants a thing then it must exist, but his sincerity is both moving and effective. The letters are extremely good rhetoric, and an excellent presentation of the problem of the idealist in wartime. They also contain the first expression of an idea which was to become central to Camus's subsequent moral and political philosophy and to dominate his discussion of Communism in *L'Homme révolté*.

The *Lettres à un ami allemand* differ from Camus's early works by introducing a criticism of the 'absurdist attitude' which is absent from *Le Mythe de Sisyphe* and *L'Etranger* and different in nature from the nostalgia for a reasonable world expressed in *Caligula* and *Le Malentendu*. The absence of all belief in moral principles can, Camus argues, lead very easily to a worship of force and success for their own sake. Man needs something to fill in the void left by the disappearance of traditional religious or humanist values, and he finds it most easily in extreme patriotism or in a political creed. This is a betrayal of the one valid lesson which could be drawn from the absurd, and the German who was prepared to sacrifice everything to the glory of his country is guilty of a 'leap' more dangerous than that criticised in Kierkegaard and Husserl. 'You supposed that, in the absence of all human and divine morality, the only values were those which dominated the animal world: violence and cunning. You concluded that man was nothing and that one could kill his soul: that in the midst of an absurd history, the task of an individual could be only the adventure of power and the realism of conquests.' This attitude—which the German might, it is true, have partly justified by reference to the passage on the conqueror in *Le Mythe de Sisyphe*—is one which Camus denounced with even more vigour and intellectual certainty when he came to discuss the problem of the relationship between Communism and nihilism after the war. Indeed, he once remarked that this relationship formed the whole subject of *L'Homme révolté*, and the filiation here between these letters and the rest of his political thought is very strong.

There is one important criticism which has been made of these letters: it is that Camus too frequently claims to be expressing the attitude of the French people as a whole when he is discussing his own personal doubts and scruples. Thus, in the first letter, he explains that the French began the war by a defeat because 'we were taken up, when you suddenly attacked us, with searching in our own hearts to discover whether or not right was on our side.' It is, he continues, 'this time lost and now regained, these scruples paid for in blood, which give us French the right to think that we entered the war with clean hands—with the purity of victims and of the condemned—and that we shall emerge from it with clean hands, but this time with the purity of a great victory won over injustice and over ourselves'. One would like these ideas to have been true of the French nation as well as of Camus himself, but historical facts are hard to change. Camus himself volunteered for military service the moment war broke out, and was only prevented from joining the army by the refusal of the medical authorities to accept a man as ill as he was. His words surely apply even less accurately to the mass of the French nation, who were held back from fighting energetically against the Germans not by doubts as to 'whether we had the right to kill men, whether we had the right to add to the atrocious suffering of the world' but by their own indifference and the military incompetence of their leaders. Such a criticism is, however, justified only if one judges the *Lettres à un ami allemand* by standards perhaps unsuited to a piece of *littérature engagée*. Their immediate object was not to give an accurate historical account of why France was defeated, but to combat the doubts of those who might still be influenced by the propaganda of the Vichy government. Judged on this level, they do present effective arguments.

The criticism just made of them takes on a relevance to Camus's literary work when *La Peste* is studied as an allegory of the Occupation and the Resistance movement. *La Peste*, it is true, insists upon the mediocrity of the inhabitants of Oran and upon the limitations of their blindly optimistic humanism, and Camus's notebooks for December 1942 shows how important this theme was in his original conception of the work. 'Develop the social criticism and the idea of revolt', he writes. 'What they (the inhabitants of Oran) lack is imagination. They treat epic happenings as if they were a picnic, and are not thinking on the scale of catastrophe. The remedies they think of are scarcely suitable even to a cold in the nose. They will die.' Nevertheless, there is no suggestion either in Camus's notebooks or in *La Peste* itself that they are in any way responsible for what happens to them or that they are going to be able to change things in such a way as to make a return of the plague more difficult. Camus's own remarks, both in the novel itself and in various interviews, stress the innocence of the people of Oran in very much the same way as the *Lettres à un ami allemand* emphasise the innocence of the people of France in the 1939–1945 war. The *Lettres à un ami allemand* thus contain, in germ, the weakness of the humanism which Camus developed in *La Peste* and *L'Homme révolté*: the notion that man is essentially an innocent victim of a hostile universe, and that he increases his sufferings only when misled by certain ideas. It was not, in fact, until the publication of *La Chute* in 1956 that Camus began to

83

correct the view of man as a largely innocent victim of events which he put forward for the first time in these four letters.

It would be wrong, however, to conclude a discussion of the *Lettres à un ami allemand* on a note of criticism. In implying, by the tone in which he addressed him, that his German friend was not a sadistic barbarian but a possibly well-meaning intellectual led astray only by a pernicious philosophy, Camus was as far removed as possible from the intolerant chauvinism which characterised the propaganda literature of the first world war. Instead of imitating the abuse and exaggeration of Barrès and Claudel, French writers between 1939 and 1945 used the problems of the Occupation and Resistance movement to underline the basic tragedy of the human condition. It is this fact which ensures for the *Lettres à un ami allemand* a greater permanent appeal than that possessed by any patriotic literature written between 1914 and 1918. When Camus writes the general profession of humanist faith already quoted—'I have chosen justice to remain faithful to the earth'—he is going beyond the question of the attitude to adopt to the German invader, and lifting the whole debate on to a higher and more interesting plane. It may be that by doing so he produces rhetoric rather than convincing arguments, but insofar as the problem of our time is a problem of recreating values, Camus provides a very moving reply to it.

These letters express only the first stage in Camus's rediscovery of values. The second stage, which culminates in the confident assertions of *La Remarque sur la Révolte* in 1945, consists of the semi-anonymous editorials published in *Combat* immediately after the Liberation. It is by a study of the new connotations with which the word '*révolte*' is used in the editorials that it is possible to trace a progression from the purely personal world of *Le Mythe de Sisyphe* to that concern with man in society which informs *La Peste* and *L'Homme révolté*. The word '*révolte*' occurs in Camus's early lyrical essays, and as has been seen, does represent one of the central ideas in *Le Mythe de Sisyphe*. In Camus's early work, however, it brings only a greater intensity to the sensation of being alive. The context in which the word is used in *Noces* and *Le Mythe de Sisyphe*, shows revolt to be a largely sterile notion, defined as 'a perpetual confrontation of man and his own obscurity . . . a demand for an impossible transcendence . . . a perpetual consciousness by man of his own being'. 'It aspires to nothing,' he says, 'and is completely without hope.' It cannot justify any kind of action undertaken in common or any kind of plans made for the future. It is completely alien to any idea of hope and can serve towards the recreation of values only by inculcating an extremely critical attitude towards any solutions proposed. In Camus's editorials of 1944, however, the word occurs with very different connotations.

On August 24th, for example, Camus juxtaposed two notions that were completely contradictory in *Le Mythe de Sisyphe* when he wrote that the reasons for which Frenchmen were fighting had 'the dimensions of hope and the depths of revolt'. On September 8th, in an article entitled *Justice et Liberté*, Camus formulated what was for him the essential objection to Christianity and gave at the same time a further resonance to the word 'revolt'. Christianity, he argued, is basically a doctrine of injustice, for it is founded upon the sacrifice of the innocent and the acceptance of this sacrifice. 'Justice, on the contrary,' he writes, '—and Paris has just experienced it in the nights lit up by the insurrection— justice is never found without revolt.' A further article published on September 19th distinguishes between the idea of revolt and that of revolution. The Resistance movement had, according to Camus, been inspired by the former and not the latter. Revolution is an intellectual idea, the passage from the instinctive movement of revolt to the realisation of its ideals in history. It is thus different from revolt, which is 'the complete and obstinate refusal, initially almost blind, of an order which wanted to bring men to their knees. . . . Revolt is first of all in the heart.' This blind instinctive refusal is very different from the lucid, personal revolt in *Le Mythe de Sisyphe*. It is unreasoned and emotional, originating in a primitive feeling of human solidarity and of human dignity. Clearly, this feeling was not one which Camus had found only in the Resistance movement. He must have experienced it in his early political activity in Algeria, and may even have developed from it the new notion of revolt expressed in the political essay which he told Francis Ponge that he had left in North Africa in 1941. The only thing one can do, at the present stage, is to note when certain words are used for the first time, in what contexts and with what connotations. And it is in these editorials and in *La Remarque sur la Révolte* that the word '*révolte*' takes on for the first time the connotations of political action and philosophical values with which it will be closely associated in Camus's major essay in political philosophy, *L'Homme révolté*. *La Remarque sur la Révolte*, which Camus was to reproduce with only a few minor changes in *L'Homme révolté* in 1951, has as its starting point exactly the movement of blind, instinctive refusal to which Camus had referred in his article of September 19th, 1944.

It is a refusal which is peculiarly suited to the mid-twentieth century, with its original combination of slavery and bureaucracy. A *fonctionnaire*—a minor civil servant—suddenly decides, after a long period of servitude, to refuse to obey an order. This refusal, argues Camus, is based upon his instinctive perception of the limit beyond which his master has trespassed. His refusal to obey the authority which transgresses this limit is one which can be inspired not only by his own experience but by that of other slaves. In other words, the rebel recognises by his first movement of refusal the existence of an inviolable frontier which he will maintain for all men. His protest is an instinctive attempt to obtain certain minimal rights, and it gives birth to the basic truth that the individual is not a zero to be ignored nor a collection of impulses to be enslaved, but a unity which has an autonomous existence. The individual, by his movement of protest, affirms his own integrity as a basic value. In maintaining his initial refusal on behalf of others as well as of himself—Camus gives a striking contemporary illustration of how this is done by mentioning the prisoners in the Russian salt mines who committed suicide to protest against the ill-treatment of their fellows— he affirms that this integrity is shared by others, both masters and slaves. 'We see already,' writes Camus on the very first page of *La Remarque sur la Révolte*, 'that the affirmation of revolt extends to something which transcends the individual, which takes him out of his supposed solitude, and which establishes a value.' The world of Meursault and Caligula, in which no individual escaped from his solitude or acted with the idea of a positive value, is invaded by a notion which will make action possible.

In the movement of revolt the individual sacrifices himself for the sake of others. Camus had already used the example of prisoners committing suicide as a protest against ill-treatment in order to show, in *Le Mythe de Sisyphe*, that suicide can be caused by things other than the indifferent tone of voice in which a man may speak to his friend. In *La Remarque sur la Révolte* this suicide of protest becomes the very basis of human solidarity. Suicide for the sake of others constitutes a movement of revolt, as does Eckhart's preference of Hell with Christ to Heaven without him. 'It is in revolt that man goes beyond himself and discovers other people,' writes Camus, 'and, from this point of view, human solidarity is a philosophical certainty.' Coming back to the same idea at the end of the essay Camus finds that it can be taken as the basis for an affirmative reply to 'the only question which seems of any importance today: can man, alone, and without the help of God, create his own values?' Revolt provides a means of transcending the world of utter loneliness and frustration which certain aspects of the absurd revealed. 'There is something beyond anguish, and which is not a religious solution, and it is revolt.' Camus had defined this revolt as 'the most relative of experiences . . . carried to the status of an absolute'.

This idea of relativity is an essential one in determining what kind of action revolt can justify. When revolt begins to act it can never aspire to the creation of an absolute in history in a revolution which is final and definite. The real value discovered in revolt is that of companionship and unity of interests among the slaves. This complicity can be maintained only by a faithfulness to the limited nature of human experience. The rebel must allow criticism and accept approximation. The only revolution which is 'adjusted to the measure of man' is to be found in 'the acceptance of relative aims and ambitions which means faithfulness to the human lot'. The attempt to attain the absolute always involves the sacrifice of the individual to a false ambition. In all revolutions there comes a moment when justice and liberty enter into conflict with each other, and when the desire for absolute justice comes into conflict with the liberty of the individual. It is here that the limit established by the first movement of revolt must be respected, and where the rebel must accept the fact that, in human experience, no absolute can be achieved without denying this first principle of the inviolability of the human personality. Revolt provides both a discipline and an inspiration. It is both a call to action and an indication of how that action should be carried on. It provides a value which revolution must try to realise but which cannot, in any circumstances, be sacrificed to expediency. Were it possible to envisage a final revolution which would realise all ideals, in which the antinomy between justice and liberty did not exist, the ruthlessness of political realism might be justified. But since this is impossible, no absolute good can be held to justify the use of all means, and the very value which revolution is striving to achieve denies it the right to be ruthless. Revolution cannot use all and every means to achieve its ends. It originates in a revolt which was the affirmation of the integrity of the individual and of the existence of limits. Revolution cannot, without betraying revolt, cease to respect this integrity and cannot deny these limits.

There are, however, two dangers which threaten revolt and destroy human solidarity. The first is what Camus calls '*une prétention à l'éternel*', the acceptance of a superhuman value which would cause men to be silent or to be nothing but 'the spokesman or echo of the divine voice', and the second the danger of political realism. Camus is far more concerned with the second than with the first—a fact which is natural in an age which has seen the replacement of religious by political persecution. Political realism justifies lying, which is a denial of the complicity created by revolt, and also justifies cruelty and the killing off of opponents. This complicity is not lost—'that is never possible,' says Camus of his newly discovered absolute, but it is denied—'and despair begins with the denial of the first truth brought by revolt, that man is not alone'. The rebel refuses the temptation of absolute Utopias which demand the sacrifice of his first value—the integrity of the individual—in order to be realised, and remains in his 'stubborn perseverance in the human being's limited status'. There is here a very close connection between the semi-political, semi-metaphysical thought of *La Remarque sur la Révolte* and the purely political thought which Camus expressed in his articles in *Combat*. There he distinguished between two forms of socialism—an indigenous French socialism, 'liberal, badly expressed, but essentially generous', which has its origins in the Resistance movement, and the orthodox Marxist social-ism. The first does not believe in doctrines which are 'ab-solute and infallible', but in 'the obstinate, disorderly but inevitable improvement of the human lot'; it thus refuses the temptation of absolute Utopias which leads Marxism to progress to the perfect city through a succession of crimes.

In politics, as in the metaphysics both of the absurd and of revolt, Camus's thought is characterised by an insistence on the limits of the human condition. In the same way as the whole argument of *Le Mythe de Sisyphe* confirmed the rejection of all non-human solutions, so revolt demands 'a human realm where all the replies are human', and, Camus adds as clarification in 1951, 'that is to say, expressed in rational terms'. The important difference between the attitude of the absurd man and that of the rebel lies in their fertility and in the realms of their application. The absurd is essentially an individual sensation. It is experienced by the individual conscience and its rules are applicable only to individual cases. Revolt, on the other hand, although at the very be-ginning an individualistic movement, can only really come to life by passing beyond the individual, and by finding its expression in political action.

This is very clearly indicated by Camus when, early on in the essay, he writes the following sentence: 'Since in the experience here described nothing can be considered outside history, the only legitimate and coherent act, for a mind outside religious solutions (*'un esprit hors du sacré'*), is revo-lution.' The articles which Camus wrote in *Combat* in 1944 and 1945 show how closely he identified political action and philosophical principles.[1] Although he did not fully share the political euphoria which immediately followed the Libera-tion, these articles do contain a note of hope and determina-tion which was never to be repeated in his political writing. For a time, he even seemed to think that there was something to be said in favour of the foreign policy of the Soviet Union. On December 18th, 1944, he wrote that 'we must never forget that Russia adopted the nationalistic policy which she now pursues only after she had in vain proposed a system of collective security. Neither must we forget that,

[1] See notes for details of these articles.

alone along all other states, she offered general disarmament.'
Camus himself, like the rest of the team of writers on *Combat*,
also seemed to have taken some time to realise the true nature
of Russian policy in Poland. On January 3rd, 1945, he supported Serge Karsky's contention that Poland was largely the
creation of the French 'Comité des Forges', and it was not
until the arrest of the Polish leaders in Russia in May 1945
that *Combat* decided that anti-capitalism was being carried a
little too far. Yet this attitude towards the Soviet Union—
surprising in someone who left the Party in 1935—was only
part of a generally extreme left-wing position adopted by
Combat and advocated at times with great enthusiasm by
Camus himself.

It was during the months immediately following the Liberation that Camus's interest in politics was most intense and
his revolutionary fervour most ardent. He maintained, in a
long polemic with François Mauriac, that the new government had both the right and the duty to be ruthless in
punishing those who had betrayed their country by working
for the Vichy régime. On three occasions he evoked the name
of Saint-Just, the most uncompromising of the leaders of the
French Revolution, as setting an example to be followed in
realising the ideals of the new revolution born of the Resistance movement. In the very first edition of *Combat* to be published openly, he demanded 'the pitiless destruction of trusts
and of the powers established on money' as the means whereby
'a true, popular, working-class democracy' could be established. The middle class, he insisted, must now hand over
power to the workers, and resign itself to being 'the witness of
a greatness it could not create itself'. On September 19th, 1944,
he even threatened that the Resistance movement might return
to violence and call its members out into the streets if the
government continued to show itself reluctant to destroy the
power of the trusts. Neither did Camus forget, in the midst
of his national and international preoccupations, to speak of
the problems of Algeria. He demanded absolute equality of
legal and political rights for the Arab population, and accused
previous governments of using the word 'assimilation' to
disguise the reality of an 'occupation that was sometimes
benevolent'. Yet the note of optimism which characterised
some of the articles in September and October 1944 soon

began to give way to one of aggrieved self-righteousness. On December 17th, for example, there appeared an article entitled 'How to ruin a revolution once it has already broken out'. The means ironically recommended were to cheer hard, tell the people that it would be dishonourable to profit too quickly from its victory, criticise the impurity of the Resistance movement, and warn the nation of the horrible violence awaiting it if this criminal conspiracy were allowed to keep its arms. It is certainly true that such methods—together with the more subtle ones of encouraging the banks to refuse credit to newly nationalised industries which *Combat* denounced on December 13th—were successful in ensuring that the revolution of 1944 was still-born. Camus continued to write frequently on political matters throughout 1945—in particular on the economic and political crisis in Algeria, to which he drew attention in a series of articles in May—but his early optimism had disappeared. When he did make a sensational return to politics in November 1946, with the articles *Ni Victimes ni Bourreaux*, it was as a man who was concerned not so much with encouraging a new revolution as with trying to ensure that politics did not simply become a pretext for intolerance and legalised murder.

It is outside the scope of this study to discuss why the Fourth French Republic, which came to life in an atmosphere of revolutionary enthusiasm, should have led so peculiarly stagnant an existence. The fact that France did not follow the path indicated by the slogan of *Combat—De la Résistance à la Révolution*—is important here principally because of the effect which it had on Camus's work. In 1945, the combined effect of the performances of *Caligula* and of his articles in *Combat* had given the impression of a Camus who violently rejected all conventional moral standards and who advocated complete revolution in both private and political life. The name of Saint-Just was frequently used to describe his own character, and he was commonly referred to as the 'apostle of the absurd'. Neither of these two public images was correct. *La Remarque sur la Révolte* had already shown that he did not hold the absurdist position described in *Le Mythe de Sisyphe*, and that he placed very definite limits, from a moral and philosophical point of view, on the type of revolutionary action to be undertaken. When it became increasingly obvious that

France was to have no revolution at all, the development of the idea of moderation in Camus's critique of Communism gave his thought a more conservative air than it would have had in a genuinely revolutionary period. In an article published after his death, Claude Bourdet argued that Camus's political ideas would be most useful in the future, when a France moving towards socialism would stand in need of the warnings he had given. While one may doubt that such a time may ever come, and also think Camus's attack on Communism an excellent thing in the Europe of the Stalinist era, there is no doubt that this is the way in which Camus himself intended his ideas to be interpreted. He did not, when he gave up his post of editor-in-chief of *Combat* late in 1945 in order to complete *La Peste*, intend to deny the ideals which had inspired him in 1944 and 1945. Like so many left-wing thinkers after 1945 he was forced to place more emphasis on the dangers presented by the perversion of the revolution in the Soviet Union than on the need for an independent socialist revolution in Western Europe. Yet insofar as *La Peste* is a political book, it does mark a movement away from the revolutionary optimism of the immediate post-Liberation period, and fits into Camus's intention of dissociating revolt from the ideas of violence and intolerance with which it had been traditionally associated. Fortunately, *La Peste* is much more than a political novel. It is an allegory firmly rooted in the reality of North Africa, a work of art which contains the essence of Camus's meditation on man's fate. 'I want to express by means of the plague', he wrote in his notebook in 1942, 'the suffocation from which we all suffered, and the atmosphere of menace and exile in which we all lived. At the same time, I want to extend this interpretation to cover the notion of existence in general. The plague will describe those whose lot in this war was one of silence, of reflection—and of moral suffering'.

Chapter Seven

THE PLAGUE

La Peste was published in June 1947 and immediately became Camus's most popular work. Over 100,000 copies were sold within a few months of publication, and by 1955 360,000 copies had been sold in various French editions. It has twice been published as a paper-back in France, once in the 'Edition Pourpre' series and once in the 'Livre de Poche', and was the first of Camus's works to appear in paper-backs in England when it was published by Penguins in 1960. This popularity can be explained both by the accessibility of its ideas and by the universality of its theme. The average reader does not need to have heard of Heidegger or Kafka to see in this account of an outbreak of plague in Oran the image and symbol of the human condition, and the morality which Camus puts forward gives *La Peste* an immediate appeal to all men of good will. The characters described are more easily understandable, as well as being more attractive to most readers, than either the Meursault of *L'Etranger* or the Jean-Baptiste Clamence of *La Chute*. In *La Peste*, Camus achieves the most difficult ambition of any writer concerned with ideas: that of writing a novel which deals with ordinary people and can be immediately appreciated by them. Descriptions of plague and pestilence have always had a universal appeal, and Camus's narration intrigues by a sufficiency of horrible details without ever nauseating by an excess. Nobility of feeling is balanced by elegance of narration, and the work is both spiritually uplifting and aesthetically satisfying. This universal appeal was, however, in the opinion of many critics, obtained by a sacrifice of the intransigent attitude which had given great value to Camus's early work and by a refusal to face the risks inseparable from any really vigorous ethical system.

In France at least, *La Peste* was one of Camus's most widely criticised works, and its publication marked the end of the period in which he received equal praise from all French thinkers with the exception of the Communists. It was the first book in which he fused the different sides of his personality together into a composite whole, allying his love of life to a philosophy of political action and using his fidelity to North Africa to illustrate a European dilemma. By a familiar paradox, he lost the support of the intellectuals at the same time as he secured that of the general reading public. This was certainly not because Camus tried to flatter popular taste and write a best-seller. It happened because the extension of his own 'philosophy of revolt' and the expression of his own views on the Resistance movement conflicted with the ideas of many intellectuals who had once been his allies, at the same time as it satisfied a more widespread general demand for moderation. The critical reception of *La Peste* was a forerunner of the intellectual storm which broke with the publication of *L'Homme révolté* in 1951, and although it is limiting to study *La Peste* principally as an illustration of the ideas expressed in *La Remarque sur la Révolte*, such an approach both illustrates the way in which the book resumed a long intellectual development on Camus's part and explains why it was so often criticised.

La Remarque sur la Révolte pointed out that the first discovery which the rebel makes, in his movement towards human solidarity, is that of a common suffering which he shares with all men. 'In an absurd world,' writes Camus, 'the rebel has still one certainty: it is the solidarity of men in the same adventure, the fact that the grocer and he are both oppressed.' The only change is that 'the evil from which one man suffered in isolation has become a collective plague'. This is the theme which runs through the whole of *La Peste*. An outbreak of plague occurs in the town of Oran, on the Algerian coast. It is preceded by the appearance of large numbers of rats which come out in their thousands to die in the streets. The town authorities hesitate to apply immediately the necessary prophylactic measures and to impose the rigorous discipline essential to prevent the plague from spreading, and it is only when the number of victims reaches thirty in a day for the second time that they decide to act. The state of siege is declared and Oran segregated from the rest of the world.

It is from their isolation that the inhabitants of Oran suffer most. The main character, Doctor Rieux, is himself separated from his wife, who leaves Oran some time before the outbreak of the plague in order to pursue a course of treatment at a sanatorium outside the town. As a doctor, Rieux naturally occupies an important place in the fight against the plague. Most of the population, however, do their best to ignore its existence or to forget about it and continue in their old life. They drink heavily, until the supply of alcohol is exhausted, and, although within a short time all the available films have been seen in all parts of the town, continue to go assiduously to the cinema. Various individuals react in different ways and are distinguished from the passive mass. Cottard, who at the beginning of the story had tried to hang himself, is pleased that the plague has come. It puts others in the same state of apprehension which had haunted him, and allows him to escape for a time from the mysterious arrest which society is preparing for him. Rambert, a journalist who had come to the town to report on the living conditions of the Arabs, attempts to escape and to rejoin the woman he loves. He finally turns down the opportunity to escape when it is provided, and joins the fight against the plague. Tarrou, whose diary is used as a means of describing the town before and during the plague, organises teams of volunteers in order to help Rieux to treat its victims. Towards the beginning of the book, after the plague has just broken out, Father Paneloux, a Jesuit priest, preaches a violent sermon in the cathedral on the theme that the plague has been sent by God as a just punishment to the inhabitants of Oran. Later in the book, after having been present at the death of a small boy who dies of the plague, he preaches a second and less confident sermon. He recognises the problem which the suffering of the innocent presents for the Christian, admits that reason is incapable of explaining the scandal, but denies that anyone has the courage completely to refuse all acceptance of God. We must accept or refuse everything, he says, for Christianity can include no half measures. He falls ill with a malady which, without quite being the plague, has many of its symptoms. Consistent with his own faith, he dies without accepting medical help.

Joseph Grand, a local government clerk, is at one point described as the true hero of the book. Unable, like Tarrou, to devote the whole of his time to fighting the plague, he helps in the evenings to keep a full statistical account of all the details of the plague's activity. For the rest of his time he is engaged in literary work—in the writing of a novel which never progresses beyond the first sentence because he can never bring this to complete perfection. Grand is a less complex character than Tarrou, whose fight against this particular plague is only a continuation of his life-long struggle against plague in general, identified by him with the existence of the death penalty. Without believing in God Tarrou wishes to become a saint, to find inner peace in his '*morale de la compréhension*'. This phrase is difficult to translate. *Compréhension* has both the idea of understanding and of *comprehending* in the sense of including everything. He dies in the last week of the plague, after Grand, who has also fallen ill, recovers.

It is never known whether the resistance to the plague and the organisation to prevent it spreading are successful. After having held the town under its domination for nearly six months, its fury gradually diminishes. The serum begins to have an effect, the death rate decreases, and the town is eventually allowed to return to normal. Its inhabitants are reunited with those they love, from whom the plague had separated them. Only those whose loved one has died know the final separation, and such is the fate of Rieux whose wife has died in the sanatorium. Cottard, exposed again to his old fears of persecution, goes mad and shoots at the crowd from his window. He is captured and taken away. Rambert is reunited with his mistress. The book ends with the revelation that it is Rieux himself who is the author of this chronicle, written to testify to the violence and injustice imposed upon his town, and to the fact that man shows, in times of tribulation, more things to admire than to despise. Rieux knows what the rejoicing crowd does not know, that the bacillus of the plague never dies and that the day will come again when, 'for the unhappiness and instruction of men, plague will once again wake up its rats and send them to die in the streets of a happy city'.

From one point of view, the attitude adopted by Rieux and the other characters towards the plague is exactly that advocated in *La Remarque sur la Révolte*. In simply doing his job well, Rieux is being faithful to the injunction always to serve man in a relative and limited way without aspiring to the eternal or the absolute. When Paneloux tells him that they are both together in working for the salvation of man, Rieux replies: 'Man's salvation is too big a word for me. I don't go as far as that. It is his health which concerns me, his health first of all.' Health is relative and attainable, salvation absolute and uncertain, and Camus's preference is given to the first. Yet it is not Rieux who is described as the true hero of the novel but Joseph Grand, who is engaged in activity as modest and unassuming as that which Camus had admired as expressing the true nature of rebellion. Joseph Grand keeps the statistics of the plague. In *La Remarque sur la Révolte* it is stated that the action of a trade union secretary who keeps his accounts up to date is 'metaphysical revolt, just as much as the spectacular daring which sets Byron up against God'. True rebellion against injustice lies in the humble task which helps man in his fight against it. *La Peste* concentrates attention on the problem of suffering, and most particularly on the problem of the suffering of the innocent. It is, as Camus himself said, the most anti-Christian of all his books, for it is the injustice of the death of the child which makes it impossible for Rieux to accept the Christian idea of an all-powerful and a good God.

In *La Remarque sur la Révolte*, Camus expressed ideas which entitle one to interpret *La Peste* as giving his own opinion on Christianity. Commenting, in a footnote, on the danger presented to revolt by a philosophy in which men become 'the echo of the Divine Voice', he wrote: 'I would insist on this point because it seems to me of capital importance. The acceptance of the Christian view seems to me to lead to despair, ("*Le monde chrétien, avec la foi, me semble désespérant*")'. This despair would spring from the need for the Christian to accept the sacrifice of the supremely innocent man, Christ, as well as the suffering of innocent children, as having been willed by God. Such a suspension of the normal standards of ethical judgment is impossible in the philosophy of revolt, since this demands, as Camus pointed out, 'a human order in which all replies shall be human, that is to say, rationally formulated'. *La Peste* continues the refusal of non-human criteria put forward in *Le Mythe de Sisyphe*, at the same time as it introduces other moral and emotional reasons for agnosticism.

Father Paneloux's second sermon defends the Christian existentialism rejected in *Le Mythe de Sisyphe*. Like Kafka and Kierkegaard, Paneloux demands that man should put aside his demand for a rational explanation, and the very words which he uses recall the '*tradition de la pensée humiliée*' and the '*saut existentiel*' described in the essay on the absurd. 'Father Paneloux said that the "total acceptance" of which he had been speaking was not to be taken in the limited sense usually given to the words; he was not thinking of mere resignation or even of that harder virtue, humility. It involved humiliation, but a humiliation to which the person humiliated gave full assent. True, the agony of a child was humiliating to the heart and mind. But that was why we had to come to terms with it. And that too was why—and here Paneloux assured those present that it was not easy to say what he was about to say—since it was God's will, we too should will it.'

La Peste adds to the critique of existentialist theology in *Le Mythe de Sisyphe* the idea that agnosticism is morally as well as intellectually justified. This is brought out in the conversation between Rieux and Paneloux which follows the death of Judge Othon's son. Paneloux suggests that 'this is revolting, because it passes our understanding. But perhaps we should love that which we cannot understand.' Rieux's immediate reply is: 'No, Father, I have another idea of love. And I shall refuse until the day I die to love this creation in which children are tortured.' Paneloux remarks that Rieux has just shown him the true meaning of the word 'Grace', and the conversation ends with Camus doing his best to suggest a Christian reply. Camus was not a militantly agnostic thinker, and never attacked religion in a violent or offensive manner. He was simply incapable of accepting it, and was almost certainly expressing a very personal attitude as well as echoing a favourite idea of Vigny's when he made Rieux say to Tarrou that 'since the order of the world is shaped by death, might it not be better for God if we did not believe in him and struggled with all our might against death, without lifting our eyes to the heavens where He keeps silent'.

To interpret *La Peste* mainly as an expression of the idea

of revolt would, however, be very misleading. When the book first appeared in 1947, most French critics greeted it as an allegorical presentation not only of '*la condition humaine*' in general, but also of the particular experience of the German Occupation. There were many reasons for doing this. The novel had been begun under the Occupation, and part of it—precisely the section which describes the feeling of separation —had first appeared in 1943. This description had an immediate relevance to people whose country was divided into an 'Occupied' and an 'Unoccupied' zone between which communication was almost impossible, and the memory was still sufficiently vivid in 1947 for readers to see the force of Camus's description. The segregation of Oran from the rest of the world, necessary from a strictly medical point of view, symbolised the separation of France from the rest of the civilised world between 1940 and 1944. A modern city would not have been so unprepared medically for an outbreak of plague as Oran, and would certainly have hesitated less in taking the necessary measures against it. The Europe of the 'thirties, however, was in exactly the same state of blindness and unreadiness as Oran, and the inhabitants of Britain and France were, like her citizens, '*enfoncés dans la stupide confiance humaine*'. In any city—especially in Africa—cinemas would certainly be closed during a period of epidemic, but they were not closed in France between 1940 and 1944. It is unlikely that in a plague a Christian, even of the most intolerant persuasion, would actually preach, 'Brethren, misfortune has come upon you: brethren, you have deserved it,' but French cathedrals in the first years of the Vichy régime were frequently witnesses to such sentiments. The impossibility for the citizens of Oran to protect themselves against the arbitrary death which it pleased the plague to send them, differed little from the helplessness of the average French citizen in face of the imprisonment as a hostage or the deportation for forced labour imposed by the German Occupation. Camus had written in 1944, that 'this time is one of separation', and he gives, in *La Peste*, the full analysis of this experience. The '*équipes sanitaires*' which Tarrou organises represent the small groups of men who originally constituted the Resistance movement, and it was in his own rebellion against the tyranny and brutality of the Occupation that Camus confirmed the moral values which form so important a part of *La Peste*. Yet here again it would be limiting to see *La Peste* as the description of a particular historical experience. Both in the insistence which Camus gives to the theme of isolation and in the moral and political implications of the activity of the *équipes sanitaires* it opens out into a much wider context.

Camus's treatment of the theme of separation is one of the most surprising and original features of *La Peste*. It is much more fully analysed than the feeling of terror which might have been expected to predominate in the minds of the citizens of Oran, and can partly be explained by Camus's personal experience. He had himself been separated from both his wife and his mother by the Allied landings in North Africa, and clearly felt the separation very intensely. It was during the war years that the theme of separation became a permanent one in his work, first appearing in *Le Malentendu* —'have pity on those who love and who are separated'—and recurring in the very titles of the last imaginative works he published, *La Chute* and *L'Exil et le Royaume*, in 1956 and 1957. Its origins are extremely varied. There is the longing for an impossible pantheistic union with the world in *Noces*, the experience of the Occupation, the regret which he frequently expressed for his native Algeria after he had settled in Paris in 1945, and the more general longing for a country of true liberty and justice which makes itself felt in all his political writing. In *La Peste*, the theme of separation is first of all linked with an idea expressed by Cherea in *Caligula* when he acknowledged that Caligula did possess the power of making people think. The inhabitants of Oran, although never as despicable as the patricians in *Caligula*, do share several of their assumptions. Like them—and like Camus himself before death separated him from the poet René Leynaud, a close personal friend killed by the Germans for taking part in the Resistance movement—they are 'sunk in stupid human confidence', and the plague teaches them the truth of the human condition: 'that reunion is only the exception, happiness an accident which has lasted'. As the narration proceeds, however, the didactic quality of the plague and the salutary effect which it might have are mentioned much less frequently. Indeed, the book closes with Doctor Rieux recognising that the 'strength and innocence of men' lie in the fact that they never really change, and that it is this which links him to them. It is in order to 'bear witness in favour of the plague-stricken, so that some memorial of the injustice and outrage done to them might endure, and to state quite simply what we learn in the time of pestilence—that there are more things in man to admire than to despise' that he decides to write his chronicle. The early reflections on the insufficiency of the philosophy adopted by the citizens of Oran gives way to an affirmation of man's innocence.

There is an apparent inconsistency here which is best illustrated by referring to the different interpretations which have been put forward of *La Peste*. Germaine Brée, basing her opinion largely on the opening chapters, writes: 'The plague is not a symbol of an outer, abstract evil; it merely applies and carries to their logical limits the values implicit in the unconscious attitudes of the people of Oran.' In her view, *La Peste* is a novel about the insufficiency of human attitudes, and her interpretation of the novel resembles that of the critic in the *Times Literary Supplement* who, seeking to define what Camus meant by 'the plague', suggested that it might be 'that penchant to injustice which, like poison, lurks in us all'. Other critics—particularly those who reproached Camus with having over-simplified the moral problems of political action—considered that the book showed man as the innocent victim of a purely external evil for which he was in no way responsible. In spite of the ambiguity which the first chapters introduce, this is probably the more correct view. Camus openly stated to Roland Barthes that he had intended the book to be read as an allegory of the Resistance movement, and in the *Lettres à un ami allemand* he does insist on the innocence of the French people as a whole. Rieux is the spokesman of Camus's own thought throughout the novel, and it is he who speaks of the 'innocence' of man. The criticism of religion which the novel contains completely ignores the problem of sin, and the emphasis throughout is on man's ability to discover moral values and act in accordance with them. Once it is accepted, however, that *La Peste* deals with the fight that men put up against an evil which is of non-human origin and which comes from outside, its value as an allegory of the Resistance movement is considerably reduced.

Jean Pouillon wrote, in *Les Temps Modernes* in 1947, that

La Peste was an idealised reconstruction of the Resistance movement such as Camus and others would have liked it to have been: the fight of a virtuous and oppressed minority against an anonymous and depersonalised aggressor. In reality, maintained Pouillon, it was a kind of civil war in which Frenchmen fought on both sides for largely political objectives. While Pouillon may have exaggerated the internecine struggle in France between 1940 and 1944, Camus certainly misrepresented the fact that the Resistance movement was a fight of men against men, in which every act of rebellion certainly caused the death of German troops and possibly that of French hostages. For critics like Pouillon and Étiemble, *La Peste* avoided the whole question of the nature of evil, which was the relationship of man to man. Instead, by representing evil as both external and inevitable—the book closes on what is almost a note of acceptance—it marked the end of Camus as a revolutionary writer. He had, according to the writers of *Les Temps Modernes*, forsaken revolution and its moral conflicts for the pleasures of a clear conscience. Etiemble pointed out that the action of simply fighting against a particular epidemic of plague was inadequate in modern times. In the next epidemic—which he suggested that the Americans were busy preparing—Rieux and Tarrou would no longer be able to wash themselves temporarily free of the plague in the sea, since it would be contaminated with radioactivity. The ordinary morality of simply doing one's job was not, he insisted, a sufficiently vigorous one for the needs of our time. After a real and recent plague had broken out in Egypt, a thorough reform of the medical services had taken place. No indication is given in *La Peste* that such a thing is going to happen in Oran or, symbolically, that it should have happened in post-war France. The political attitude implicit in *La Peste* was thus, for Etiemble, basically conservative through timidity and abstention.

This criticism was repeated by other writers apart from the socially committed revolutionaries of *Les Temps Modernes*. The Christian writer Bertrand d'Astorg admired Camus's moral integrity but noted the limitations of the attitude recommended in *La Peste*. 'The best among them attack the effects,' he wrote of the *équipes sanitaires*: 'no-one deals with the cause.' Might it not be better in some circumstances, he asked, to prefer 'the humility of the builders who are prepared to get their hands dirty' to Tarrou's attempt at sanctity? Even an academic critic like John Cruickshank, writing in an atmosphere unaffected by French political arguments, notes that: 'By using the plague as a symbol and by emphasising its arbitrary nature, Camus places political evil outside the scope of human responsibility.' These critics all agree that one cannot equate resistance to microbes with resistance to men. Were Camus writing as a pacifist and openly advocating a mixture of passive resistance and help for the International Red Cross, these objections would not arise. As it is, however, he stated on several occasions that he was not a pacifist, and maintained that the attitude in *La Peste* was that of a man who refused not violence itself but only its systematic use for political purposes.

He was, naturally, fully aware of the criticisms made of *La Peste*, and answered them in a letter to Roland Barthes in 1955. He replied to the question 'What would the combatants of *La Peste* do when faced with a human visage of pestilence?' by saying that it ought to have been couched in the past tense. 'For', he continued, 'it has already received its answer, which is a positive one. What these combatants, whose experience I have partially translated, did, they did against men, and at a price which you know well.' The reply, though undoubtedly sincere, is unconvincing. Camus chose to transfer an actual fight against men into an allegorical fight against disease. In doing so, he eliminated the problems raised by a struggle in which men have to kill their fellows. He then maintained that this new and different attitude was still valid because it was originally inspired by a fight against men. The allegory of the Resistance movement is not, however, the only political theme in the book. The attack on capital punishment introduced by Tarrou's confession is closely related with the political problems to which Camus gave most of his attention after 1945 and does much to dispel the objections made to the ideas of the novel.

Tarrou's confession takes place one evening, after a day spent with Rieux fighting the plague, in an hour which is, as Tarrou says, 'the hour of friendship'. Unlike Rieux, a workman's son who had learned the truth of the world through poverty, Tarrou was the son of a public prosecutor, who had wanted him to follow the same career. One day, in order to impress his son, Tarrou's father invited him to come and watch him in court. That day—he was seventeen—decided Tarrou's future. Only one memory remained in his mind, that of the figure of the criminal in the dock, a little red-haired man, who looked like an owl frightened by too strong a light, who bit the fingers of his right hand, who was alive and who was inevitably to be killed. Tarrou was filled with horror at this 'most abject of all murders'. Unable to bear life at home, where even the railway time-table which it was his father's hobby to learn by heart reminded him of this legalised murder, he went away and fought against the society which rested upon the institution of the death penalty. 'I did not want to be a carrier of the plague,' he says, and identifies it with the guilt which no member of a society which practises capital punishment can ever escape. But in his struggle against society and his attempts to transform it, he came upon the same plague in a new form. The revolutionaries with whom he worked themselves pronounced death sentences which Tarrou began by accepting as necessary to bring about a better world. Then, one day, he actually saw an execution by a firing-squad in Hungary. This experience revealed to him that, as he says, 'I had not ceased to be a carrier of the plague during all these long years when I had nevertheless believed, with all my soul, that I was fighting against plague.' This brings Tarrou into contact with the main moral problem of revolt. There comes a moment, in the movement of rebellion, when the rebel must face the question of his attitude towards those who might oppose him. Since he is protesting against suffering and death, has he any right to add to them by killing his enemies?

Tarrou's reply is an uncompromising 'No'. He refuses to allow that the fight for a better world can ever justify 'this disgusting butchery', and limits his revolutionary activity to seeking to abolish the specific evil of capital punishment. Not, he tells Rieux, that he himself thinks he has attained a complete innocence and is no longer responsible for the crimes which society commits. In this world, our smallest actions may bring about the death of a man, and none can claim absolute innocence. Understanding this, he has realised that all men are *dans la peste* and he has lost all peace. For the time being, his action is limited to refusing to countenance any execution and to putting himself, under all circumstances, 'on the side of the victims . . . to limit the destruction'. His more intimate and personal aim is to become 'a saint without God', to attain a peace of mind where he will no longer feel his guilt for the death of others and be a carrier of the plague.

Camus said in an interview with Claudine Chonez in 1948 that it was Rieux, the narrator, whose ideas predominated throughout La Peste, and whose 'strictly human' attitude he preferred to Tarrou's quest for sanctity. Nevertheless there is no doubt that on this question Tarrou is speaking very much in Camus's own name. His emotional reaction against capital punishment is Camus's own, and his remark that 'it seems to me that history has borne me out; to-day there's a sort of competition as to who will kill the most' reflects Camus's own horrified vision of mid-twentieth-century politics. The ideas put forward in Tarrou's confession give La Peste an obvious political message. They also offer a more convincing reply than that directly given by Camus himself to the criticisms that its moral implications were inadequate.

From 19th to 30th November, 1946, there appeared in Combat a series of articles by Camus entitled Ni Victimes ni Bourreaux (Neither Victims nor Hangmen). Beginning with the epigram that: 'the seventeenth century was the century of mathematics, the eighteenth that of physics; our century is the century of fear,' Camus made these articles into an impassioned protest against the use of murder as a political weapon. The century of fear, he argued, had been created by 'a world where murder is made legal and where human life is considered as worthless'. This had happened because the long tradition which accepted dialogues and approximations, reasonable discussions and rational arguments, had given way to the domination of abstract ideologies. Both La Peste and Ni Victimes ni Bourreaux are protests against the acceptance of this world, and particularly against what seemed to be taking the place of Fascism as its supreme incarnation: Stalinist Communism. Camus had already written in January 1946, that 'when one believes, like Hegel and the whole of modern philosophy, that man is made for history and not history for man, one cannot believe in dialogue: one believes in efficacity and in the will to power. Ultimately, one believes in murder.'

Seen in this light, Tarrou's and Rieux's struggle against the plague—frequently referred to in the novel as '*l'abstraction*'—is Camus's own fight against the abstract logic of the Marxist-Hegelian theory of history and against totalitarianism in all its forms. Rieux's attitude corresponds to the 'modest political thought' which Camus is trying to formulate. Translated into political terms it is a plea for tolerance and liberalism, an argument for Popper's 'piece-meal social engineering' as against Lenin's idea of a violent revolution followed by a complete reorganisation of society. Revolutions, in Camus's view, are too expensive. However high the ideals of those who conduct them, they cost more in human lives than they create in social improvement. 'Good intentions can do as much damage as wickedness if they are not enlightened,' thinks Rieux, and in this he is very much the spokesman of Camus's own thought. 'What strikes me in the midst of all these polemics, threats and violent outbreaks,' writes Camus in the second article of *Ni Victimes ni Bourreaux*, '*Sauver les Corps*', 'are the obvious good intentions of everybody. All of them, except for a few crooks on the Right as on the Left, think that their truth is the one which will make men happy.' *La Peste* is an attempt to show that totalitarianism inevitably relies on mass-murder to impose its rule and therefore can only increase human misery. It also points out that there are other, more modest ways, of trying to improve society. The book extols, in fact, the virtue of those who 'simply try to be doctors', that is to say, who are prepared to carry out piece-meal social reforms on the body politic without trying to cure it of all its ills by drastic surgery.

An interpretation of *La Peste* as an attack on Communist totalitarianism is the best reply to the criticism that its implicit plea for non-violence makes it an inaccurate allegory of the Resistance movement. It is a book written in reaction against a prevailing climate of thought, and as such goes perhaps too far in the opposite direction. What Camus is arguing against in *La Peste* is the myth of violent revolution prevalent in post-war France, a myth with which he himself had briefly sympathised, but which he was to attack in much more detail in *L'Homme révolté*. *La Peste* announces the ideas later developed in *L'Homme révolté* not only in Tarrou's confession but also in several of its other themes. When heroism is placed 'just after, and never before, the generous demand for happiness'; when Rieux acquiesces in Rambert's attempt to escape and rejoin his mistress in Paris; when the narrator refuses to condemn the black-marketeer Cottard by anything more than the phrase that 'he had an ignorant, that is to say a lonely heart', Camus is arguing against the myth that all personal considerations must be sacrificed to the cause of the revolution. When the insignificant and at times almost ridiculous character of Grand is presented as the true hero of the book, Camus's reaction against the ideas of Saint-Just, Robespierre and Lenin reaches its highest point. Yet although he made Tarrou say 'it is other people who will make history', Camus did not intend La Peste to be read as an apology for political inactivity. The choice which Tarrou made to 'put himself on the side of the victims in order to limit the damage' was one which Camus tried to follow out in his own political activity—and in particular on the problems of North Africa— during the rest of his life. La Peste is a plea for moderation, not for quietism, in the political struggles of the twentieth century.

None of the critics who attacked La Peste for the inadequacy of the remedies it proposed for the plagues of war, exploitation and injustice, ever denied the great value which the book had as a work of art. Even Jean-Paul Sartre, whose general views were certainly reflected by Pouillon's and Etiemble's articles, referred to La Peste at the end of Qu'est-ce que la littérature? as the perfect novel of the future. Critics all agreed that Camus had combined allegory with what Roger Stéphane called 'the most faithful depiction of daily life under the Occupation' in a most skilful and intelligent manner. Detailed aesthetic considerations, however, gave way in most reviews to arguments for and against Camus's moral and political ideas, and Camus himself remarked in a radio interview in 1955 that his careful composition of the novel had passed almost without comment. This was, he added, a sign that he had done his work almost too well, since no one noticed that the book's division into five parts expressed the invasion, triumph, and eventual departure of the plague.

In the first part, Camus remarked in conversation in 1956, the style illustrated how individual actions still prevailed in a city as yet untouched by the plague, and he quoted the following passage to illustrate his point, stressing as he did so the number of singular past definites:

'*Le matin du seize avril, le docteur Bernard Rieux sortit de son cabinet et buta sur un rat mort au milieu du palier. Sur le moment, il écarta la bête sans y prendre garde, et descendit l'escalier. Mais, arrivé dans la rue, la pensée lui vint que ce rat n'était pas à sa place, et il retourna sur ses pas pour avertir le concierge.*'

('On the morning of April 16th, Dr. Bernard Rieux came out of his surgery and stubbed his foot against a dead rat lying in the middle of the landing. On the spur of the moment, he kicked it aside and continued on his way downstairs without thinking any more about it. But, once he was in the street, the thought struck him that the rat had no business to be on his landing, and he retraced his steps to go and tell the hall porter.')

After the official declaration of the state of siege, a long passage analysing the feeling of separation in general terms introduces the idea that the plague 'began by making our fellow-citizens act as if they had no individual feelings'. The style continues to reflect this idea, for as the plague kills more and more people, the description of Rambert's attempt to escape and the reproduction of the conversations between Tarrou and Cottard give way to an analysis of feelings shared by all. In the third and shortest section, when the plague makes all individual feelings disappear, almost no isolated actions are described. What is evoked is the 'reign of immobility imposed upon us, or, rather, its final aspect, that of a city of the dead where plague, stone and darkness had effectively silenced every voice'. Then, at the beginning of the fourth section, individual actions reappear, as Castel's serum is tried out for the first time and the death of the child introduces a change in Paneloux's attitude. The plague then begins gradually to decrease in intensity, until, at the end of the fourth part, live rats make a sudden and unexpected return to the streets of the city, and the brief fifth section describes the reunion of lovers and the return to normal.

Although these variations of style do exist in the book, it is easy to see why the majority of critics failed to notice them. Camus was not, in fact, wholly consistent in allowing his style to reflect the importance of individuals in the first part and their growing insignificance in the second and third, since the book opens with a general, impersonal account of life in Oran, and the descriptions of Rambert's various attempts to escape do take up long sections of part two. What is more noticeable is the careful construction which places the three most moving episodes—the death of the child, Paneloux's sermon and Tarrou's confession—as a series of climaxes towards the end of the book. Tarrou's death and the news that Rieux's wife has died in a sanitorium then follow as a reminder that whatever the nobility and heroism of certain acts, the truth of the fight against the plague lies in the dull pain of death and loneliness. Just as the variations of style aim at underlining the abstraction and impersonality of the plague, so the construction of the book indicates that Camus is not just talking about what happened on a particular occasion. The plague is always with us, and it is a power as mysterious and irresistible as a force of nature or as life itself. It is by his style as much as by his subject-matter that Camus makes *La Peste* into both a modern myth of impotence and imprisonment and an allegory of man's permanent fight against the natural order of creation. 'What is natural,' says Rieux 'is the microbe. All the rest, health, integrity, purity, if you like, is an effect of our will, and of a will that must never weaken.' By causing the book to close upon Tarrou's death and Rieux's loss of his wife, Camus is emphasising that man lives in a condition where suffering predominates.

Camus obtains his effects in *La Peste* not only by carefully relating style to construction, but also by choosing a style peculiarly suited to the events described. The constant understatement in the descriptive style of *La Peste*, the precise use of administrative terms and official language, the deliberate banality of the words, are essential elements in the final effect which the chronicle makes. The impersonal mode of narration allows the author to act on the reader's sensitivity without revealing his own, to create emotion in the reader's mind by forcing him to project his own feelings on to the extraordinary events so calmly described. The irony of Camus's style is the most important factor in bringing out the full horror of the situation, and his use of understatement plays an essential rôle in establishing the relationship between reality and allegory. His aim is to equate plague with the bureaucratic tyranny of a modern dictatorship, and he does it by describing plague as manifesting itself in the same way and having the very same effects as bureaucracy.

A good example of this is in his evocation of the monotony of the period of plague.

'*Dans le souvenir de ceux qui les ont vécues, les journées terribles de la peste n'apparaissent pas comme de grandes flammes interminables et cruelles, mais plutôt comme un immense piétinement qui écrasait tout sur son passage.*'

('In the memory of those who lived through them, the terrible days of the plague do not seem like great, cruel, interminable flames, but rather like an endless movement of feet which crushed everything it passed over.')

Here his words apply exactly both to the period of German occupation and to the effect which a plague would have upon a modern city. The essential services would be maintained, as they were maintained in occupied France. The primitive terror of plague would bring a reinforcement in the discipline of the day-to-day government of the city. The horror of pestilence would be hidden for the most part under a monotonous administration and reveal itself only suddenly and in unexpected places—at the theatre, where an actor is stricken down in the middle of his rôle, in a restaurant where a diner is suddenly taken ill. In earlier plagues, in more primitive times, the carts went round the streets to collect the dead, whose bodies were heaped in confusion one upon another. In Oran, the dead are scientifically collected, disinfected, loaded into trams and carried by night to the pits of quicklime. The excellence of Camus's description lies precisely in the contrast which he maintains between the physical, primitive horror of the plague, and the quiet, scientific administration of the modern city, between the awfulness of the events and the everyday places where they occur. His skill in alternating them—evident in the description of the incident at the theatre and of the sudden shock when Rieux's foot squelches upon the dead rat in the middle of his landing—is combined with an extremely effective style. When Rieux discovers the rat on his landing, the incident is described as '*insolite*'. Camus's deliberate refusal to use any other but the most precise and

simple words in most of the descriptive passages enables him
to throw into high relief those scenes to which he wishes to
attach a special significance.

One of the important minor themes of the 'chronicle' is that
of the weather, and the relationship which it has with the progress of the plague. Towards the beginning of the second section, the narrator remarks that each inhabitant of Oran was
forced to 'live a day-to-day existence, alone in face of the
heavens', with the result that they were all 'given over to its
caprices'. The weather does indeed play an essential part in *La
Peste*, encouraging the progress of the epidemic as the heat of
the summer grows more intense, and, perhaps, leading to its
departure when the cold months of January and February
arrive. When Rieux's concierge dies, thick mists cover the
sky and are followed by downpours of rain and a heavy
stormy heat. Then, as the sea loses its blueness and 'takes on
flashes of silver and steel painful to the eyes', people feel that
they are held prisoner by the sky. As the plague strengthens its
hold over the town the link with the weather becomes stronger.
'A scorching wind blew steadily for a whole day and dried up
the walls. Then the sun shone steadily. Ceaseless waves of heat
and light poured daylong on to the town, and, but for arcaded
streets and interiors of houses, everywhere lay bathed in the
dazzling impact of the light.' The summer, normally the time
when the people of Oran feel most in tune with the universe,
becomes the season when 'the sun of the plague had killed
all colours and sent all joy into exile', and when, in the hot
afternoon's silence 'sunlight, dust and plague have the streets
to themselves'. The town 'warms up to boiling-point under
a sultry sky' and there is no means of knowing 'if the air is
heavy with menace or merely with dust and heat'. At the
beginning of the third section, when the rule of the plague
becomes absolute, the wind returns and blows steadily
through the town. 'A smell of brine and seaweed came from
the unseen and storm-tossed sea. And the city, emptied of all
its inhabitants, palled in dust and loud with the shrilling of
the wind, groaned like a lost island of the damned.' Then,
when the plague has finally gone, the weather is again
favourable to man, and the sun returns 'dispersing the cold
winds that had been fighting in the air since morning and
pouring out on to the town a steady flood of tranquil light'.

This linking-up of the progress of the plague with the changes in the weather is important for two main reasons: it helps to keep the reader conscious of the passage of time, and thus make him realise how interminable the period of plague must have seemed to the inhabitants of Oran; it links up with the ideas of the novel in showing that 'this external world which can always be a salvation against everything' is not always the ally of man's happiness. It can, as when the sun made Meursault kill the Arab, bring suffering as well as happiness. This idea is particularly emphasised in *La Peste* when Camus uses one of his own most characteristic images, that of the wind, in order to personalise the plague.

One of the best essays in *Noces* is entitled *Le Vent à Djémila*, and describes how Camus 'bent over in the middle, eyes burning, lips cracking, skin drying until it was no longer his', felt himself 'flapping in the wind like a sail' until he almost lost the feeling of his own identity. The image of the wind occurs at the crucial points in *L'Étranger*. Just before Meursault kills the Arab it engulfs him with its 'hot, thick breath', and in his final outburst to the priest the image which comes to his mind is that of the 'dark wind' of death which, blowing through his whole future, sweeps all meaning from his life. In *La Peste*, the wind is evoked early in the book when Rieux, recalling the description of the great plagues of history, remembers the construction in Provence of an enormous wall which was to have stopped 'the furious wind of the plague' blowing from the South. When Paneloux is giving his first sermon, and using for the first time the image of the flail, 'a damp wind swept up the nave and made the candle flames crackle and splutter'. From this point onwards the wind is linked with the images of the flail, and of the great spear which Paneloux describes as striking the houses of those afflicted and pointing out to others the path of salvation. Rieux, drinking in a café with Grand, feels that the night is full of the groans of dying men and thinks that 'somewhere in the dark sky, above the street-lamps, the invisible flail tirelessly beating the air is making a dull whistling sound above their heads'. In September and October it is as if this flail were 'tirelessly whistling above the houses', and turning the flocks of birds away from the town. It is in the description of the child's death that the wind, having 'risen and blown for several days on the plague-stricken city' shows itself most closely linked with the forces of evil. Like Meursault's shooting of the Arab, the death of Judge Othon's son is described in an intensely poetic passage where the image of the wind predominates over everything else.

'*Il resta creusé ainsi pendant de longues secondes, secoué de frissons et de tremblements convulsifs, comme si sa frêle carcasse pliait sous le vent furieux de la peste et craquait sous les souffles répétés de la fièvre. La bourrasque passée, il se détendit un peu, la fièvre sembla se retirer et l'abandonner, haletant, sur une grève humide et empoisonnée où le repos ressemblait déjà à la mort.*'

('The child remained bent over for long moments, quivering and shuddering in long trembling fits, as if his frail body were bending beneath the furious wind of the plague and cracking beneath the repeated gusts of fever. The squall ceased, he relaxed a little, the fever seemed to withdraw and leave him, panting, on a damp and poisoned bank where rest was already like death.')

Tarrou's death is described in similar terms, and also marks the final union of the two images of the flail and of the wind.

'*L'orage qui secouait ce corps de soubresauts convulsifs l'illuminait d'éclairs de plus en plus rares, et Tarrou dérivait lentement au fond de cette tempête. Rieux n'avait plus devant lui qu'un masque désormais inerte où le sourire avait disparu. Cette forme humaine qui lui avait été si proche, percée maintenant de coups d'épieu, brûlée par un mal surhumain, tordue par tous les vents haineux du ciel, s'immergeait à ses yeux dans les eaux de la peste et il ne pouvait rien contre ce naufrage. Il devait rester sur le rivage, les mains vides et le coeur tordu, sans armes et sans recours, une fois de plus, contre le désastre.*'

('The storm, lashing his body into convulsive movement, lit it up with ever rarer flashes, and in the heart of the tempest he was slowly drifting, derelict. And now Rieux had before him only a masklike face, inert, from which the smile had gone for ever. This human form, his friend's, lacerated by the spear-thrusts of the plague, consumed by searing superhuman fires, buffeted by all the ravaging winds of heaven, was foundering under his eyes in the dark flood of the pestilence, and he could do nothing to avert the wreck. He could only stand, unavailing, on the shore, empty-handed and sick at heart, unarmed and helpless yet again under the onslaught of calamity.')

The excellence of *La Peste* as a work of art is, like that of *L'Etranger*, the result of both planning and inspiration, of the contrast between the vivid images which come naturally and spontaneously to Camus and a style which he deliberately adopts for a particular purpose. The restraint which Camus shows in describing the plague as 'primarily a prudent and impeccable administration' enables him to bring out, by contrast, the force of the images personifying it as a flail or a violent, irresistible wind. The advantage which he derives from his refusal to dramatise the plague when it is seen as a symbol of bureaucracy can best be appreciated by comparing the style of *La Peste* with that of the *Discours de la Peste à ses Administrés* which, published separately in 1947, was later incorporated in *L'Etat de Siège*. There, as in Camus's play, the plague is a bombastic dictator who proclaims, 'I have assumed the appearance of a junior officer to vex you and because it is good for you to be vexed.' Whereas in *L'Etat de Siège* totalitarianism is given the deliberate intention of making people unhappy, Camus's representation of it in *La Peste* is much more subtle and much more convincing. In the novel, the plague is seen as imposing separation, rationing and bureaucratic controls on the inhabitants of Oran because these are 'in their own best interests'. The allegory of modern totalitarianism which imprisons men only for their own good is here made much more effective by Camus's restraint in not attributing to the plague the purely mischievous intentions that it has in *L'Etat de Siège*. His description goes beyond the mere evocation of the spirit of totalitarianism, for when Rieux stands 'on the shore, empty-handed, sick at heart, unarmed and helpless yet again under the onslaught of calamity' he foreshadows the whole situation of democratic liberalism in the modern world: its inability to do anything to save Hungary in 1956.

Camus himself affirmed that *La Peste* marked the progress from 'an attitude of solitary revolt to the recognition of a community whose struggles all must share'. Its publication, however, coincided with a narrowing-down of his own political activity and preoccupations. He had given up the editorship of *Combat* in 1945 in order to complete *La Peste*, and early in 1947 *Combat* ran into financial difficulties. A businessman called Henri Smadja then bought the newspaper, and Camus withdrew from the editorial committee to be replaced by Claude Bourdet. According to an article which M. Bourdet wrote in 1960, Camus did little to fight against this take-over, and thereby made the task of those who were trying to keep the newspaper independent more difficult. Later, in 1949, when M. Bourdet received an offer from another businessman who was prepared to buy out M. Smadja and enable Camus to return and take control of *Combat*, Camus again refused the offer. The reason offered by M. Bourdet for Camus's strange indifference towards the fight to preserve the newspaper which had once been so dear to him was that by this time he was too far removed from the practical considerations of day-to-day politics. He argued that Camus had taken so idealistic a view of the Resistance movement that he became unable to accept the compromises, bargainings and bitter internal disputes which characterise any revolutionary movement in its attempt to seize power or exercise political influence. 'Little by little,' he wrote, 'Camus grew more and more bitter, and closed his newspaper experience on a note of Olympian loss of illusions.'

This account lends weight to those critics who saw in *La Peste* Camus's renunciation of the ideal '*De La Résistance à la Révolution*' which had so well summed up both his own attitude and that of *Combat*. From 1945 onwards, Camus did in fact become increasingly obsessed with one political problem: totalitarianism. By concentrating upon it, however, he gave his political thought a narrowness of application which is disappointing when compared with the articles he published in *Combat* in 1944 and 1945. It is true that he did write on other political matters: he protested against the violent repression by the French authorities of a revolt in Madagascar in 1947, supported Garry Davies's 'Citizens of the World' movement in 1948, and intervened on behalf of Greek Communists sentenced to death in 1948 and 1949. Yet the limits which he himself placed on his political activity, combined with the apparent rejection of revolution as a means of social progress in *La Peste*, seemed to Camus's left-wing critics a sign that he was falling into the systematic anti-Communism which, on October 10th, 1944, he had denounced as 'the beginning of dictatorship'. A study of his next two plays and of the political implications of *L'Homme révolté* will show whether or not this was a correct impression.

Chapter Eight

THE DIDACTIC THEATRE

ON October 27th, 1948, Jean-Louis Barrault produced Camus's fourth play, *L'Etat de Siège* (*State of Siege*), at the Théâtre Marigny. The *Avertissement*, written by Camus himself, and printed at the front of the published version, informs the reader that although the subject is the same as that of *La Peste*, the play is by no means an adaptation of the novel. This warning applies on the plane of ideas as well as on that of aesthetics. From a theatrical point of view, Camus is trying to mingle 'all the different forms of dramatic expression, from the lyrical monologue to the collective theatre, through dumb show, straightforward dialogue, farce and the use of the chorus'. Nothing could form a stronger contrast to the deliberately restrained narration of *La Peste*. On the plane of ideas, Camus selects some of the themes of his novel and gives them greater importance, just as he completely omits others and introduces new ideas not expressed in the novel. While in *La Peste* the wind was generally represented as a hostile force, in *L'Etat de Siège* it is wholly on the side of the forces of freedom and individuality. In this respect, *L'Etat de Siège* shows how Camus returned to nature, his first love, as a refuge from the deadening abstraction of his time and a final means of conquering them.

La Peste does indeed announce this idea when, after Tarrou's confession, he and Rieux go down and bathe in the sea together. They find a temporary escape from the plague, and renew their strength for the fight against it. Yet, as has been seen, the wind and the natural elements are an ambiguous force in *La Peste*, and are shown for the most part as being hostile to man. In *L'Etat de Siège*, where the complex symbolism of *La Peste* is narrowed down to the expression of

116

one specific idea, this ambiguity disappears. Thus, when the plague establishes its dominion over Cadiz, the town people know that when the wind blows from off the sea their liberation will come. The close identification of the plague with totalitarianism was emphasised in the actual production of the play when the character who represented it wore the uniform of a Nazi officer. The plague takes over the town and makes a long speech—the '*Discours de la Peste à ses Administrés*' from '*Les Archives de la Peste*'—in which Camus expresses all his hatred of totalitarianism and all his admiration for the simple human values that it threatens. The official authorities of the town, a group of cowardly non-entities symbolising the selfishness and stupidity of bourgeois society, begin by trying to pretend that nothing is happening, but as soon as they themselves are threatened by the plague they submit to its power. The plague then explains to the townspeople why it has come. Its aim is to replace 'the ridiculous anguish of happiness, the stupid faces of lovers, the selfish contemplation of the countryside and punishable irony' by an efficient organisation. Now that order has been imposed, and the confusion of happiness and individuality banished, even death can be rationalised and made part of a system. 'You have your card index numbers,' says the plague to its subjects, 'you will no longer die by caprice. Destiny has grown wise, henceforth, and has installed itself in its offices. You will form part of statistics, and you will finally be of use to something.' The plague brings with it, as its gift to the inhabitants of Cadiz, 'silence, order and absolute justice'. The symbolism which remained ambiguous in the novel is here made explicit and obvious, and the attack against all forms of dictatorship deliberately made the centre of the play.

The plague recruits, in the place of the old authorities, the services of Nada, a drunken nihilist. It is he who is given the task of justifying, often in a highly ironic tone, the dictates of the plague to the townspeople. A mere buffoon if the play is read or seen by itself, Nada becomes a symbolic figure if he is studied side by side with Camus's other more philosophical writings. He represents the intellectual nihilism which, in the absence of all other values, justifies totalitarianism in order to satisfy its yearnings for destruction. 'Suppression, that is my gospel,' says Nada, 'but until now I had no good reasons to justify it. Now I have the reasons which the regulations provide.' For Camus, the absolute philosophies of history have been able to establish such a hold on European thought because they have based themselves upon its nihilism and despair. Camus's German friend had adopted the reasons for living and acting offered by Nazism because no others were available. In the absence of other values to oppose to them, abstract ideologies, with their denial of life, have triumphed. This idea, central to the argument of *L'Homme révolté*, is here expressed in the rather crude symbolism of the character of Nada.

The revolt of the inhabitants of Cadiz against the plague is led by Diego, who has to struggle between his love for Victoria and his duty towards his fellow-men. His revolt has not the quiet perseverance of Rieux and Tarrou, but more of the rhetorical protest of the Orestes in Sartre's *Les Mouches*. As soon as he rebels against the plague's secretary—a white-cuffed young lady symbolising death—she realises that she no longer has any power over him. 'As long as I can remember,' she says, 'it has always been enough for a man to overcome his fear for the machine to start to go wrong.' As soon as Diego takes consciousness of his power of revolt and achieves his freedom, the wind blows from the sea and the liberation of the town is at hand. Diego, like Sartre's Orestes, argues with the oppressor and in his argument expresses the author's own ideas. Like Sartre's Jupiter, Camus's plague has no power over the man who claims his own freedom. In the last scene of the play, the plague holds Diego's fiancée, Victoria, prisoner, and offers to exchange her life either for the liberty of the town, or for Diego's own life. Diego refuses the exchange, rejecting the realist argument of the plague that 'one cannot be happy without consenting to the death of other people. It is the justice of this earth'. 'I was not born to consent to that justice,' he proclaims, and follows his refusal by a violent denunciation of the logic on which the political realism of the plague is based. 'I know the formula,' he says, this time completely the spokesman of Camus's own thought. 'We must kill to abolish murder, break laws to cure injustice. And this has been going on for centuries. For centuries the lords of your race have been infecting the world's wounds under the pretext of curing them, and still continue to boast about their remedy, since no one laughs at them to their face.' Diego's outburst is, like the whole of *La Peste*, a plea that ordinary people, with ordinary limited ambitions and qualities, should replace the hangmen of absolute justice. 'I hate only hangmen,' proclaim both Diego and Camus. Both plead that revolt should remain faithful to its origins, to the limit which it discovered as its first value and to the essential modesty which characterises it.

Diego wins his argument with the plague, not because the plague recognises that its attempt to impose absolute order and justice by using all and every means is wrong, but because death, which had been at the orders of the plague, grows tired of killing. She had been, in the past, sometimes welcomed as a reliever, sometimes merciful. Since she has been placed at the service of logic and reason, she says, 'I have ruined the skill of my once helpful hand.' Frustrated, deprived of his power by the revolt of death, the plague departs, and the wind blows again from the sea. Nada, as the plague goes away, throws himself into the sea, unable to bear the return of the justice which he hates. He is weary of everything, and cries out: 'I know too many things. Even scorn has had its day. Farewell, good people, you will one day learn that one cannot live well, knowing that man is nothing and that the face of God is terrible.' *L'Etat de Siège* is as much a refusal and criticism of nihilism as it is of totalitarianism.

It also contains, exaggerating a mere tendency of *La Peste* but continuing a central theme of *L'Etranger*, an extremely biting satire against the hypocrisy of bourgeois morality. In *La Peste*, the Judge Othon and his family form the subject of a satirical little portrait in Tarrou's diary, and, after the death of the judge's little boy, Tarrou feels sympathetic to his father but asks bitterly, 'Who can help a judge?' It is in keeping with the more violent tone of *L'Etat de Siège* that Victoria's father, who is a judge, should be a thorough hypocrite and should wish to betray Diego to the plague. It is his duty, he claims, to give Diego up, as he will then be acting in accordance with the law. But his wife revolts against him, pointing out that he had not the law on his side when he seduced a young girl who was attempting to obtain judgment against an unjust master, and claiming that, even if he has the law on his side, she has right on hers. The right she has is 'the right of those who love not to be separated, the right of the guilty to be pardoned, and the penitent to be honoured'. The normal human values of goodness and forgiveness are shown to be menaced not only by the excesses of revolutionary or fascist dictatorships, but also by the hypocrisy of outworn bourgeois morality. Such a direct attack on the hypocrisy which has perverted humanism in modern society is rare in Camus's work, for he is in general far more concerned with the criticism of revolution than of bourgeois society. For Camus, orthodox humanism as it is expressed in conventional middle-class morality is so definitely dead and discredited that it is no longer necessary to satirise or attack it. He does so only in *L'Etranger* and in *L'Etat de Siège*. In *L'Etranger* his satire is used principally for artistic purposes, to show the contrast between the absurd man and conventional society, and in *L'Etat de Siège* to liberate an instinctive hatred of judges which is only latent in *La Peste* but which is given full scope in *La Chute*. The morality expressed by the formal laws of society is at the greatest possible distance from the true object of his admiration, the beauty and freedom of the sea and nature. Throughout the play, the richness and diversity of the natural world form a contrast with the meanness of bourgeois morality and the terrible monotony of the totalitarian state.

It is impossible not to admire the beauty and nobility of the ideas that Camus expresses in *L'Etat de Siège*, and equally impossible to claim that the play was an artistic success. One of the most attractive features of the whole of Camus's thought was his detestation of totalitarianism and the determined fight which he put up against it. In this respect, he was the welcome spokesman of all those who, in mid-twentieth-century Europe, were haunted by the betrayal of revolutions and their tendency to become one-party states based on police terror. Camus's insistence that Communism has never been established by genuinely democratic processes anywhere in the world is central to an understanding of *L'Etat de Siège*, and it is excellent that he should have chosen to base a whole play on this theme. Unfortunately, good intentions do not always make good works of art. Rarely has a work by an important modern author, produced by one of France's leading actor-managers, had such a disastrous critical reception as *L'Etat de Siège*. Bernard Simiot expressed the general reaction when he wrote that it was 'a spectacle that is often boring, wordy and grandiloquent, interspersed with bad revue scenes or incomprehensible ballets, animated by symbolic characters in whose suffering or loves it is extremely difficult to take any interest'.

A number of critics writing in 1948 suggested that most of the blame for the failure of the play should be attributed to Jean-Louis Barrault, who, it was said, had seduced Camus from his natural sobriety and restraint and enveigled him into writing an extravaganza suited to Barrault's production methods and Pierre Brasseur's style of acting. This is a suggestion which Camus himself firmly denied, and which cannot be seriously entertained once the play has been read. The crudeness, the over-simplification, the empty characters, are all there in the text itself, and Camus's decision to allow it to be published in that form indicates that *L'Etat de Siège* was entirely his own work. The principal reason for the failure of the play can be found in Camus's over-simplified approach to political problems. All the good is on one side and all the bad on the other. The simple townsfolk and the attractive lovers stand in the same relation to the hypocritical bourgeoisie and the wicked totalitarians as the hero does to the villain in nineteenth-century melodrama. The good triumph too easily over the wicked, whose motives are nothing more complicated than the desire to inflict suffering. One has only to compare *L'Etat de Siège* with Koestler's *Darkness at Noon*, a work of equally anti-Communist inspiration, to see how Camus has failed to recognise that, in spite of all the suffering it causes, totalitarianism is not always born of wholly despicable motives. It may be argued that the play is a satire, and that Camus's aim is not so much to study totalitarianism as to present it as ridiculous. Here again, however, his over-simplification prevents him from carrying out his purpose. The subtlety of approach demanded by satire is destroyed by the intrusion of emotion in the characters of Victoria and Diego, and by the sheer caricature of Nada. The audience must be able to accept that the character satirised does believe in his own ideas, and it is impossible to do this when the character speaks with the exaggerated sentiments which Camus puts in the mouth of the plague. Yet although *L'Etat de Siège* was a failure from a dramatic point of view, it is not true to say that it represented a movement towards an acceptance of bourgeois society or a readiness to accept any ally as long as he is staunchly anti-Communist.

This was emphasised when Gabriel Marcel attacked Camus for having set his play in Spain. Camus replied, in a public letter in 1948, that 'I will not excuse this hideous plague in the West just because it is ravaging the East', and violently attacked Franco's dictatorship. His fidelity to the cause of Spanish freedom shows the continued radicalism of his political outlook, for he never ceased to defend what he called 'free and suffering Spain' against 'the Spain of churches and prisons'. From his earliest published newspaper article defending the International Brigade, through his appeal for the united diplomatic pressure which could have brought about the collapse of the Franco régime in 1945, through his resignation from UNESCO in 1952 because of the admission of Spain, he argued in favour of Spanish republicanism and democracy. Both in 1948 and in 1952 he linked his attack on Spain with a more general condemnation of Western political society, protesting in both cases against the increasing readiness to sacrifice democracy's moral assets by accepting any allies who were anti-Communist. He himself never intended his denunciation of Communist dictatorship to be associated with conservatism or reaction, and always protested that he was as much the enemy of 'the society of merchants as of the society of policemen'. Nevertheless, his further concentration on the betrayal of the revolution in his next play, *Les Justes*, and his long essay *L'Homme révolté* showed that although he was prepared to condemn Western society in general terms, his detailed criticisms were still aimed at Communism.

Les Justes, which was first performed on December 15th, 1949, at the Théâtre Hébertot, was one of the two more successful of Camus's plays, and, like *Caligula*, ran for over four hundred performances. It also resembled *Caligula* in being based upon a story and characters not invented by Camus but taken from another writer—in this case, from Savinkov's *Souvenirs d'un Terroriste*, translated into French in 1931. Camus had again been very ill in 1949, and was not able, as he would have liked, to produce the play himself. *Les Justes* came at a moment when, after the success of *La*

Peste and the failure of *L'Etat de Siège*, there was intense curiosity to see what Camus would write next. In general, the play was well received, with critics giving to Camus's noble intentions the praise which they could not bestow upon his skill as a dramatist. Its theme led many critics to compare it with Sartre's *Les Mains Sales* (*Crime Passionnel*), but in spite of their general preference for Camus's ideas, few maintained that *Les Justes* was the better play. The most frequently expressed criticism was that all the characters talked far too much, that for most of the time they seemed little more than marionettes representing particular intellectual attitudes, and that, as Gabriel Marcel put it, Camus's political ideas were 'sympathetically naive'. It is certain that, compared to *Les Mains Sales*, *Les Justes* is a rather dull play both to watch and to read, and it illustrates a curious paradox in the frequently made comparison between Camus and Sartre: that Camus, a passionate enthusiast for all things theatrical, a producer and actor of wide experience, was far less successful as a playwright than Sartre, whose own theatrical interests are so much more restricted. *Les Justes* has in its purest form the main defect of all Camus's plays: that of having been written expressly to illustrate a particular thesis. Camus's evident intention in this play is to preach political morality by holding up the Russian revolutionaries of 1905 as heroes whose example ought to be imitated in 1949.

This was made clear in an article published in *La Table Ronde* in 1948. There, Camus discussed the answer which '*Les Meurtriers délicats*' ('*The Scrupulous Assassins*') gave to the gravest problem of revolt: have we the right, by killing our opponents in a just cause, to add to the sum total of human suffering which we are trying to reduce? It is an eternal problem, but one which has an especial importance in view of Camus's own conception of revolt. For him, revolt is not a demand for absolute freedom or for the complete liberation of the individual from all constraint, but a protest against an excess of suffering and injustice. It has as its first concern the protection of the basic rights of the individual against violence. How can it, then, without denying its origins, be held to justify killing? In *La Peste* Tarrou had unconditionally denied that anyone had the right to kill for any reason whatsoever. In *Les Justes* Camus proposes a different answer to the problem, and one which he will offer as a possible solution in *L'Homme révolté*.

An extract from Camus's article on '*Les Meurtriers délicats*' affirming that these revolutionaries had 'lived out the rebel's destiny in all its contradictions' was printed in a programme note on sale in the theatre. Very wisely, Camus took from Savinkov's description of the assassination of Grand Duke Sergei Alexandrovitch in 1905 only the central and most dramatic incidents: the failure of the student Kaliayev to throw the bomb when he saw that the Grand Duke was accompanied by his niece and nephew, his later success in throwing the bomb, and his execution. In the first act, Kaliayev returns to tell his comrades that he was not able to throw the bomb when he saw the children in the carriage. His failure brings him into conflict with Stepan, the revolutionary who, embittered by his years of imprisonment, believes that all means which lead to the triumph of the revolution are good. Stepan is prepared to sacrifice the lives and happiness of the men who are living today in return for the perfect happiness which the revolution will achieve in the future. Kaliayev, on the contrary, loves 'those who are living today on the same earth as I', and refuses, he says, 'for a distant country of which I am not certain, to strike my brothers in the face'. 'I will not add to living injustice for a dead justice,' he says, preferring, as for Camus the true rebel should, the immediate but limited justice which can be attained in the present, to the absolute justice which can exist only in the future. The scene between Dora, Kaliayev's mistress, Kaliayev and Stepan, is, in its confrontation of the true rebel and the absolute revolutionary, at the centre of the play. It is not based upon Savinkov's account of the incident, for in the *Souvenirs d'un terroriste* the revolutionaries are shown as having all agreed that under no circumstances was the killing of children justifiable. It is a debate, however, which contains the essence of Camus's thought in *Les Justes*, for it deals with that observance of limits which characterises true revolt as Camus defines it.

For Dora and Kaliayev there are, even in assassination and destruction, limits which must be observed. Stepan recognises no such limits and maintains that they are incompatible with a belief in the revolution. For those who are certain that the revolution will destroy despotism and build 'a land of liberty that will finally cover the whole world', the death of two children has simply no importance. For him, 'we sometimes kill for nothing if we do not kill enough', and the revolutionary must be prepared to will the means at the same time as he wills the end. Kaliayev's solution to the problem of revolt, which Camus himself recognises as the only valid one, is that the assassin should pay with his own life for the life he has taken. He will thus show, by his two actions, that murder is both inevitable and impossible, and will illustrate the impossible tension 'between the yes and the no' of revolt. There was no question, Camus wrote in the programme note to *Les Justes*, to which we in the mid-twentieth century could not find an answer in the lives and examples of the scrupulous assassins. The fact that the original action took place in Russia enables Camus to point an obvious moral: compared to the revolutionaries of 1905, those of 1950 are brutal fanatics, disregarding all moral limits in their mad pursuit of the classless society. The didactic note which made itself felt in *L'Etat de Siège* is even more apparent here, and both plays openly express Camus's own views on political questions.

Like *L'Etat de Siège*, *Les Justes* is a highly rhetorical and romantic play. Kaliayev, condemned to death, proclaims as he did in real life, that 'death will be my supreme protest against a world made of tears and blood'. Death is for him the easiest solution to his problems. 'It is easy, so much more easy, to die of one's contradictions than to live with them'— and both he and Dora are more than half in love with death. The play has as its epigraph a quotation from *Romeo and Juliet*, which sets the tone for the love between Kaliayev and Dora. They are haunted perpetually by the idea of death, torn between a longing for this solution to all their problems and the insistent appeal of life and happiness. 'I love beauty and happiness,' says Kaliayev, 'and it is for this reason that I hate despotism.' This conflict between their love of life and need for death separates them from the rest of the world. Like Moses in Alfred de Vigny's poem, they can never know the warmth of normal human affection. 'We are not of this world, we are the just,' is Dora's cry. 'There is a warmth which is not for us. Ah, have pity on the just.' Theirs is the fate of separation from which the victims of the absurd and of the plague also suffered, and in death Kaliayev knows that he will find the solution to this as well as to other problems. In his cell, after he has been condemned, the Grand Duchess comes to try to persuade him to repent and seek Christian forgiveness for his crime. Kaliayev refuses to accept the idea of his guilt, insisting that he has killed an idea and not a man. He has killed for love, he says, and will die for this same love of humanity. His death will be the final resolution of separation. 'Those who love today must die together if they wish to be reunited. Injustice separates, shame separates, suffering, the ill one does to others, living itself separates. Living is torture since being alive is separation.'

Kaliayev's solution to the problem of separation is perhaps more in keeping with his own character than with that of Camus himself, but apart from that he is the complete spokesman for Camus's ideas. In particular, his solution to the problem of political murder—that the assassin should demonstrate the injustice of his necessary act by committing suicide —is especially praised by Camus in *L'Homme révolté*. It was not an idea which Camus took from Savinkov, who simply quotes Kaliayev's remark that 'now I am near to death, everything is narrowed down for me to one question: my honour as a revolutionary'. It was one of Camus's own ideas, and one which, as was to be expected, laid him open to a good deal of criticism from the Left. J.-F. Rolland, in the fellow-travelling *Action*, expressed this criticism in its most extreme form when he wrote: 'Monsieur Camus is a professional advocate of purity. And, naturally, all the bourgeois critics are delighted with him. "Oh, how good, how pure, how *moving* revolutionaries were in those days! How tender and touching compared to those of today!" Monsieur Camus offers the bourgeoisie the kind of revolutionaries it likes: those who get themselves killed for nothing. Those who seize power and retain it, on the other hand, are unnatural monsters.'

In spite of the violence and exaggeration with which they are expressed, such criticisms do contain some truth. However great the horror one feels at the systematic execution of political prisoners behind the Iron Curtain, the message of *Les Justes* is not a convincing one. Certainly, the admirers of Stalinist methods did need reminding, in 1950, that the quality of an omelette could not be judged by the number of eggs broken to make it. Yet to recommend that all conscientious rebels commit suicide after they have been obliged to kill in the service of the revolution is rather an impractical suggestion. No political organisation fighting against a tyranny could possibly succeed if its leaders followed Kaliayev's example. Camus's own obsession with capital punishment combined with the history of Europe in the nineteen-forties and nineteen-fifties to make him see all political problems in the relation to the problem of killing. While this led to the admirable series of political articles already mentioned—*Ni Victimes ni Bourreaux*—and gave *La Peste* a very definite political significance, it had less fortunate results when Camus tried to base his attitude towards political action on this obsession with killing. Several critics asked what good the killing of the Grand Duke would do anyway, and the comparison with *Les Mains Sales*, where murder was shown to have been both necessary and futile, was largely to Sartre's advantage. That *Les Justes* should have run for such a long time shows that Camus was treating a subject which was of immediate and vital importance for his audience. It is also true that *Les Justes*, when its immediate political message is not taken too closely into account, has certain qualities which compensate for its defects.

One of Camus's own major ambitions in the theatre was to write a modern tragedy. He had already tried to do this in *Le Malentendu*[1] and was to repeat his attempt, with considerably more success, when he adapted William Faulkner's *Requiem for a Nun* in 1956. *Les Justes* has a potentially tragic note, especially in the portrayal of characters who, like Kaliayev and Dora, are placed in a situation where the action they are forced to take contradicts their ideals. The scene in Act III between Stepan and Kaliayev captures something of the argument between Cassius and Brutus in *Julius Caesar*, but Camus transforms what was for Shakespeare a question of temperament and character into a conflict between two sets of political and philosophical principles. In spite of the passion which Serge Reggiani put into the part of Kaliayev in the Paris production, he could not quite overcome the stilted note that Camus's didactic intention had introduced into the play. It seemed at times, as one hostile critic remarked, as if Camus

[1] See notes.

'had undertaken to present both sides of the realist/idealist view of political action in five acts'. This is not a universally held view, and John Cruickshank writes that: 'In its dramatic appeal and moral strength *Les Justes* is, in some degree, a modern successor to the Cornelian tradition of the seventeenth-century French theatre. Honour, nobility and moral conscience combine in a moving struggle to realise high human ideals.' It is easier to share this opinion if one forgets the political overtones of the play and treats it as a work of pure literature, but it is not always possible to do this. Even in the very moving last scene, where the conversation of Dora, Stepan, Voinov and Annenkov forms a lyrical chorus accompanying Kaliayev's death, the moralising tone is still there. Dora looks forward with horror to the time when Stepan's ideas will dominate and men will come who, lacking Kaliayev's scruples, 'will use our example and will not pay with their life', and Camus the didactic writer comes to deprive Camus the artist of a complete theatrical triumph.

He nevertheless comes so close to it partly through his intense sincerity and partly because of the noble and moving actions which he chose to describe. As in *Le Malentendu* his language gives the play a nobility and elevation which is fully in keeping with the themes he has chosen to treat: man's attitude towards his destiny and towards his fellow-men. The scrupulous assassins are people whose lives were admirable, and all one's intellectual doubts about the ultimate value of their attitude must not be allowed to come in the way of an appreciation of the ideal which they represented. As an antidote to the casual and bureaucratic killings of modern dictators the respect which they showed for human life was truly heroic. One does feel, in *Les Justes*, a note of heroism which is almost completely lacking in the French theatre of the present day. If this note does not quite lead to the modern tragedy that Camus wished to write, the reason lies perhaps in the fact that the creator of tragic characters must combine sympathy for his heroes with a full realisation of the faults which lead them to their doom. It is because Camus shows himself too completely an admirer of Kaliayev's attitude that the play does not produce the exact note of ironic compassion which can be found in genuine tragedy. Kaliayev's death is, for both him and his creator, the result solely of his virtue and not of his faults. It is the difference between the portrayal of willing martyrdom and the creation of tragic characters which turns *Les Justes* into the highest form of didactic drama and away from the realms of tragedy.

The insufficiency of any approach which treats Camus exclusively as a literary artist is most evident when one studies *L'Etat de Siège*, *Les Justes*, and *L'Homme révolté*. In this, which might for the purposes of convenience be called his middle period, Camus was very concerned with political problems, and this concern spread into almost everything he wrote. The dichotomy between his literary and political activity which had persisted until 1945 had given way to a desire to use literature to influence men's political ideas. This was in no way accompanied by a deliberate sacrifice of aesthetic to political considerations, and Camus never formally adhered to Sartre's thesis that good writing was the fruit of good, left-wing sentiments. Nevertheless, the Camus who wrote *L'Etat de Siège* and *Les Justes* is in striking contrast both to the author of *Noces* and *L'Etranger* and to the author of *La Chute* and *L'Exil et le Royaume*. The Camus of *L'Etranger* or of *La Chute* can be adequately judged by purely literary standards. The Camus of *L'Homme révolté* cannot, and it is misleading to study this part of his work outside the context of the French intellectual and political scene of the nineteen-forties and the nineteen-fifties. Claude Roy, one of the best critics of modern French literature, wrote of Camus after his death that 'his importance is also to be measured by the keenness of the discussions which he had with the best minds of our time. His long and no doubt necessary polemic with Communism, his arguments with Mauriac, Sartre and André Bréton, are as much a witness of his stature as his most perfectly finished literary works'. Although this is naturally less true for the Anglo-Saxon than for the French reader, it must be remembered that the Nobel Prize citation praised Camus for having, 'with clear-sighted earnestness, illuminated the problem of the human conscience in our time'. For French readers, he did this by arguing with other writers preoccupied by moral and political problems as well as by creating works of art. For English or American readers interested primarily in Camus as a literary figure, the polemics which followed the publication of *L'Homme révolté* in 1951 are, inevitably, much less interesting. They do, however, throw considerable light on his later literary work, to such an extent that the atmosphere of *La Chute* is almost a direct reflection of Camus's reaction to the political and intellectual atmosphere of Paris.

Chapter Nine

THE REBEL

THE publication of *L'Homme révolté* in November 1951 marked a turning point in Camus's career. Both its extreme popularity—over 70,000 copies were sold within a year of publication—and the controversies to which it gave rise confirmed his position as one of France's most important writers. The arguments that the essay provoked continued well on into 1952, and convinced Camus that polemical 'open letters' and fierce intellectual controversy were a waste of the time that could be more profitably spent on artistic creation. After *L'Homme révolté*, he turned his back on political philosophy and ambitious attempts to improve the intellectual climate of his time. And, although one cannot but admire the perseverance and energy with which he played the rôle of 'director of conscience to a stricken Europe', he was undoubtedly wise to do so. In spite of the praise which *L'Homme révolté* received from critics in France, England and America, it is doubtful whether his future reputation will ever depend upon this particular book. It was, it is true, his most highly praised as well as his most controversial work. In France, thinkers from both the Right and the Left welcomed it with enthusiasm. The Catholic and conservative André Rousseaux found it an excellent criticism of revolutions and wrote: 'The moment has perhaps come for the man of the twentieth century when anguish as to his destiny gives way before a consciousness of his real situation.' Claude Bourdet found it an 'invaluable' book, whose analysis 'contained almost nothing with which one could disagree.' It was, he wrote, 'a work from which there might one day be born a truly scientific and "probabilist" Marxism, as effective as the first in destroying social hypocrisy, and better adapted to use, for its social planning, not

131

fleeting and murderous dogmas but the working hypotheses which true scientists employ'. In England, Sir Herbert Read stated in his preface to the 1953 translation: 'With the publication of this book, a cloud which has oppressed the European mind for more than a century begins to lift. Once again it becomes possible to hope—to have confidence again in man and in the future.' Philip Toynbee gave it equally high praise, and wrote that it was 'more than a brilliant essay in political philosophy; it is a balanced and conscious work of art'. In America, Waldo Frank received it with great enthusiasm, and Charles Rolo called it 'the most intellectually exciting and most rewarding essay that has come my way for a long time'. Yet there were dissenting voices in all three countries, and, for reasons that will be studied, it is not easy to agree with these very high estimates of its value.

The main argument in *L'Homme révolté* is based upon the idea of revolt which Camus first elaborated in *La Remarque sur la Révolte* in 1945, and which he expressed in different ways in *La Peste* and *Les Justes*. Revolt protests against absurdity, suffering and injustice and creates a moral value based on the idea of moderation. Since it is founded on the protest of the slave against the infraction of limits, it is perpetually concerned with ensuring that a limit is respected. It implies the recognition of the integrity of the individual as the basic value, and the acceptance, in politics, of relative aims that will respect this integrity. If an aim is postulated as absolute, then this integrity is relegated to second place and revolt is betrayed. This is Camus's attitude, and one which he is concerned with propagating. Were it to be universally accepted, then European politics would cease to be characterised by executions, massacres and concentration camps, all justified in the name of revolt. What Camus is doing in *L'Homme révolté* is showing that any revolt which does not recognise that it should transcend nihilism and establish this limit is doomed to justify murder and lead to dictatorship. So far, he argues, revolt and revolution have failed. They have set out with the highest ideals of liberty and justice, and have culminated in the police state. If revolt is to avoid doing this, then it must see where it has gone wrong. *L'Homme révolté* is a diagnosis of the sickness of revolt, a sickness which comes from several sources.

First of all, it comes from a failure to go beyond nihilism. This is best illustrated by the example of Ivan Karamazov, who protests against the world because it is full of unjustifiable and inexplicable suffering and maintains at the same time that 'If God does not exist, then everything is permitted'. In other words, he is a rebel in his protest against suffering and injustice, but remains a nihilist in his ideas. Because of his nihilism, he betrays his revolt. Inspired by Ivan's teaching that 'If God does not exist, then everything is permitted', his repulsive double, Smerdyakov, murders his father. Is Ivan to accept this crime which his own nihilism has brought about, and which it is incapable of condemning? The contradiction drives him mad, and his revolt has failed because it remained basically nihilistic. It did not recognise that it existed primarily in the name of something, and that unless it recognised this value it was predestined to failure. The revolt of Nietzsche and of the Russian nihilists Bakunin and Netchaev had little of Ivan's protest against suffering but was deeply infected with the same nihilism. It was thus that Nietzsche's thought was perverted to justify National Socialism, while that of Netchaev led, as Dostoievsky pointed out, to a cult of murder for political ends. Since there are no values, then it is permissible to sacrifice everything to the development of the Superman or to the coming of the revolution. It is basically its failure to escape from nihilism which has caused revolt, in the twentieth century, to be so turned from its generous origins. There are, nevertheless, other reasons for its betrayal.

One of the most important is to be found in its purest form in Sade, Lautréamont, Rimbaud and the surrealists, and lies in a striving after the absolute. Sade demanded absolute liberty for himself in order to satisfy his desires. In this he is unfaithful to the teachings of true revolt which demands for each man only so much liberty as is consistent with the liberty of his neighbour. Because of this desire, Sade is led, in spite of his own generous nature—revealed by his constant opposition to the death penalty—to the establishment, albeit in imagination only, of absolute dictatorships. In his elaborate formulation of his erotic day-dreams he creates situations in which large numbers of people are subject to the whim of a few all-powerful individuals. The dictatorships which purely political rebels come to create are foreshadowed in Sade's 'kingdoms of absolute necessity', for it is as a result of this false idea of absolute liberty that rebels create dictatorships. The poetry of Lautréamont and the life of Rimbaud are also illustrations of this. Lautréamont is the author of two books, of which the first, *Les Chants de Maldoror*, is a long litany of revolt, and the second, *Les Poésies*, a manual of conformity to established rules and traditions. This passage from absolute revolt to absolute acceptance is, for Camus, typical of the failure of revolt. The rebel who aspires after an absolute excludes all limits from his first revolt. When he wearies of the effort which this absolute revolt demands—and, argues Camus, weary he inevitably will—he falls automatically into the arms of conformity. Unable to bear liberty, he voluntarily enslaves himself. The fate of many revolutionary intellectuals is announced by Lautréamont. They too will go from absolute revolt to complete conformity, from anarchistic rebellion to Communist discipline.

Rimbaud and surrealism reveal, though to a lesser extent, the same characteristics. The true significance of the second half of Rimbaud's life, where he abandons poetry for gun-running in Abyssinia, lies in the illustration which it gives of this same movement. Rimbaud gave revolt the purest poetic expression which it had yet received. After that, he abandoned poetry completely and his letters from Harar show him obsessed exclusively by thoughts of money. His initial refusal of all the commercial and materialistic values of the nineteenth century is thus followed by their complete acceptance. Surrealism, continuing where Rimbaud left off, shared the same basic fault. Several of the surrealists found their way so easily to Communism because, unable to obtain the best, 'they preferred the worst. In this, they were nihilists. . . . The true destruction of language which surrealism desired with such obstinacy, is to be found not in incoherence or in automatic writing. It is to be found in the party line'. In art, as in politics and in philosophy, a desire for the absolute is the ruin of revolt. This was something of which Camus had been aware in 1945 when he wrote that 'the only revolution which is adjusted to the measure of man is to be found in the acceptance of relative aims and ambitions, which means fidelity to the human lot'. In seeking to change life fundamentally, Rimbaud and surrealism were false rebels, and failing to escape from the nihilism of our time, plunged into absolute conformity.

In the French Revolution, revolt was betrayed by too absolute a reliance on formalistic virtue. Saint-Just and the Jacobins killed, in the person of Louis XVI, the last representative of God's law on earth. Their ambition was to replace this with the perfect city of man. They failed because they did not take into account the complexity of human nature, and tried instead to make all men conform to a preexisting model of virtue. They were unable to understand the attitude of those who might oppose them, deeming all critics automatically wicked. They could not accept the approximations and the need for compromise which the truly modest rebel will recognise. Their excess of virtue was as destructive of the individual as is the complete lack of moral standards which characterises nihilism. They sacrificed man to a formalistic morality, while nihilism sacrifices him to expediency. They were, in a way, the precursors of Hegelianism, which was to sacrifice him no less completely to the process of history.

It is with the advent of Hegelianism that revolt is, from a philosophical point of view, turned from its origins. Hegelianism is nihilistic because it recognises no other values but those which will finally be produced by history. It destroys the formal values of the French revolutionaries and of the bourgeois thinkers who followed them, at the same time as it inherits and develops their destruction of divine morality. It abolishes all values in order that the process of history may be more easily accomplished. Having dispensed with all other standards, it postulates the creation of an Absolute when the Idea realises itself at the end of history. It doubly betrays revolt, both in maintaining nihilism and in setting up the Absolute as a final goal. It can thus justify the constant sacrifice of the individual in the name of an eventual good. Since it has been the dominating philosophy in the twentieth century, it is not surprising that this has witnessed an unprecedented disregard for the importance of the individual. Russian and Marxist totalitarianism, the constant justification of ignoble means by a noble end, and the systematic use of murder as a political weapon, all come, for Camus, from the influence of Hegel on Russian and European thought. The

Hegelian dialectic is the philosophical basis of Communism, and Communism is therefore infected with its indifference to individual life.

Hegel is the real villain of *L'Homme révolté*. It is under his influence that Marxism ceases to be an empirical science and becomes a prophetic and intolerant religion. Communism developed, under the influence of Hegel, the idea that the workers' state was the realisation of the Idea in history, and therefore that the workers' state was bound inevitably to come into being. Thus it systematically ignores any historical developments which might disprove its prophecy. Because Marxist Communism is no longer a science but a religion, it persecutes those who do not conform, and finds its historical expression in the police state of the Soviet Union. In Communism, Prometheus effects his final metamorphosis. He has abandoned all that first characterised him—his love of men and of justice, his hatred of the cruelty of divine and earthly rulers—and has become Caesar. 'The true, the eternal Prometheus has now taken on the face of one of Caesar's victims. The same cry, from the depths of ages, echoes in the Scythian desert.' The wheel has come full circle, and the rebel has become the tyrant.

L'Homme révolté thus contains a criticism of some of the forms which revolt has taken up to the present day, and an explanation of their failure. It also considers the question why revolt should occupy so important a place in contemporary thought, and proposes a way by which man can escape from the impasse into which the betrayals of revolt have led him. The way of escape consists of a return to the *mesure* which, in Greek thought, originally made the idea of absolute revolt impossible.

Camus points out that since revolt is necessarily against something or someone, it does not make its appearance as a metaphysical idea until a religious tradition teaches that one God is responsible for the whole of creation. In classical thought, it is only with Epicurus and Lucretius that the idea of the revolt of mortals against the Heavens comes to be expressed. Before them there was no rigid division between the gods on one side and unfortunate mortals on the other. Consequently, for the Greeks, 'the idea of innocence opposed to guilt, the vision of history reduced to the fight between good and evil, was foreign to them. In their universe, there were more mistakes than crimes, and the only final crime that of excess.' Having thus, in the early part of the book, announced his conclusions in advance, Camus develops this idea, determined to lose no opportunity to castigate the thought of the twentieth century. 'In the completely historical world which threatens to become our own,' he continues, 'there are no more mistakes, but only crimes, of which the first is moderation.' In a world governed by generally accepted moral values there is no place either for the virtues or for the perversions of revolt.

It is with the idea of the God of the Old Testament that revolt such as we know it makes its first real appearance. He alone is responsible for the Creation, and the New Testament is an attempt to explain and justify this God to man. Christ justifies the existence of suffering by assuming himself the rôle of greatest pain, and to all potential rebels Christianity replies that man must accept because Christ accepted before him. When, from the eighteenth century onwards, the divinity of Christ is increasingly denied, he becomes 'just one more innocent victim, whom the representatives of the God of Abraham have sacrificed in a rather spectacular manner'. Christ no longer intercedes but seems instead, by the cruelty and pointlessness of his crucifixion, a greater proof of the cruelty of God, so that 'the ground is prepared for the great attack against the hostile heavens'. The figure of God as moral ruler of the civilisation against which revolt is directed must be destroyed before revolt can assume its full task of reorganising civilisation on the new basis of human justice. The failure of the revolt of Spartacus is an illustration of this. Spartacus, able if he so wished to capture and destroy Rome, refrained at the last moment from doing so. His ambition did not extend to abolishing the city against whose injustices he rebelled, for he had not the necessary metaphysical assurance and justification. He did not try to do so, and his revolt was mercilessly crushed. It is only when the French revolutionaries kill the king, the representative figure of God's law on earth, that revolt assumes its ambition to be a revolution. 1793 is the true beginning of the modern era, the beginning of the attempt to construct the city of man without, and against, God.

Revolt is so important in our own time because belief in a God whose existence justifies our civilisation and our values has disappeared. With the disappearance of religious faith, the world becomes absurd. Camus's point of departure is in Dostoievsky's 'If God does not exist, then everything is permitted', and the Nietzschean realisation that God is dead. The aim of Camus's revolt, like that of Dostoievsky's Christianity, is to show that this is not true, and that values do exist. The revolutions which have taken place in history may have denied them, but they can never be quite destroyed. In the realm of action, it is the example of the Russian revolutionaries of 1905, whose story Camus had already told in *Les Justes*, which guarantees their continued vitality. They consented to pay with their own life for the life they had to take. In doing so, they proclaimed and maintained the limit which the first movement of revolt brought into being, and their example is one which can restore the standards needed by European thinkers and men of action. 'All can live again by the side of those who sacrificed themselves in 1905, but on condition that they correct one another, and that there is, under the sun, a limit which controls them all. Each tells the other that he is not God; this is the end of Romanticism.' *L'Homme révolté* closes with this thought, with the hope that Europe has now outgrown its stage of nihilism and absolute revolt, and that it is going to adopt an adult attitude.

The principal value of *L'Homme révolté* lies more in its central theme than in the detail of its argumentation. In assuming, by the very act of writing this book, that men may still be influenced in their political actions by reason and moderation, Camus helped to keep alive the much needed tradition of liberalism, and his general argument is still useful in the present context of European thought. The tradition and idea of revolt have been associated with violence, excess, nihilism, hatred and provocation of God, and indifference to man for far too long. Camus, like George Orwell, had the feelings of the common man and the mind of an intellectual. He saw revolt as it really is for the ordinary person—a protest against suffering and injustice and not an attempt radically to transform the nature of the world—and pointed out that the right way to protest against the injustice, the cruelty and the disorder of nature is to try to realise the specifically human qualities of order, mercy and justice.

His obsession with the murderous visage which politics has assumed in the twentieth century, his evocation in *L'Homme révolté* of the utter destruction of Lidice, his intense concern for the seventy million people killed in the name of patriotism, liberty and justice, give the book a note of urgency and compassion, lacking in most pleas for political agnosticism. His criticism that 'Marx allied the most valid critical method with the most contestable Utopian Messianism' is one with which most liberal thinkers would unhesitatingly agree. His demonstration of the danger to personal liberty implicit in the Hegelian philosophy of history contains little that can be seriously contested. Only the fanatics of the French literary world would—and did—disagree with the excellent pages on the Marquis de Sade and Rimbaud, while his views on the true nature of art deserve the most serious discussion. Considered as a set of isolated essays, *L'Homme révolté* is a most interesting book. Judged for what Camus himself said it was —a personal confession—it offers valuable if fleeting insights into both his intellectual biography and the aims of his literary activity. It is when it is studied in the context of Camus's other statement that 'this is an attempt to understand my time' or analysed, in Richard Wollheim's words, as 'a great service to liberal thought', that its weaknesses become apparent.

The two most serious criticisms to be made of *L'Homme révolté* are that it is too ambitious in its aims and too consistently negative in its recommendations. In order to express the idea that revolt is betrayed from the moment it abandons the idea of moderation, Camus finds it necessary to study its history from the Greeks right through to modern times. This obscures rather than clarifies the issue, and the vast number of different people and events which the book mentions merely confuses the average reader. When a book of three hundred and seventy-eight pages refers to one hundred and sixty different writers, ranging from Rimbaud to Milton and from Petrus Borel to Bossuet; when it adds to these the names of ninety-six historical characters—including Christ, Stalin, Saint Paul, Ford and Napoleon—and supplements its argument by quoting the names of twenty fictional and mythical personalities, much of what is said must inevitably be very superficial. When, among all this plethora of proper names, only the *meurtriers délicats* of 1905 and the anarcho-syndical- ists of the present day are shown as having made any positive contribution to the largely unsuccessful tradition of revolt, the solutions which Camus proposes for the evils of his time seem far removed from practical reality.

In his review of the English translation of *L'Homme révolté* in January 1954, R. H. S. Crossman put Camus firmly in his place as a distinguished literary man whose opinions on politics deserved about as much attention as Crossman's own views on Proust. Pointing out how little anything seemed to matter in Camus's eyes except the French and Russian revo- lutions, he noted how strange it was that *L'Homme révolté* should ignore not only the tradition of bourgeois revolt repre- sented by 1688 and 1767, but also the whole history of the British Labour Party and the American trade-union move- ment. These were revolts which had avoided the passage to totalitarianism noted by Camus, and his failure to discuss them gives the book a very one-sided appearance. Camus does, it is true, express great admiration for the social justice realised by the Scandinavian democracies, but this is as far as he is prepared to go in making any positive suggestions to supplement his vague appeal for a return to the tradition of moderation represented by Mediterranean thought. What is even more serious than this neglect of revolutions that succeeded is, however, the frequency with which Camus refers in scornful terms to the whole history of Europe in the last fifty years.

Discussing the *meurtriers délicats*, he insists that it is in their case alone that 'the spirit of revolt encounters com- passion for the last time in our history': it is 'Kaliayev and his brothers', he writes, 'be they German or Russian, who are the true opponents of Hegel in the history of our time', and it is because their example was not followed that, 'the prole- tariat has had, since the Commune of 1871, no historical mission but to be betrayed'. Camus is not prepared to accept that Western industrial society is in any way preferable to that set up in the East, and writes that 'in 1950, the fate of the world will not be decided by the fight between bourgeois and revolutionary production, because their aims are the

same, but by the fight between the Caesarian revolution and
the forces of revolt'. This statement is acceptable when the
word 'revolt' is being used to speak of the general liberal
values with which it is associated in Camus's later thought.
It is less acceptable when 'revolt' refers only to the attitude
of the very small number of people of whom Camus is prepared to approve. His condemnation of the intellectual and
moral atmosphere of Europe is frequently so complete that
he rejects any allies whom he might otherwise have. Europe
is 'ignoble', it is the place where 'petty-minded people show
us their mean faces' and where 'the sniggering cohorts of
petty rebels, the stuff of which slaves are made, offer themselves to any slavery on all its markets'. Elsewhere in the book,
he writes contemptuously that 'the only true passion of the
twentieth century is for slavery' and that 'our civilisation lives
on in the complacency of cowardly souls full of hatred and
in the boasting vows of ageing adolescents'. It is impossible
to see what positive attitude Camus was trying to encourage
when he wrote these sentences, and how he thought they
could fit into a book which set out to defend intellectual
tolerance.

These sweeping statements strike a particularly unfortunate
note when they are contrasted with what Camus did and said
both before and after he had published *L'Homme révolté*. In
1948, for example, he joined a tradition admirably represented by Mr. E. M. Forster's *Two Cheers for Democracy*,
when he wrote: 'Democracy is not the best of all forms of
government; it is the least objectionable.' In 1953 he wrote:
'The few democratic liberties that we still enjoy are not
unimportant trifles that we can allow to be taken away from
us. They represent what we still retain of the great revolutionary conquests of the past two centuries.' In 1955, he was
quite ready to ally himself to someone who had nothing of
the anarcho-syndicalist about him when he wrote regularly
in *L'Express* to support the electoral campaign of Pierre
Mendès-France. Like George Orwell, whom he resembled
both in his humanism and in his obsession with totalitarianism, Camus was not—except in *L'Homme révolté*—prepared
to argue that bourgeois democracy was a complete illusion
and that half a loaf was better than no bread. Like Orwell, he
saw that the most important single political event of the first

half of the twentieth century was the abandonment of liberty by left-wing thinkers, and, like Orwell, he was not prepared to imitate them. Where he differed from Orwell—and where he resembled most of his French contemporaries—was in the attitude of romantic refusal which he at times adopted towards bourgeois society as a whole. It is this attitude which makes *L'Homme révolté*, for an English reader, so unsatisfying a work of political argument. It may be, of course, that such a refusal is the only attitude that could be adopted in France, and that Camus was fully justified when he wrote in 1952, that 'If there were anything worth keeping in our society, I should be a conservative. Unfortunately, that is not the case'. It is this 'all or nothing' approach, so untypical of Camus in the rest of his political thought, that causes his general defence of liberal values in politics in *L'Homme révolté* to take place in so curious an intellectual and social vacuum.

This gap between certain aspects of *L'Homme révolté* and the political reality of Camus's time would not matter if the book were, as Germaine Brée has suggested, a primarily literary essay, which, like Camus's other works, was 'addressed to the layman and not to the professional philosopher'. While it is certainly not a professional's book, it was nevertheless both intended by Camus and received by the vast majority of his critics as a contribution to political philosophy. It consequently deserves to be judged by higher standards than are usually applied to the political ideas of an eminent man of letters. Camus himself defined his aims when he wrote: 'The aim of this essay is not to repeat for the hundredth time the description of the phenomenon of revolution, nor to repeat yet again the historical and economic causes of past revolutions. It is to discover, by the analysis of revolutionary events, what are the manifestations, the constant themes, and the logical consequences of metaphysical revolt.' This statement was intended primarily as a defence against the criticism that he had attributed too great an importance to the influence of ideas on political action, but it does indicate that he wanted to do a good deal more than simply write a general essay on 'revolutions in history and revolutions in literature'.

For a number of reasons, however, the criticism that it was meant to anticipate remains a valid one. Camus does represent both the Russian and French revolutionaries whom he discusses as always guided by ideas and never influenced by circumstances, and this again considerably weakens the value of his book as a piece of historical analysis. When he maintains that the bloodthirsty course of the French Revolution was the result of the ambition to change men into gods, or when he writes that Russian Communism has 'taken up the metaphysical ambition which this essay describes: the construction, after the death of God, of a city where man himself shall become God', one does expect some kind of corrective in the way of a reference to the possible social, economic or historical causes of tyranny. His essay would be much more convincing if he were at least to consider the possibility that Communist imperialism is but old style Russian expansionism writ large, and that Robespierre and Saint-Just were acting under the pressure of events. The fact that he does not do so lays him open to the reproach of having given far too much importance to ideas and not nearly enough to circumstances.

It has also been suggested that *L'Homme révolté* should be looked upon as a highly personal history of revolutions, valuable precisely because of the limited but extremely acute personal vision which it offers. Camus, it is argued, has hit upon two hitherto neglected truths: the relationship of Communism to nihilism and the importance of the cult of the historical process in Marxist thought. This would be an excellent reason for admiring *L'Homme révolté* if Camus had really been the first person to put forward these ideas and had they consequently been really original. The fact is, however, that long passages of *L'Homme révolté* merely summarise or reproduce the conclusions of a number of thinkers whom Camus had read—Jean Grenier, Wladimir Weidlé, Jules Monnerot, Nicholas Berdiaeff—and that his analysis is not a particularly new one.[1] The English reader can find most of it in the second volume of Professor Popper's *The Open Society and its Enemies* or in the passage of Koestler's *Darkness at Noon* where Rubashov, meditating on his past career and on his present condemnation, realises that a worship of history was one of the causes which had led him to betray others and be accused of treachery himself. The French reader can find almost all Camus's analysis of Marx in the works of Raymond Aron, Roger Caillois or Jules Monnerot, while the theme of

[1] See notes.

the 'divinisation of man' is very reminiscent of Father Delubac's *Le Drame de l'Humanisme athée*. When critically analysed *L'Homme révolté* shows itself to be a curious hotchpotch of sincere feelings and secondhand ideas. Intelligent but unoriginal criticism of Marx mingles with an obsession about nihilism reinforced by reference to selected authorities, and with ideas about the divinisation of man borrowed from a wide variety of conservative thinkers, to make it into one of the least personal books that Camus ever published.

Transposed from the high plane of metaphysics on which the book is constructed, the *mesure* which Camus advocates can be rather crudely expressed in the anecdote about the Englishman and the nihilist. 'My liberty is absolute,' claimed the nihilist. 'There is no value at all to prevent me from punching you on the nose if I wish to do so.' 'Oh yes there is,' replied the Englishman. 'Your liberty ends where my nose begins.' As Kant expressed it in more philosophical terms: 'Every man should be treated as an end in himself and never as a means to an end.' Camus's revolt creates no philosophical principle which is not shared by liberal humanists. In fact, when he criticises both Hegelianism and Christianity for sacrificing human nature and the individual to a supposedly higher good, he is going further back than liberal humanism and restating the Gospel truth that the Sabbath is made for man and not man for the Sabbath. Such conclusions were inevitable from the moment he argued, in *La Remarque sur la Révolte*, that the first refusal of the slave created the right of each man to be respected and treated as an individual. His originality lies in the way in which he comes to the same conclusions as the liberal humanist while setting out from absolutely different premises.

For traditional humanism, the world is not absurd, but basically rational. Man is at home in it, and the values which cause him to be respected as an individual are certain and absolute. In some way, the non-existence of God does not invalidate the normal rules of moral conduct. Camus does not go so far as the existentialist and say that values do not exist, but insists that they can only have reality insofar as man discovers them by his own efforts. The death of God which, in company with Nietzsche, Malraux, Sartre and other thinkers of his time, he experienced as the birth of the absurd, threw him back on the individual as the only possible source of new values. Setting out from a philosophical *tabula rasa*, he recreated a humanism which starts out from the loss of faith which characterises our time. He was impelled into doing so by the intellectual and historical atmosphere in which he came into consciousness. It is difficult for an ordinary English reader, protected by the lay morality still implicitly accepted in England, to understand the complete inability to justify moral values which has characterised French thought in the twentieth century. It is in the context of Malraux's *La Tentation de l'Occident* and *La Condition Humaine*, of Nietzsche's *Beyond Good and Evil*, Sartre's *La Nausée* and *L'Être et le Néant*, and, most of all, of Dostoievsky's *The Brothers Karamazov* and *The Possessed*, that *L'Homme révolté* must be placed if it is to be understood. It is authors and books such as these, together with Hegel and Marx, that dominate political and philosophical thinking among contemporary left-wing French intellectuals. The premisses which all these intellectuals share—the rottenness of bourgeois society and of the values on which it supposedly rests, the absence of all divine or transcendent morality— were automatically accepted by Camus in his first works, *L'Etranger* and *Le Mythe de Sisyphe*. He did not need to elaborate an attack upon bourgeois principles of morality or spend any time proving the absurdity of the world. These were ideas commonly accepted among French intellectuals, and Camus simply had to make his own position clear. Once he had done this, Camus could begin the long and difficult task of rehabilitating normal values in the context of French intellectual society. He was, however, more successful in doing this in *La Peste* than in *L'Homme révolté*, because he was better as a literary artist than as a political philosopher.

His intention was the same in both books and the difference between them lies in the fact that one is a work of art and the other is not. It is one of the most serious defects of *L'Homme révolté* that, in spite of the formal perfection of its prose, it has neither the rigorous composition nor the poetic quality of *Le Mythe de Sisyphe*. The lyricism of its closing pages—'We shall choose Ithaca, the faithful earth, audacious and frugal thought, the generosity of the man who knows'—is forced and pompous when compared to that of *Le Mythe de Sisyphe*.

145

When carefully analysed, it means very little indeed, and, in John Cruickshank's words 'it strikes one as an unsuccessful attempt to turn a fundamentally negative argument into a positive one'. Aesthetically, *L'Homme révolté* is Camus's least satisfying prose work. Politically, it suffers from an impatience with traditional liberal democracy which makes it impossible to tell just what Camus is advocating as a practical alternative to Communism.

It was partly the vagueness of Camus's actual recommendations which led to the famous dispute with Jean-Paul Sartre in August 1952, although Sartre would probably have had even less sympathy for a book which explicitly maintained that there was something to be said in favour of bourgeois democracy. Yet the actual debate between Sartre and Camus did centre round a specific political problem: What should be the attitude of the left-wing intellectual towards the Communist Party? Camus maintained that any honest left-wing movement must begin by making it quite clear that it would have nothing at all to do with Stalinism. Sartre insisted that one had to be content with what one could get, and that no working class movement could, in the France of the early nineteen-fifties, ever hope to achieve anything if it cut itself off from the only political party which had the support of the vast majority of the French working class.

Most French, English and American critics who have written on *L'Homme révolté* have taken Camus's side against Sartre, and their reaction is fully understandable. Sartre's flirtation with Communism, which had begun seriously in July 1952 with the publication of the first part of *Les Communistes et la Paix*, has naturally alienated most liberal-minded critics. If one shares neither Sartre's obsessional hatred of the middle-class nor his perception that politics is the science of the practical, his attitude towards the French Communist Party is difficult to understand. He has always been a less attractive figure than Camus, whose high moral integrity and compassion for suffering earned him the general sympathy which Sartre's more intellectual approach cannot hope to rival. Sartre is clever, physically rather ugly, obviously very much the intellectual and apparently very much the misanthrope. Camus was handsome, a married man with two attractive children, intelligent but of the highest character, and an open defender of basic human decency. Yet he was also, as Sartre pointed out, becoming rather over-conscious of his mission to reform French intellectual life, and had recently shown that his zeal for truth was not always free from a certain high-handed attitude.

Having systematically ignored *L'Homme révolté* for over five months, the Communist press eventually condescended to discuss it. In the intellectual monthly *La Nouvelle Critique*, Pierre Hervé, who has since left the party, wrote a long article called *La Révolté Camuse*—a title which was probably a pun, since *camus* means flat-nosed. In many ways it was a silly and inaccurate article, for Hervé alleged that Camus had no interest in colonial affairs and no awareness of the dangers of nuclear war. If he had tried deliberately, he could not have chosen two subjects on which Camus had written more sincerely. In a phrase which might have referred to either Camus himself or to the anarcho-syndicalists whom he admired, Hervé spoke of 'crooks who receive dollar subsidies to pretend that they inherit the tradition of revolutionary trade-unionism'. Altogether, the article was, as Jean Lebar noted in *France-Observateur*, 'remarquable'. Unfortunately Camus misread the adjective for 'belle', and wrote an indignant letter demanding that it be withdrawn. Roger Stéphane replied that Camus had made a mistake—which he had—and that in any case his demand that *France-Observateur* should in all cases ally itself with his views was quite unacceptable. Both this incident and the general tone of Camus's letter gave Sartre an excellent opportunity to begin his reply by attacking him on his weakest point: the intolerant attitude he was beginning to adopt towards those who disagreed with him.

Both Sartre's and Francis Jeanson's replies did indeed concentrate on Camus's personal attitude to such an extent that they seemed to by-pass his main argument. In his original article in May 1952, Francis Jeanson had maintained that *L'Homme révolté* ignored the struggles of men and concentrated revolt upon a non-existent God; that Camus's book amounted to a refusal of 'history' and of concrete political action; and that, by emphasising the crimes committed by revolutionaries, it restored the bourgeoisie's confidence in itself and condemned revolt to permanent impotence. Camus replied to Jeanson's criticism, on Sartre's own invitation, and addressed his letter to the 'Editor of *Les Temps Modernes*', in August 1952. He insisted that Jeanson's article had completely misrepresented the main theme of *L'Homme révolté*. This was not the refusal of 'history' or of political action in a particular historical context. It was the attack on a worship of 'the Movement of History' which justified using all means to create the classless society. What Camus wanted Jeanson to do, and what he maintained that any self-respecting critic who disagreed with *L'Homme révolté* ought to do, was to argue that 'history has a necessary meaning and a final end, that the atrocious and confused face which it presents is an illusion, and that, on the contrary, it progresses towards a moment of reconciliation when we shall be able to leap into final liberty'. Because Jeanson had not done this, Camus maintained in his letter to Sartre that 'your contributor'—he did not actually mention Jeanson by name—had systematically misunderstood and misrepresented the argument of *L'Homme révolté*, and had been unjust, 'not towards myself, but towards our reasons for living and fighting, and the legitimate hope that we shall go beyond our contradictions'.

It is undeniable that neither Sartre nor Jeanson did discuss the main thesis of *L'Homme révolté* and that, for this reason alone, Camus may be said to have won the argument. Nevertheless, his opponents did mark up a number of points. The sentence quoted above and the previous dispute with *L'Observateur* laid Camus wide open to Sartre's taunt of 'Tell me, Camus, by what strange miracle can one not criticise your books without depriving humanity of its reasons for living?' Camus's conscious intention was certainly to denounce the Marxist-Hegelian theory of history, but certain phrases in *L'Homme révolté* did reveal the more 'transcendental' attitude which Jeanson had criticised. When Camus writes, for example, that 'true liberty is an interior submission to a value which faces up to history and its triumphs', and when he states in his closing peroration that 'at this hour when each of us must bend his bow to prove himself again and conquer, in and against history, that which he already possesses, the slender harvest of his fields, the brief love of this earth, at this hour when a man is truly born, we must leave our time and its adolescent furies' he is showing that

Jeanson's criticism is not wholly unjustified. He is turning his back on our time—'and its adolescent furies'—and is trying to go back either to the classical ideal of Greece or the more Romantic attitude of the *meurtriers délicats*. Camus's attitude towards Communism was a very noble one, and was founded on a genuine horror of totalitarian oppression. One wonders, however, since both he and Sartre continually asserted that they were serving the cause of the working class and striving to improve its lot, whether Sartre's attitude was not, in the France of 1952, a more positive and possibly a more fruitful one.

It is not quite true to say that Sartre and Jeanson accepted the identification of the workers with the Communist Party 'as an article of faith'. They did so because, then as now, there was no other party which both represented the interests and received the support of the French working class. One may profoundly regret this fact and contest the legitimacy of Sartre's attempt to draw general and international conclusions from it. The attitude of the French Communist Party towards the repression of the Hungarian revolt shows that Sartre was perhaps wrong to argue as he did, but he was at least ready to assume the risks of being proved wrong by events. It is the willingness to run risks of this nature which distinguishes Sartre's political attitude from that of Camus and makes him, from this particular point of view, a more attractive thinker. The principal objection to Camus's political writing is the paradoxical one that he was always right. He was right to denounce tyranny in Spain and Hungary, right to attack the obscurantist philosophy of contemporary Communism, right to oppose the death penalty, right to appeal for a civil truce in Algeria, right to support Mendès-France in 1955, right to insist that nuclear weapons had fundamentally changed the nature of international problems, right to maintain that the rivalry between France and Germany was no longer the central issue in European politics. On matters more controversial, where the truth stood out less clearly, he either said nothing or was vague. On Suez, on the 1958 coup d'état and referendum, on German rearmament, on the Korean war, he was silent. On the use of torture in Algeria and on the Indo-Chinese war his remarks were so general as to give no indication of what *political* attitude he recommended.[1] Were Camus purely an

[1] See notes.

artist, or were he an 'ordinary' writer whose views on politics were of as little importance as Mr. Crossman's views on Proust, this criticism would be of no importance. But in the late nineteen-forties and early nineteen-fifties he was a political writer as well as a literary artist, and a writer who did try to influence men in their political opinions by the books which he wrote. He should therefore be judged by standards appropriate to what he was trying to do.

Although neither Sartre nor Jeanson was prepared to discuss Camus's main argument in *L'Homme révolté*—'Does or does not the *Phenomenology of the Mind* authorise a theory of political cynicism? Have there or have there not been left-wing Hegelians who have influenced the development of Communism in this direction?'—they were prepared to put forward their own view of history and compare it with Camus's. In so doing they provided a convincing if indirect reply to his criticism. Sartre insisted that nobody acts merely out of a consideration for the meaning of history. 'In fact,' he wrote, 'men are engaged in short-term projects which are inspired by long-term hopes. And there is nothing at all absurd about these projects: here, Tunisians rebel against colonial authority; there, miners express their financial demands or their solidarity with other workers by going on strike. I will not discuss whether history has or has not transcendental values: I will simply point out that *if there are values*, they express themselves through human activities which are historical by definition.' Francis Jeanson clarified his own attitude and expressed his major objection to *L'Homme révolté* when he asked the following long rhetorical question: 'But finally, Camus, perhaps revolutions are also made by men, perhaps they are above all made by men, by ordinary men who try—working together, some well, some ill —to conquer the right to exist as men. Perhaps it has not been possible for them to get better results up to now, using the resources which they have and the situation imposed on them from the very beginning. Perhaps one never does find the ideal conditions of pure revolt when real men are in fact rebelling against real social structures?' And *was* it, he asked, really the 'grandiose or terrifying aim' of making men into Gods that had both caused revolts to go wrong, and which still inspired the millions who voted Communist in France?

It is no real reply to these objections to say that Camus had wanted to insist upon the way in which these men who were struggling for their freedom were consistently betrayed by their leaders. This is a good answer to Jeanson's question, but the distinction is not clearly made in *L'Homme révolté*, for nowhere in the book is there the suggestion that some Communists might have been good but misguided men. Jeanson concluded by giving a definition of his own and Sartre's attitude which was, perhaps, in France in 1952, a more intelligent if less moral way of looking at politics than the empty rhetoric which concluded *L'Homme révolté*. 'The Stalinist movement throughout the world does not seem to us to be genuinely revolutionary, but it is the only one which maintains that it is revolutionary, and, in France, it groups the great majority of the proletariat behind it; we are at one and the same time against it because we criticise its methods, and for it because we simply do not know whether pure revolution is not simply an illusion, and because we do not know whether, after all, the revolutionary enterprise does not have to take this kind of road before it establishes a more humane social order; and because we do not know whether, in the present context, the perversions of the revolutionary enterprise are not preferable to its complete and utter annihilation'.

The English critics who have followed the discussion of *L'Homme révolté* to this point will probably be divided into two categories; those who say: 'Why waste so much time discussing the political opinions of a man who was first and foremost an artist?'; and those who ask: 'Why write a book on Camus if one is determined to adopt the point of view of his opponents?' The answer to the first objection is that *L'Homme révolté* was both written as a political book and welcomed as such. It would be unfair to discuss it without giving some considerations to the views of those who, like Philip Toynbee, Sir Herbert Read, Richard Wollheim, Waldo Frank, Leon Roth, André Rousseaux and Claude Bourdet, considered *L'Homme révolté* to be an important contribution to political thought. The answer to the second objection is that no critic can be content with saying, of an author whom he greatly admires, 'This is not a good book and it would have been better if my author had not written it. I will therefore not waste my own or my readers' time by discussing it'. Camus's political ideas deserve serious discussion for two reasons, even if one cannot agree that his analysis of political events is particularly accurate. They are inspired by that compassion for human suffering which was his finest characteristic, and they offer a way of considering politics which runs the risk of being neglected by the Anglo-Saxon empirical tradition. A study of political philosophy is most important at a time when philosophers have become kings and when, as Camus himself remarked, 'they are not quite as nice as people expected them to be' (*Ils n'ont pas la tête qu'on croyait*). The ideas which he puts forward in *L'Homme révolté*, however, do need counterbalancing by the stress which a writer like Sartre lays upon the fact that politics is the science of the possible. Where Sartre completes rather than contradicts Camus's moral approach to politics is in his insistence that political problems can be solved only by political measures, and that political measures are always disagreeable to some, unpalatable to others and unjust in the eyes of their opponents. Where Camus corrects Sartre—and the correction is possibly a more important one—is in the idea that the individual can never be justly sacrificed to the accomplishment of any overall historical plan, however admirable it may seem. Both represent an essential part of the European revolutionary tradition, Sartre by his intellectual fervour and practical approach, Camus by his deep moral concern for man the individual. It is only unfortunate that each should have shown himself so extreme a representative of the attitude he adopted.

For the literary critic, the most interesting feature of *L'Homme révolté* is not the content of its political and philosophical sections but the light which it throws upon Camus as an artist. *La Remarque sur la Révolte* ended with the promise that the nature of man's revolt, the attempt to create order, unity and justice, could take the form either of political action or of artistic creation, and the aim of art was there defined as the construction of 'an ideal work in which natural creation would be corrected'. This already showed, as early as 1945, a distinct movement away from the ideas expressed in *Le Mythe de Sisyphe*, where artistic creation is simply another attempt to get the most out of life. 'To create' writes

Camus in 1943, 'is to live twice. The groping, anxious quest of a Proust, his meticulous collecting of flowers, wallpapers and anxieties, has no other significance. At the same time, it has no more importance than the continuous and infinitely valuable creation in which the conqueror, the actor, and all absurd men indulge every day of their lives.' The 'absurd work of art', argues Camus, can have no final significance and 'cannot be the final end, the meaning or the consolation for a life'. Like all the other activities described in *Le Mythe de Sisyphe*, artistic creation is sterile, without ultimate value and in no way an attempt to remodel the universe in a manner more satisfying to the 'demand for clarity which echoes in the deepest heart of man'.

This is precisely what the theory of art put forward in *L'Homme révolté* does set out to do, for it develops the implications of Camus's statement in *La Remarque sur la Révolte* by presenting art as the 'transforming of natural disorder into a unity satisfying for the heart and mind'. Camus illustrates his point by quoting Van Gogh's remark: 'I am more and more convinced that we should not judge God on this world. It is one of his badly conceived sketches.' He argues that art improves upon natural creation and 'tries to give form to a value which escapes in the perpetual flow of becoming, and which the artist feels and tries to wrench from the movement of history'. Without art there would be no form and no permanence in anything. It is art which corrects natural disorder and provides man with a refuge from the all-consuming movement of time. It is thus partly because it represents a triumph over time that the world created by Proust 'has the ambition of being a closed perfection and of giving eternity a human face'.

Like the political ideas of *L'Homme révolté*, this affirmation of the value of art is a theme which develops in Camus's thought from 1944 onwards. He himself did not try to compose an 'absurd work of art'—indeed, his failure to find a really satisfactory one to discuss is a weakness in the chapter on art in *Le Mythe de Sisyphe*—and it has already been argued that *L'Etranger* can be seen as the putting into practice of the ideas on stylisation described in *L'Homme révolté*. It is also unlikely that he intended the ideas expressed in *Le Mythe de Sisyphe* to be taken as representing his own point of view on art, since he was already writing, in his preface to *Maximes et Anecdotes* of Chamfort in 1944, that 'art is the opposite of silence, for it is one of the signs of that complicity which links us to men in our common struggle'. *Le Mythe de Sisyphe* was certainly the product of Camus's own personal experiences, but he himself always emphasised that the attitude which it described was essentially a provisional one. As Professor Viggiani has recently shown, this is nowhere more true than in the discussion on art, for at the age of nineteen, Camus was already expressing one of the basic ideas of *L'Homme révolté* in an essay on the nature of music which he wrote for the short-lived periodical *Sud*, published in Algiers in 1932.[1] All art, he then argued, was basically anti-rational, but all true art showed an effort to bring about 'the objectivisation of things such as we should like them to be'. A similar but more virile idea also occurs in 1943, in an article entitled *L'Intelligence et l'Echafaud*, in which Camus maintains that the attempt to give form to one's passions which constituted the great tradition of the French novel was 'a kind of revenge, a way of overcoming the difficulties of fate by imposing a form upon them'. It is a very similar view which is put forward in *L'Homme révolté* when Camus discusses the aims and nature of the novel. All men, he argues, yearn for a life which is moulded, harmonious, and saved from the disorder and incompleteness of nature. 'Whether it takes the form of religion or crime' he writes 'all human effort finally obeys this unreasonable desire and tries to give life the form which it lacks. The same movement which can lead to the worship of heaven or the destruction of man, can equally well lead to the writing of novels, which thus becomes a worthwhile activity.'

To write a good novel is to revolt against the natural formlessness of life and present experience as a coherent and unified whole. Normally, argues Camus, both our day-to-day experience of events and the succession of happenings which make up our lives are without pattern or unity. We rarely if ever take a decision whose consequences are both immediate and foreseeable, and although we may think that we have decided to change the direction of our life by performing a particular action, we realise, when we look back upon events, that they can never have the definitive quality which we would

[1] See notes.

like to give them. The writing of novels is one of the ways by which we try to give life the fixed and irredeemable quality which we long for but which is unattainable in reality. In Gobineau's *Les Pléiades*, he remarks, the hero Casimir does succeed in dying of hopeless love in Vilna when, in reality, he would have merely stayed in the dull provincial town for a few weeks before getting bored and coming home. Ordinary life, Camus suggests, is essentially unsatisfying, and remarks, in a paraphrase of Nietzche's words, we have art in order not to die of life.

His choice of two types of fiction to illustrate this theory of the novel shows how *L'Homme révolté* is both the 'confessional' work that he said it was and an essay written in deliberate reaction against certain prevailing French intellectual fashions. He changed his mind about Proust between 1943 and 1951, and it was his new attitude which enabled him to see how *À La Recherche du Temps Perdu* fitted into the idea of revolt. He then proceeded to compare the true revolt of Proust's work with the unauthentic revolt of the 'tough' school of American novelists in order to make his ideas stand out by contrast with commonly accepted views. During the vogue of Hemingway, Steinbeck, Faulkner, Dos Passos and Caldwell in France in the nineteen-thirties and nineteen-forties, certain critics had maintained that the cruel and brutal universe which they portrayed had metaphysical overtones. Armand Hoog argued that 'the so-called observance of reality by Hemingway and Caldwell' was 'a form of revolt', and Claude Edmonde Magny was even more specific about the work of John Dos Passos. The U.S.A. trilogy, was, she wrote in 1946, 'a silent protestation not only against capitalism, but also against the human lot, against the world as it is, and, finally against the very Structure of Being'. It was, it may be noted, against similar interpretations of other writers that Camus was reacting in many other sections of *L'Homme révolté*. His long criticism of Sade was an attack on those who, like Maurice Nadeau, considered that the Marquis 'carried in him the image of tomorrow's humanity, which will have thrown off all codes and all morality, all religions and all taboos, and will be concerned solely with creating its own happiness'. The long discussion of Saint-Just—mentioned far more frequently in *L'Homme révolté* than any other leader of the French Revolution—may have been an attempt on Camus's part to atone for the admiration he had expressed in 1944. It was more probably inspired by the desire to react against the myth propagated by numerous fellow-travelling editions of Saint-Just's work that had been published since the war, and against the views of those who, like Jacques Gaucheron, maintained that 'by choosing Terror, Saint-Just chose the only possible way to Virtue'. The literary passages in *L'Homme révolté* have in general, however, a more authentic and a more personal note than the sections where Camus is mainly concerned with reacting against fashion, and this is particularly true of his theory of the novel.

In the section on the novel, Camus writes: 'It seems that great souls are often struck with terror less by suffering itself than by the fact that it does not last. If we cannot have unceasing happiness, a long period of suffering would at least make life into a destiny. But this does not happen, and our worst torments one day come to an end. One morning, after so much despair, an irresistible desire for life tells us that all is over and that suffering has no more meaning than happiness.' This sentence has an unmistakably personal note, and its autobiographical quality is even more marked when one remembers that Caligula had been made to suffer from exactly the same feeling when he realised that he would one day forget even his pain at Drusilla's death. Unfortunately, the didactic tone rapidly returns to *L'Homme révolté*, and brings with it a sweeping condemnation of modern art which parallels the other remarks about 'ignoble Europe' and its 'passion for slavery': 'Whether it gives way to the dizziness of abstraction and formal obscurity or whether it appeals to the whip of the crudest and most naive realism, almost the whole of modern art is an art of tyrants and slaves, not of creators.' It is true that in the passages on Proust Camus does show himself capable both of the admiration for genius which he maintains is the highest quality of the true artist, and of interesting though rather high-flown literary criticism. 'His difficult victory is to have been able, on the very threshold of death, and using only memory and intelligence, to extract from the transcience of forms the quivering and living symbols of human unity. The surest challenge which a work of this sort can offer to the God-created world is to present itself as a whole, as a close and unified world.' It is unfortunate that Camus was so preoccupied with the need to insist on how most writers failed to represent true revolt that he wrote so little positive literary criticism in this essay. It is his desire to prove his point which again spoils the value of his discussion of Rimbaud, Lautré-amont and the Surrealists.

His analysis of Rimbaud begins very well, and gives the temporary impression that here at least is someone of whom Camus approves. 'The greatness of Rimbaud,' he writes, 'bursts out at the moment when, giving revolt the most strangely accurate expression it has ever received, he speaks at one and the same time of his triumph and his anguish, of true life absent from the world and this same world's inescapable nature, the cry for the impossible and the need to embrace rough reality, the refusal of morality and the irresistible nostalgia for duty.' Very soon, however, he is using Rimbaud simply as an example to prove his thesis. Refusing to consider the possibility that Rimbaud's farewell to poetry may well have been an attempt to attain reality by other means, an inevitable result of mere adolescent impatience or an intensely honest attempt at moral repentance, he sees it as a sign of the danger of nihilism and as a warning not to begin revolt by excess. The same desire to illustrate a thesis falsifies his treatment of Sade and Lautréamont in a very similar manner. He says what can be said in favour of both writers—and it is not very much—but then goes on to treat them like a doctor diagnosing the same disease in all his patients. He completely neglects the fact that it was Sade's own peculiar temperament which led him to establish his 'kingdoms of absolute necessity' and emprison his victims far from the sight of men. Had he compared Sade with other erotic authors, he would have seen that the theme of imprisonment occurs with monotonous regularity in all sado-masochistic fantasies. In his discussion of Lautréamont, he pays no attention at all to the very strong possibility that the apparent volte-face between *Les Chants de Maldoror* and *Les Poésies* was merely an attempt at an ironical mystification of the bourgeois reader. When he suggests that so many surrealist poets later went over to Communism because 'these drawing-room nihilists were clearly destined to provide servants for the strictest orthodoxies' he is again oversimplifying a complex phenomenon, and, what is even worse, making a very sweeping statement without mentioning any specific names to prove his point. Yet in spite of the superficiality of many of the remarks which he made about the heroes and practitioners of surrealism, it is impossible not to take his side in the controversy into which he was drawn with André Breton in *Arts*.

Before *L'Homme révolté* was published as a whole in November 1951, the extract *Lautréamont et la Banalité* appeared in *Les Cahiers du Sud*. This criticism of Lautréamont, and of the revolt expressed in his work, stimulated André Breton, the most faithful representative of the surrealist movement, to make a violent attack on Camus. The work of Lautréamont, he wrote, was 'that of the greatest genius of modern times', because it was one which systematically denied all rational explanation. In his criticism of it, Camus had put himself on the side of 'the worst kind of conservatism and conformity with accepted opinion' and had tried to bring down to his own level something a thousand times greater than him. In the exchange of letters which followed this reply by Breton, Camus insisted once again upon the confessional aspect of *L'Homme révolté*. What he criticised in Lautréamont and the surrealist movement was, he said, a tendency which he recognised in his own character and which he realised was responsible for much of the disorder and intellectual mystification of his time—nihilism. Breton, in his view, had reason to regret certain of his early nihilist declarations in the surrealist movement, because he must have realised, after 1933, that they opened the way to Hitlerian barbarism. 'It was then that we all understood,' he writes, 'that a certain nihilism which we all more or less shared, left us defenceless against an enterprise which we detested with all our being.' Such a remark throws an interesting light on the *Lettres à un ami allemand*, in the same way that Camus's other statement to Gaston Leval that 'I have lived through nihilism, contradiction, violence and the dizziness of destruction' indicates how closely autobiographical a play *Caligula* might be. It is unfortunate, however, that *L'Homme révolté* itself contains so little explicit and detailed reference to the intellectual temptations which Camus had undergone, for it would certainly have been a more interesting book if the confession had been more direct.

The argument with Breton was less serious intellectually and less important than the disagreement with Sartre. The periodical *Arts*, where it took place, took a childish pleasure in encouraging the bitter personal quarrels which are so regrettable a feature of French literary life, and was later to show an unbelievable degree of frivolity and personal spite in attacking Camus. What this controversy does show, however, is the extreme popularity of the word 'révolte' and the immense variety of usages to which it was put. For Camus, it was an attempt to protect the individual against the absurd and the irrational, and to preserve something which he himself found infinitely valuable: human life as it naturally is. For Breton, the purest surrealist act—the definition had existed since 1922—was to go down into the street and shoot at random into the crowd. There was no doubt in his own mind, Breton informed Camus in 1952, that the author of such an attempt would be lynched on the spot. 'It was a question, metaphysically speaking, of a deliberate attack against man, which was capable of reaching at one and the same time both the "I" and the "Other".' The implied quotation in Breton's statement is from Rimbaud's *La Lettre du Voyant*—'Car Je est un autre'—and it fits in with the avowed aim of surrealism of obliterating the existence of all opposites. It is also a good summary of what the surrealists understood by 'révolte', which was, for them, a movement which aimed at exalting the desires of the individual above the needs of society and above the restraint imposed by any form of law, religion, morality, reason or common sense. Although not himself a Surrealist, George Bataille showed how different most writers' connotation of revolt was from Camus's own when he compared it—in a phrase with which Breton must surely have agreed—with the 'running amok' of the Malayan native. For Bataille, revolt is essentially 'refusal to obey, uncontrolled and unsubdued passion'. His and other writers' idea of what the word meant differed so completely from the associations of moderation and reason which Camus had given to it from 1945 onwards that it is scarcely surprising that so many of the disputes aroused by *L'Homme révolté* seem like a dialogue of the deaf.

It has already been suggested that the principal value of the sections of *L'Homme révolté* which are concerned with art lies in the indication which they give of Camus's own ambitions and experience as an artist. This is true not only of his theory of the novel but also of his general reflections on what he calls 'stylisation'. The fact that *L'Etranger* and *La Chute* were described by Camus himself as 'récits' and *La Peste* as a 'chronique' makes it difficult to judge them by the standards of the ideal 'roman' which Camus discusses in *L'Homme révolté*. Like André Gide, Camus was acutely conscious that the word 'novel' should be applied only to works of art which satisfied certain conditions, and it may be that he did not think that any one of his completed works of fiction had the necessary depth and complexity to justify being called a 'novel'. Nevertheless, each of his prose fictions does show that stylisation of reality which he found characteristic of the greatest art. He remarked to Jean-Claude Brisville in 1959 that the actual writing of his books was always a slow and painful process, made even longer by the 'profound anarchy' of his own temperament. In this respect, his remark that 'true classicism is nothing more than a Romanticism brought under control' may be a far more personal one than its echo of the ideas of André Gide and Professor Peyre might lead one to think. The contrast already mentioned between the apparent formlessness of *La Mort Heureuse* and the perfect finish of *L'Etranger* is another pointer in the same direction, and critics who have access to Camus's other unpublished manuscripts may be able to judge how far his fiction did represent the attempt to stylise reality which he described in *L'Homme révolté*. The subtle way in which he translated his own experiences and ideas into *La Chute* and *L'Etranger* is certainly a proof that the passages on stylisation in *L'Homme révolté* are to be read as statements of his aims.

In spite of the interesting light which it throws upon Camus's ambitions as a writer and in spite of its very laudable central idea, *L'Homme révolté* nevertheless remains his most unsatisfying prose work. This is very probably because it was not the kind of book that his natural talent fitted him to write. It has already been suggested that the expression which Camus's work gave to the problems of his time was most convincing when he was expressing his purely personal experiences. This is especially true of *La Peste*, where Camus exploits his own preoccupation with separation, with suffering and with the forces of nature in such a way as to give a most moving picture of man's fate in the twentieth century. The strongly personal note in *L'Etranger*, *Caligula* and *Le Mythe de Sisyphe* has been sufficiently emphasised to need no detailed repetition here. It will later be argued that although Camus in no way intended the hero of *La Chute* to be either an exemplary or an autobiographical figure, it is very much his own experience which brings Jean-Baptiste Clamence to life. All his other works apart from *L'Homme révolté* give the impression of having been born of a kind of inner necessity, where the difficulties of composition were overcome by the impulse which he felt to express what was in him. He referred on one occasion, however, to the *decision* which he had had to take to write *L'Homme révolté*—implying that he wrote it almost through a sense of moral duty and that he had some difficulty in bringing himself to do so. Camus's natural talent as a writer led him to talk about nature, about physical pleasure, about the beauty of North Africa and about the strange lessons of the sun and of poverty. When he describes the effect of the sun and heat in North Africa—'A certaines heures, la campagne est noire de soleil. Les yeux tentent vainement de saisir autre chose que les gouttes de lumière qui tremblent au bord des cils.' ('At certain times of day, the countryside is black with sunlight. The eyes strive in vain to hold on to anything but the drops of light which tremble on the eyelashes.')—he is writing most naturally and making his most immediate and unsophisticated appeal. The intellectual-isation of his North African experience left enough of the original passion for life that had inspired them to make *L'Etranger* and *Le Mythe de Sisyphe* into intensely living as well as perfectly finished works of art. The moral impulse which drove him to write *L'Homme révolté* lost itself in the mass of ideological and historical detail which Camus felt he had to incorporate into his essay. The Camus who had himself so vivid and intense an appreciation of physical life was admirably suited to write the defence of happiness and normality in *La Peste* or the impassioned appeal for tolerance of *Ni Victimes ni Bourreaux*. The Camus who grew convinced that the political evils of his time were the result of a pernicious philosophy of history and of an all-pervasive nihilism was too intolerant of other people's ideas to express the humanism of *La Peste* convincingly in the medium of the philosophical essay. In *L'Etat de Siège*, *Les Justes* and *L'Homme révolté* it is Camus the didactic writer who stands in the way of Camus the artist, and important though his political ideas were both for himself and for many of his contemporaries, it is a relief to turn once again to his work as a creative writer.

Chapter Ten

THE CREATIVE REVIVAL

BETWEEN 1951 and 1956 Camus published no major work. He limited his activity to clarifying the intentions of what he had already written, to collecting polemical texts in the second volume of *Actuelles* and lyrical texts in *L'Eté*, and to beginning his career as a translator, adapter and producer of plays. It has already been noted how Camus preferred to take the subjects for his own plays from texts by other writers, and the task of adapting and presenting other men's plays enabled him to continue work in the theatre at a time when he apparently found it impossible to write a new play of his own. In limiting himself to the purely technical aspect of the theatre he was, of course, continuing an earlier feature of his career, since he had produced plays for the Théâtre de l'Equipe in Algiers, and the 1953 adaptation of Pierre Larivey's *Les Esprits* had originally been made as early as 1940. His adaptation of Calderón de la Barca's *La Devoción de la Cruz*, which was produced at the Festival d'Angers in June 1953 together with *Les Esprits*, was an act of homage to the writer whom he called in his preface 'the greatest theatrical genius that Spain has produced'. Both adaptations are very skilfully made and enjoyed great success at the Festival d'Angers where Camus himself produced them after the original producer, Marcel Herrand, had fallen ill. Although it is perhaps exaggerated to describe Camus, as Robert Kemp did in his favourable review of *La Devotion à la Croix*, as 'a writer whose atheism is as hard as a block of ice', there seems little point in studying either this or any other adaptation which Camus made in order to find out anything about his own personal ideas. It was perhaps in his later theatrical work that he was most exclusively an artist, working with no ambition other than the purely aesthetic one of producing a good play.

His adaptation in 1955, of Dino Buzzati's *Un caso clinico* (*Un cas intéressant*) at the Théâtre de la Bruyère was enthusiastically received and widely discussed. Critics saw in this story of a healthy man so convinced by the staff of a sinister hospital that he was 'really' ill that he died, the sign that Camus was returning to the Kafka-like atmosphere of *Le Malentendu*, but they were wrong. Camus had been struck by the vitality of Buzzati's work, and had wished to express his admiration for it. Similarly, when he produced his excellent version of Faulkner's *Requiem for a Nun* in May 1956, he made it clear in his later preface to the translation of the novel that it was Faulkner's attempt to write modern tragedy which really interested him, and not his rather strange religious views. He remarked in 1956 that he considered the theatre to be the highest form of literary art. It was an opinion which, he admitted, had originally been a highly personal and emotional one, but which he had confirmed intellectually by considering that the greatest writers had all been dramatists. This is a curious reflection on the aesthetic theories of *L'Homme révolté*, where the theatre is mentioned hardly at all, but perhaps explains why Camus preferred to devote most of his energy in the last years of his life to the theatre and not to the writing of his promised novel, *Le Premier Homme*.

His adaptation of Dostoievsky's *The Possessed* in January 1959 was, like his version of *Requiem for a Nun*, remarkable in that it showed with what skill he could make a complicated or difficult novel into a clear and exciting play. Alone among his adaptations, *Les Possédés* may have been intended to have a political significance, for it deals with the nihilism which is discussed in such detail in *L'Homme révolté*, and it was a novel written by Dostoievsky himself as a piece of *littérature engagée*. Nevertheless, no didactic purpose is allowed to interfere with Camus's attempt to recapture the atmosphere of Dostoievsky's work, and re-create in the medium of the theatre the feeling of mystery which hangs about Stravrogin in the novel. Like *Requiem for a Nun*, *The Possessed* was an extremely successful adaptation and ran for a long time. Yet although Camus left excellent texts of both plays, his tragic death does leave us with a special feeling of regret that he chose to follow out the aesthetic of *Le Mythe de Sisyphe* and do so much work in a medium that was essentially perishable. If only, one is tempted to say, he had devoted less time to what he himself referred to as his hobby, and had instead added to the remarkable evidence of his continued powers as a creative artist given by *La Chute* and *L'Exil et le Royaume*. His experience in adapting other men's work may possibly have enabled him to write the really great play which somehow, in spite of all his enthusiasm for the theatre, he had failed to produce, but such speculation is pointless since we shall never know. His return to creative writing after he had recovered from *L'Homme révolté*, was, however, extremely fruitful and contains four very different types of text that show how vital an artist he was and had remained: his prefaces, the lyrical essays in *L'Eté*, *La Chute* and *L'Exil et le Royaume*.

The two most important prefaces which Camus wrote after 1951 were the introduction to a new translation of Oscar Wilde's *The Ballad of Reading Gaol* and a long article presenting the complete works of Roger Martin du Gard in the *Bibliothèque de la Pléiade*. The introduction to *The Ballad of Reading Gaol* is interesting in that it showed how Camus's sense of the importance of art enabled him to give a different tone to the legend of Oscar Wilde in French literature. Rather strangely for an amateur of the theatre, Camus apparently had little taste for *The Importance of Being Earnest*, since he did not distinguish it from the other works written during the period when, in his view, Wilde was the 'pharisee' of the religion of art. Once Wilde had been sent to prison, however, Camus considered that he became a true artist. He then wrote *The Ballad of Reading Gaol* and *De Profundis* and showed that 'the supreme aim of art is to confound all judges, to abolish all accusations, and to justify everything, life and mankind, in a light which is the light of beauty only because it is the light of truth'. The Camus who, in Roger Quilliot's phrase, tried never to separate the sea and prisons, natural beauty and the suffering of men, was admittedly expressing a very personal attitude when he divided Wilde's work so sharply into two parts, one almost worthless and the other immensely valuable. Nevertheless his preface is a welcome change from those French and English critics who treat

Wilde simply as a victim of English hypocrisy or as a charming dilettante.

The preface to the works of Martin du Gard is one of the most sympathetic that Camus ever wrote or that Roger Martin du Gard has so far received. It shows that Camus had nothing of the Romantic rebel about him by marking a preference for Antoine over Jacques Thibault and for Tolstoy over Dostoievsky, and indicates how Camus came to regard literature not so much as a means of protesting against life as of proceeding towards a deeper understanding of it. It also marked a renewed interest in the technique of novel writing which was to give birth to *La Chute* and *L'Exil et le Royaume* in the same way as Camus's earlier reading of Hemingway had suggested what technique could be best used in *L'Etranger*, and his study of Defoe and Melville had showed him how to use symbolism in *La Peste*. Camus's return to imaginative writing was particularly welcome after *L'Homme révolté*, which marked a stage beyond which it was difficult to make any progress in the same direction. Before *La Chute* was published, however, Camus made available for the first time in book form a number of essays which had been written between 1939 and 1953. These supplement the self-portrait which he gave in *Noces* and *L'Envers et l'Endroit*, at the same time as they contain a number of passages illustrating the aspect of Camus's work which, in his own view, had been most consistently neglected by his commentators: his humour.

There are, of course, touches of humour in most of Camus's works, but they are generally there to fulfil a particular purpose. *L'Etranger* reproduces some of the North African comedy of speech and manners of which Camus had already given examples in *Noces*, and also has the description of the 'petite femme automate'. One day, when Meursault is lunching at his usual restaurant, a strange little lady comes and sits at his table. She feverishly takes off her coat, sits down, orders her meal in sharp, staccato accents, adds up the bill, lays out the money to pay it, together with the exact tip, on the table, and then proceeds to tick off the radio programmes in her magazine. Meursault watches her for a while after she has left the restaurant, weaving her way precisely in and out of the traffic, until she disappears. She comes to watch him at his trial, but gives no sign that she recognises him.

Her appearances simply add to the strange, almost Kafka-like atmosphere which pervades part of *L'Etranger*, and she is obviously put in to serve two purposes. First of all, as Robert Champigny pointed out, she gives Camus the opportunity to show that Meursault thinks of himself as normal, since he finds her way of behaving 'bizarre'. Secondly, she illustrates the idea that the absurdity of the world can show itself in a comic as well as in a tragic manner.

There is a similar character in *La Peste*, a retired grocer who, having retired from business at the age of fifty, passes the whole of his time in bed. There he spends his days methodically transferring one potful of peas to another pot. He never, apparently, gets bored, and finds the arrangement an eminently satisfactory one since it does away with all need for a clock; at every second transference, he needs a meal. He is a character carried over from the atmosphere of *L'Etranger*, and one can easily imagine a middle-aged Meursault doing the same thing. In *La Peste*, however, he provides a valuable touch of humour, and like Grand, is almost a chorus figure, a reminder that in the midst of the greatest catastrophes, odd people still continue to be odd in their own particular way. *Caligula* has something of the *humour noir* of Jarry and the Surrealists, but here again it obviously serves the purpose of underlining the absurdity of the world. *L'Etat de Siège* contains a number of time-honoured jokes about bureaucracy, while in *Les Justes* there is rather a grim example of humour in one of the prison scenes. The idealistic Kaliayev is there brought face to face with the working class criminal Foka, one of those for whom he has committed murder, but who, in prison, has turned hangman for personal profit. The humour in *L'Eté* differs from that of all Camus's other works in having no illustrative function and in being simply the expression of a personality attuned to the laughable side of human nature.

Camus's humour depends for the most part on an ironic contrast between the events described and the style used, and consequently evokes a quietly intellectual smile rather than outright laughter. Occasionally, however, his humour is more open and direct, and shows that he had nothing of the rigorous and austere attitude which was sometimes attributed to him. In the first essay reprinted in *L'Eté*, *Le Minotaure ou la Halte d'Oran*, Camus turns a more critical eye upon his native North Africa than he had done in *Noces*. Oran is a city whose inhabitants have all been eaten up by the Minotaur of boredom; they live in a city made of stone, and yet are so fond of it that 'shopkeepers put it in their windows to hold papers or simply to display it. Men heap it up by the road-side, doubtless for the delight of contemplating it, since a year later the heaps are still there'. It is a city where 'all the bad taste of Europe and of the East have come together in the shopwindows. You find there, heaped together at random, marble greyhounds, ballerinas with swans, versions of Diana the Huntress in green galalith, disc-throwers and reapers, everything that is used for birthdays and wedding gifts, the whole race of painful figurines constantly called forth on to our chimney-pieces by the practical jokes of a commercial genie'. The cinema advertisements in Oran have a particular charm. 'I read in a hand-bill of an Oran cinema,' writes Camus, 'the advertisements for a third-rate film. I note the adjectives "sumptuous", "splendid", "extraordinary", "amazing", and "tremendous". At the end, the management informs the public of the considerable sacrifices it has undertaken to present this "startling realisation". Nevertheless, the price of the tickets will not be increased.'

The more sophisticated tone of *Le Minotaure ou la Halte d'Oran* is a pleasant change after the rather uncritical enthusiasm for all aspects of North African life expressed in *L'Eté à Alger*. Its highlight is the description of the boxing display 'which will be appreciated by true amateurs'— 'more clearly expressed', Camus remarks, 'this means that the boxers are far from being champions, that many of them will be going into the ring for the first time, and that, as a result, one can count on their enthusiasm if not their skill'. It is here that Camus's pseudo-heroic style achieves its best effects, as the crowd 'breathing in the sacred aroma of embrocation' watches 'these series of slow rites and unregulated sacrifices' which are 'the deliberate ceremonial prologues of a savage religion'. As a French sailor and the local champion, 'covered with sweat beneath the pitiless light, open their guard, shut their eyes and hit out, shove with shoulders and knees, swap their blood and snort with rage', the spectators' enthusiasm reaches its climax. 'Every blow that gives a dull sound on the shining pectorals echoes in vast vibrations in the very body of the crowd, which, together with the boxers, is making its last effort.' The Manichean atmosphere in which there is 'Good and Evil, the Conqueror and the Conquered' gives a bad reception to the referee's decision of a draw, until, climbing into the ring, the sailor 'throws his arm round his opponent's neck and drinks in his fraternal sweat'. The applause bursts out as the crowd proves what Camus's neighbour had been telling him all along—that, whatever the more sophisticated inhabitants of Algiers might think, the men of Oran are 'not savages'.

While Camus's humour is at its best when he is talking about life in North Africa, it also recurs in his description of French literary life. The essay *L'Enigme*, written in 1950 after Camus had been particularly annoyed by an article which insisted on still treating him as the 'prophet of the absurd', contains, together with one delightful explanatory parallel, some entertaining reflections on the modest attitude which certain aspects of French journalism cannot fail to inculcate into a successful writer.

'You no longer need to write books to make a name for yourself in literature. All you need to have done is written one book which has been discussed in the evening papers and you can rest on this laurel for the remainder of your life. . . . Doctors know that some illnesses should be wished for rather than avoided; they are, as it were, a compensation for a functional disorder which, without them, might give rise to the most serious consequences. Thus there are blessèd constipations and providential attacks of arthritis. The flood of words and hasty judgements which today drowns all activity in an ocean of frivolity can at least teach the French writer a modesty which he constantly needs in a nation which gives an exaggerated importance to his calling. To see one's name in two or three newspapers we know of is so hard a trial that it must perforce have some benefits for the soul.' It was Camus's ability not to take his rôle of 'Director of conscience' too seriously which almost deserted him at the time of *L'Homme révolté* but which, returning in a rather different form in *La Chute*, showed that he was not always the pompous pilot that Sartre had accused him of being.

L'Eté has other qualities which, in addition to its humour, make it one of the best minor works that Camus published. There are only two 'moralising' essays—*Prométhée aux Enfers* and *L'Exil d'Hélène*—where Camus's tendency to use the example of classical Greek as a stick with which to beat the modern world strikes a jarring note, but even there his description of the physical atmosphere of the Mediterranean is very adequate compensation. *Les Amandiers*, an essay first written in 1940, is an excellent example of the way in which two moods could co-exist in Camus's mind. At the same time as he was publishing the very pessimistic editorials in *Le Soir Républicain*, he also wrote what was probably the best short statement of his attitude towards literature and towards political problems:

'What we want is for the mind never again to bow down before the sword, and never again for force to be triumphant when it is not serving the interests of the mind. This is, it is true, a task that has no end, but it is we who must continue it. I have not sufficient faith in reason to believe in progress, or in any philosophy of history. But I believe that men have never ceased to go forward in the consciousness which they have of their destiny. We have not overcome our condition, and yet we have come to know it better. We know that we are living in contradiction, but that we must refuse this contradiction and do what we can to reduce it. Our task, as men, is to find the few expressions of belief that will ease the infinite anguish of free souls. We have to knit together that which has been destroyed, to make justice possible in so obviously unjust a world, to give meaning to happiness for men poisoned by the suffering of the century. This is naturally a superhuman task. But tasks are called superhuman when men take a long time to complete them, that is all.'

It is a curious reflection on what can happen when literature takes sides to think that the seven pages of *Les Amandiers* are an incomparably more persuasive expression of the validity of Camus's attitude than the three hundred and seventy-eight pages of *L'Homme révolté*.

Retour à Tipasa, the description of two visits made to Algeria after a long absence, is another essay which is interesting both from a biographical point of view and as a statement of Camus's conception of his rôle as an artist and thinker. The first 'pèlerinage aux sources' was unsuccessful.

It rained for five days without stopping and Camus sought refuge in the cafés where, as he said, 'I could read my age on faces which I recognised without being able to put a name to them'. Then he returned to Paris, thinking that the barbed wire which surrounded the ruins of Tipasa under the pouring rain symbolised all the changes which had come over the world since the days of his youth. It was on his second visit that, one fine morning, he set out for Tipasa and found there the experience which he had been seeking.

'It seemed as though the morning had cast anchor and the sun had stopped moving for an immeasurable moment. In this light and this silence, the years of darkness and fury melted slowly away. I listened to a sound within me which I had almost forgotten, and it was as if my heart had long since been stopped and had begun to beat again. And, now awakened, I recognised, one by one, the sounds that made up this silence: the ceaseless background of the birds, the light, short breaths of the sea at the foot of the rocks, the trembling of the trees, the blind song of the columns, the sound of the absinth plants rustling in the breeze and the lizards slipping furtively over the stones. I could hear all this, and I also listened to the waves of joy which now rose within me.'

It is this moment of rediscovered happiness which taught him, as he says, that 'in the midst of winter, there was in me an unconquerable summer' and which gave the title of *L'Eté* to the book in which it was described. 'Yes,' he wrote, 'there is beauty and there are men who suffer in humiliation. Whatever may be my faults as a man or as a writer, I would like never to have been unfaithful either to the one or to the others.' It was through experiences such as these that Camus was able to continue his activity as a creative writer, and their inspiration must never be forgotten when, in *La Chute*, there are signs which seem to suggest that he is on the point of denying almost everything that he previously admired.

When *La Chute* was first published in Paris in May 1956, critics paid more attention to its possible meaning than to the indication it gave that a new phase had begun in Camus's career as a creative writer. Many saw it as a self-portrait and as the direct description of a new pessimism and awareness of sin which probably foreshadowed a conversion to Christianity. In England, Donnat O'Donnell carried this interpretation to the point of suggesting that the book marked the end of Camus's 'liberal progressive' attitude, and revealed a concern for theological problems which contradicted the whole atmosphere of his earlier work. Similar ideas had, of course, been put forward in France, with the result that Camus decided to preface the English translation with the following quotation from Lermontov's novel, *A Hero of our Time*: 'Some were dreadfully insulted, and quite seriously thought the author to have held up as a model such an immoral character as *A Hero of Our Time*; others shrewdly noticed that the author had portrayed himself and his acquaintances . . . *A Hero of Our Time*, gentlemen, is in fact a portrait, but not of an individual; it is the aggregate of the vices of our generation in their fullest expression.' Camus thus emphasised that neither his general philosophy nor his attitude towards his work had changed. He was still trying to be 'an objective writer . . . who chooses themes without ever taking himself as subject'. A study of the novel will show, however, that although Camus was by no means proposing its hero, Jean-Baptiste Clamence, as an example to be followed, he had nevertheless used much of his own experience in creating him.

La Chute like L'Etranger, is a monologue, and is the shortest 'novel' that Camus published. It describes in six parts the life and attitude of Jean-Baptiste Clamence, 'judge-penitent'. It is addressed to an unnamed listener whose reactions are sometimes indicated by the narrator's comments, and who finally turns out to be what Clamence himself was before coming to live in Amsterdam: an eminent Parisian lawyer. Before he made the alarming discovery of his own cowardice and duplicity, Clamence was the defender of all noble causes, the humanitarian advocate who rushed to the help of widows and orphans—although, as he now admits, 'there are widows who cheat and orphans who are quite savage'. He radiated friendliness, generosity and charity, 'spoke of justice as if I slept with her every night', helped blind men across the street and rejoiced when a beggar approached his house. He was perfectly at home in the physical life, and had so complete and so charming a self-confidence that people sought out his company and absolute strangers often had the impression of having already met him.

After some time, however, he began to have doubts about the reality of his own radiant perfection. An incident with a motor-cyclist in which he was publicly humiliated showed him that, when he himself was threatened, he became 'an irascible master who wanted, regardless of all laws, to strike down the offender and bring him to his knees'. After that discovery, he remarks, 'it is very hard to continue seriously believing that one has a vocation for justice and is the pre-destined defender of the widow and the orphan'. He begins to have the illusion that people are laughing at him, and then, one night, does something which destroys his self-satisfaction for ever. Returning home from a visit to one of his mistresses, he notices, as he is crossing the Pont des Arts, a young girl leaning over the parapet and looking down into the Seine. As he leaves the bridge and walks along the quai, he hears a noise which might be that of a body falling into the water, and hears the cry for help which follows it. He stands still for a moment, overcome by a strange weakness, and then continues on his way. When no one is there to watch him he is a coward, and it is this incident which, on top of his growing realisation that what he really wants is to dominate others, which leads him to exercise in the bars of Amsterdam 'the strange calling of judge-penitent'.

His technique, as he explains to his listener, is to confess all his crimes and weaknesses in the utmost detail and without the slightest reticence. Once he has managed to persuade his listener—who must, as he himself admits, be an intelligent bourgeois like himself—that all men are equally guilty, then his pride can once again be satisfied:

'Covered with ashes, tearing my hair, my face scored by clawing, but with piercing eyes, I stand before all humanity recapitulating my own disgrace without losing sight of the effect I am producing, and saying: "I was the lowest of the low". Then, imperceptibly, I pass from the "I" to the "We". When I get to the "This is what we are", the game is over and I can tell them all about themselves. I am just like them of course: we're all tarred with the same brush. However, I have a superiority in the I know it and this gives me the right to speak. You see the advantage, I am sure. The more I accuse myself, the more I have the right to judge you. Even better, I make you judge yourself, which makes it that much less necessary for me to do it.'

Already, he remarks at the end of the last section, his listener will be feeling slightly less pleased with himself than he did when the monologue began five days earlier. Already, by looking into the mirror of Clamence's own duplicity and *libido dominandi*, he has begun to recognise his own face. Once this has happened, Clamence's triumph is complete.

His motives are made clear at several points in the book. He has always wanted to look down on people from the heights of his own perfection and be able to despise them because of his own virtue. He has always been a monster of pride, and when he could no longer feel that he was superior to all other men, he was forced to make them feel their guilt so that he could still continue to despise them. 'You see in me, *très cher*,' he remarks to his listener, 'an enlightened prophet of slavery.' It is in this respect that, in Camus's own opinion, he is the 'aggregate of the vices of a whole generation in their fullest expression', for both his original good intentions and his present desire to convince others of their guilt express that desire to enslave others which Camus found so characteristic of his time.

In an interview which he gave to the *Gazette de Lausanne* in March 1954, Camus made a remark which provides a clue as to the real meaning of *La Chute*. 'Many modern writers,' he said, 'and among them the atheist existentialists, have denied the existence of God; but they have kept the notion of original sin. People have insisted too much on the innocence of creation; now they want to crush us with the feeling of our own guilt.' In private conversation in August 1956, Camus said that what he was principally satirising in *La Chute* was the attempt by certain writers to bring middle class people to the Communist party by making them feel how deeply they shared the guilt of bourgeois society. From this point of view, Clamence is expressing his motives with almost as much openness as the character who represented the plague in *L'Etat de Siège*, and there is a similarity between Camus's views on the aims of totalitarian politics in both books. Far from seriously expressing a belief in universal human wickedness in *La Chute*, Camus is satirising and attacking it. He sees it as a weapon for enslaving men, in the same way as, in *L'Homme révolté*, he showed that nihilism and the Hegelian theory of history could be used for the same purpose. In the *prière d'insérer*—the little explanatory note that French authors sometimes slip into their books—Camus remarked that Clamence 'has a modern heart, that is to say that he cannot bear to be judged. He thus hastens to accuse himself, but it is so that he may more easily judge other people'.

Although it would be unwise to stress the political significance of *La Chute*—which is, to tell the truth, rather esoteric and very dependent upon Camus's own idiosyncratic view of the motives of left-wing intellectuals—critics like Robert Kanters were certainly wrong when they thought that Camus was presenting Jean-Baptiste Clamence as a model. Neither was he indicating that he now accepted the idea that all men are sinful and was therefore coming nearer to Christianity. In his preface to the translation of *Requiem for a Nun* in 1957, Camus commented on the number of times he had been asked whether he was now a convert, and remarked with some asperity that 'if I had translated and produced a Greek tragedy, no one would have asked me if I believed in Zeus'. He added a footnote which protested against the French intellectual habit of attacking those who did not reject Christianity with sufficient violence, and indicated that his own attitude was one of polite disbelief. In an interview published in *Le Monde* in August 1956 he told Claude Sarraute: 'I don't believe in God, it is true: but this does not make me an atheist. I would even agree with Benjamin Constant that irreligion is something rather vulgar and, yes, something rather worn out.' As to the meaning of *La Chute*, he remarked that nothing at all authorised critics to interpret it as the sign of a coming conversion, and added: 'Does my judge-penitent not say that he is a Sicilian and a Javanese? Nothing Christian about him at all. Like him, I have a great feeling of friendship for the first Christian. I admire the way he lived and the way he died. My lack of imagination prevents me from going any further than this. And that, I may say, is the only point which I have in common with this Jean-Baptiste Clamence with whom people want to identify me.'

All Camus's published statements on *La Chute* thus invite the reader to look upon it as an objective and ironic novel.

Clamence recalls not only John the Baptist and the 'vox clamens in deserto', but also *clémence*, mercy, the virtue he lacks most. Yet the very frequency with which Camus said that people must not identify him with his hero may as easily indicate an uneasy conscience as a legitimate impatience with the modern habit of treating every book as a thinly disguised autobiography. There are, in addition, more solid reasons for thinking that, like all Camus's fiction, *La Chute* may have been intended as an objective novel, but that it was in fact a work which presents much of his own character and experience. The book was originally intended to be one of the short stories in *L'Exil et le Royaume*—it is easy to see how Clamence's nostalgia for his youth and for the islands where the Trade Winds blow could fit into the theme of exile—but while Camus was writing it, the central character became big enough to fill a short novel. It may be, of course, that there were purely aesthetic reasons for this; that Camus became so interested in the technical problems of using the monologue to express the universal egotism of all men that he felt he needed a wider canvas; and that there is no need to assume that, because he used his own experience as raw material, he was necessarily obsessed by it. Yet the temptation to see *La Chute* as something more than an exercise in narrative technique or an objective denunciation of the sins of our time is a strong one. Jean-Paul Sartre called *La Chute* 'perhaps the finest' of Camus's works, and 'certainly the least understood'. He may perhaps have meant by this that Camus had now exorcised all the faults which had shown themselves in *L'Homme révolté* and in the open letter to *Les Temps Modernes*. What is certain is that Camus did put a great deal of himself into the character of Jean-Baptiste Clamence.

Like Camus, Clamence feels innocent 'only at Sunday football matches and in the theatre', which, like Camus, he 'loves with an unrivalled passion'; he is, as Camus was, a good dancer, a charming person to be with, and a strong critic of General Franco; if the rumours which one circulated about Camus's private life are true, Clamence's success as a Don Juan may also have reflected something of his creator's character: like Camus, he despises judges, espouses the cause of the oppressed, and, again like Camus, is very conscious of the elegance and purity of the language which he uses. Two passages in particular can be quoted to show how Camus incorporated his own character and experience into this particular novel. In the essay *Retour à Tipasa*, Camus writes: 'There is thus a will to live without refusing anything that life offers which is the virtue that I honour most in the world.' Clamence is made to remark: 'I was altogether in harmony with life, fitting into it from top to bottom without refusing anything of its ironies, its grandeur or its servitudes.' In a different tone, Clamence describes how his vanity enabled him to forget other people's insults, with the result that, as he says, 'someone who thought I hated him could not recover from his surprise when I greeted him with a broad smile'. In his introduction to the essay *La Mer au plus près*, written in 1953 and published in *L'Eté* in 1954, Camus wrote: 'Men praise me, I dream a little, they insult me and I am scarcely surprised. Then I forget, and I smile at someone who has insulted me, or greet someone I like with too much ceremony.' By themselves, of course, such coincidences merely show that Camus is using his own experience just a little more obviously than one would expect an 'objective' writer to do. It is when the more important resemblance between Clamence and his creator is examined in some detail that the 'confessional' aspect of *La Chute* becomes more intriguing and more significant.

Clamence is a severe judge of his time, and makes a number of remarks which, like his scorn for judges and dislike of General Franco, echo Camus's own opinions. For example, he tells his listener: 'You must have noticed how Europe has at last learned to philosophise in the right way. We no longer say, as in simpler times; "This is my opinion. What are your objections?" We have become lucid. For the dialogue we have substituted the communiqué. "This is the truth", we say. "We can discuss it if you want; we aren't interested. But in a few years there'll be the police to show you that I'm right".' In passages like this Camus seems to be using Clamence as a mouthpiece for his own opinions, for it is his own burning awareness of the need to re-establish the tradition of dialogues and approximations which Clamence is ironically expressing. When Clamence makes a little joke about a prostitute who 'wrote her mémoires for a confessional journal quite open to modern ideas', it is quite obvious that Camus is getting in a little dig at Sartre's review *Les Temps Modernes*, which published exactly such an autobiography in 1948. The description by Clamence of his mistress who had 'read the sentimental press with such assiduity that she spoke of love with the assurance and conviction of an intellectual announcing the classless society' is again the exact expression of the ideas which Camus put forward at the time of *L'Homme révolté*. When Clamence suggests the various possible means whereby man tries to satisfy his desire to dominate others, he remarks that 'some people go in for politics and run directly to the cruellest party'. In the *avant-propos* to *Actuelles III*, the collection of articles on Algeria which he published in 1958, Camus suggested a very similar reason for the popularity of certain French political attitudes when he wrote of those who 'went with no transition at all from speeches about honour and brotherhood to the worship of the *fait accompli* and of the cruellest party'.

This similarity should not, of course, be pushed too far and Clamence is not always the spokesman for Camus's views. It is easy to see how, in the following passage, Camus deliberately exaggerates his own lack of enthusiasm for Parisian life and suspicion of the intellectual habits of his contemporaries into an attitude of absolute condemnation which is exclusively Clamence's own:

> 'Paris is a real *trompe-l'oeil*, a magnificent dummy setting inhabited by four million silhouettes. Nearly five million at the last census? Why, they must have been fruitful and multiplied. And that would not surprise me. It always seemed to me that our fellow citizens had two passions: ideas and fornication. Without rhyme or reason, so to speak. Still, let us take care not to condemn them; they are not the only ones, for all Europe is in the same boat. I sometimes think of what future historians will say of us. A single sentence will suffice for modern man: he fornicated and he read the papers.'

Nevertheless, when one remembers the sweeping statements in *L'Homme révolté* and reflects that Camus wrote in his preface to *The Ballad of Reading Gaol* that it was the fault of 'servile societies like ours' to be able to see beauty only in suffering; when Clamence's denunciations of modern intellectual habits are put side by side with Camus's own remark that 'contemporary intelligence no longer seems to measure the truth of doctrines otherwise than by the number of armoured divisions which they can put into the field'; and when, finally, Camus speaks in Clamentian accents of the 'mercantile and vulgarly cruel face of the last just men that we have', the tone in which both author and fictional character speak makes it hard to tell where one ends and the other begins.

The difficulty here is partly the traditional one of distinguishing the author from the narrator in almost any novel written in the first person. The repetition by Clamence of Camus's own tendency to extreme intolerance is, however, more interesting than the normal coincidence between an author's own views and those of his main character. It is certainly Camus's intention to satirise people who pass unmerciful judgments on their fellows, and he had no sympathy for Clamence's general approach. He stated in his second Nobel Prize speech that 'at the end of his journey, the artist absolves instead of condemning. He is not a judge but a justifier'. And also wrote that Roger Martin du Gard was 'our perpetual contemporary' because he was 'a man of pardon and of justice'. It was certainly Camus's *intention* to demonstrate the need for pardon, compassion and sympathetic understanding by showing the extremes to which their neglect can give rise. Emotionally, however, he seems to have shared many of Clamence's attitudes—his remark about 'the atrocious intellectual societies in which we live, where nastiness tries to pass itself off as intelligence' is one which it is easy to imagine in Clamence's mouth—and it is tempting to think that it is himself he is satirising in those passages where Clamence is made to speak scornfully of the society he has abandoned. In this interpretation, he would stand in the same relation to Clamence as Gide does to the Michel of *L'Immoraliste* or the Alissa of *La Porte Etroite*. The problem of Camus's relationship with Clamence is not, however, quite as easily solved as that. There are so many cases where Clamence is expressing Camus's own ideas that it is impossible to see at what point we should start to reject his views because, after all, he is intended to be a false prophet. Professor Hanna expresses it neatly when, after asserting that 'it is Camus himself who, very clearly, has raised his voice in confession', he writes: 'And it is just as clear (and this is the difficulty) that it is uncertain whose history and sins he is confessing.'

Such problems do not, however, in any way diminish the literary value of *La Chute*. On the contrary, by prolonging the ambiguity of the novel they add to the deliberate half-light in which the story is told. It might be argued that *La Chute* is principally a study in the 'spirit of place', and that its evocation of the mists and fogs of Amsterdam is mainly a deliberate artistic contrast to the blazing sunlight of North Africa in *L'Etranger* and *La Peste*. In the first two novels, the clear sunlight of Algeria formed an appropriate background for the discussion of definite questions—life and death, solitude and communion, good and evil, suffering and happiness. The sun dominates the whole of the action in *L'Etranger*, obsessing Meursault at his mother's funeral, giving him pleasure when he is with Marie, making him kill the Arab, reminding him at his trial that a year has passed since his adventure first started, and pouring in through the windows of the court-room. In the same way, rain and mist determine the psychological atmosphere of *La Chute*, casting a strange light in which guilt and innocence, pride and humility, irony and deadly seriousness, are impossible to identify and distinguish one from the other. At Amsterdam, the sea is no longer shimmering under the powerful sun, but 'steaming like a laundry', stretching without limits around Clamence and his listener as they sail across the Zuydersee. In this respect it is the atmosphere as well as the technique of narration in *La Chute* which reflects the ideas which the book expresses. It is a work of art whose principal value lies in its ambiguity, in the picture which it gives of man as a creature of duplicity, whose bad faith can poison all his enterprises and good intentions. The setting of Amsterdam admirably reflects the idea which Camus put forward in his preface to the poetry of Rene Char. 'We live in the time of damp souls; the damp smell which rises from the ruins covers the whole of Europe.'

When Sartre said that *La Chute* was Camus's 'best and least understood work' it was also perhaps because he had been struck by the remarkable resemblance between the means which Clamence uses to enthral his listener and the theory of literature which he himself put forward in 1952 in the long essay *Saint-Genet Comédien et Martyr*. There, he argued that Genet's intention in writing his books was to make the middle-class reader lose his self-confidence and instil in him the poison of reflective self-awareness. When the honest middle-class reader makes the necessary effort to understand a novel by Genet, he uses his own powers of sympathy to give life and reality to all the acts of theft, homosexuality and betrayal that are described. He is then like the peasant who picked up a sleeping serpent and warmed it in his bosom: the serpent came to life and stung him. The person who listens to Clamence is very like Sartre's 'good man'— defined as 'the average bourgeois reader'—who is shocked and horrified at the sudden discovery which he makes about himself when he realises that, reading Genet's work, he has been sharing the criminal and homosexual desires that Genet describes. When Clamence holds up his self-portrait so that his listener may recognise his own features in it, he is also setting a trap to catch clear consciences and destroy the peace of mind of the bourgeoisie. With a characteristic openness, Clamence describes to his victim just exactly how he intends to catch him:

'I accuse myself up hill and down dale. It's not hard, for I have now acquired a memory. But let me point out that I don't accuse myself crudely, beating my breast. No, I navigate skilfully, multiplying distinctions and digressions—in short I adapt my words to my listener and lead him to go one better. I mingle what concerns me and what concerns others. I choose the features we have in common, the experiences we have endured together, the failings we share—good form, the man of the moment, in fact, such as he reigns in me and in others. With all that I construct a portrait which is the image of all and of no one. A mask, in short, rather like those carnival masks which are both lifelike and stylised so that they make people say: "Why, surely I've met him!" When the portrait is finished, as it is this evening, I show it with great sorrow: "This, alas, is what I am!" The prosecutor's charge is finished. But at the same time the portrait I hold out to my contemporaries becomes a mirror.'

What is essential in both *La Chute* and in Sartre's ideas in *Saint-Genet Comédien et Martyr* is that the listener or reader must be an intelligent and analytically minded member of the bourgeoisie. The aristocrat and the happy proletarian are both immune from the poison of modern literature.

La Chute is not only an exercise in a particular narrative technique and a brilliant example of how the spirit of a place can contribute towards the portrayal of a particular psychological characteristic. It is also, especially in the first sections, a very funny novel. The humour admittedly becomes less marked as Clamence comes to describe his sinister ambitions, but it nevertheless plays a more important part in *La Chute* than in any other of Camus's major works. This humour depends less upon the witty and epigrammatic quality of the prose—'When you have no character, you need to give yourself a method'—as in the incidental touches which bring Clamence to life. The description of how Clamence went about doing good, for example, is a delightful portrait of the daily pleasures of the affable man.

> 'Indeed, good manners provided me with the greatest of pleasures. If I had the luck, on certain mornings, to give up my seat in the bus or the underground to someone who obviously deserved it, to pick up some object an old lady had dropped and return it to her with a smile I knew well, or merely to surrender my taxi to someone in a greater hurry than I, it was a red letter day. I even rejoiced, I must admit, on those days when, because the public transport system was on strike, I had a chance to load into my car at the bus stops some of my unfortunate fellow-citizens unable to get home. Giving up my seat in the theatre to allow a couple to sit together, lifting a girl's suitcases on to the rack in a train—these were all deeds I performed more often than others because I paid more attention to the opportunities and was better able to relish the pleasure they gave.'

Occasionally, of course, the mask slips, and a Freudian lapse in Clamence's normally self-assured speech reveals his true motives. 'Another day during the same period, when a motorist thanked me for helping him, I replied that no one would have done so much. I meant, of course, anyone. But that unfortunate slip weighed heavily on me. At modesty I really was a champion.' One of his judgments in particular is funny because it is so absolutely true. Many of the criminals whom he defended, remarks Clamence, were inspired by a desire for fame. 'And,' he continues, 'to achieve notoriety it is enough, after all, to kill one's concierge. Unhappily, this is usually an ephemeral reputation, for there are so many concierges who deserve to have their throats slit and who receive their deserts.'

Yet the humour, the political implications and the excellence of Camus's literary technique should not be allowed to distract attention from the essential contribution which *La Chute* makes to his thought. Camus himself was the first to admit that, in his own phrase, he was 'not a philosopher', but he immediately showed where his real interest lay when he added: 'What interests me is to know how we should behave.' He was essentially a moralist, and it is his awareness of the close relationship between ideas and actions in the sphere of ethics that inspires much of his work. It was because it seemed to him that wrong attitudes contributed greatly towards increasing human suffering that he thought it so important to use his powers as an artist to point out the dangers implicit in certain ways of thinking. This concern is present in *La Chute* which, perhaps more than any other of his books, 'illuminates the problem of the human conscience in the present time'. Like Camus's other books, it is a work with an essentially humanist theme. The hardest trial for any humanist is to admit that man is cruel, hypocritical and self-centred and yet not to despair in him. What Camus did in *La Chute* was to face up to this problem and indicate what disastrous results could follow the denial of man's *relative* innocence. In this book, Camus remains faithful to his idea that no attitude can be so absolutely true as to deserve our complete allegiance. Once we forget limits, whether in our political life or in our judgments on ourselves and other men, we are encouraging tyranny and all the suffering it causes. At the same time as *La Chute* indicates how Camus faced up to and overcame the problem of human duplicity and wickedness, it also provides a most valuable corrective to the ideas which he expressed in his earlier work.

It has already been noted how *La Peste* suffers from Camus's presentation of man largely as the innocent victim of events. It is also one of Camus's noblest characteristics—his refusal to believe that men are naturally wicked—which leads him to the over-simplification which is one of the faults of *L'Homme révolté*. Since men are good, the evil they do comes from the fact that they are misled. A philosopher must therefore be found whose influence is likely to have misled them. Hegel is conveniently there as a philosopher who influenced certain early Communists, and whose thought can be used to justify almost any political pretensions. He is therefore, argues Camus, responsible for the crimes which

Communism commits. *La Chute* corrects this point of view by emphasising the very human origin of certain kinds of tyranny. Clamence has chosen to enslave other men, and has thus committed a crime for which he is morally responsible. As several critics have suggested, *La Chute* can be read as a kind of *critique* of *La Peste*, for until he discovered how impure his motives were, Clamence had been living as a legal equivalent of Doctor Rieux. It would thus be true to apply to his most ambiguous and fascinating novel the remark which Camus made about his own work in 1950 and which has already been quoted: 'In some writers, it seems to me that their works form a whole in which each is to be understood in relation to the others, and in which they are all interdependent.'

The volume of short stories entitled *L'Exil et le Royaume*, which Camus published in March 1957, is linked to the rest of his work in two principal ways: all the stories treat the theme of separation, and they all show that care for style and literary composition which, more than anything else, distinguishes him from Sartre and makes him a more satisfying writer. They differ from the rest of his work, however, by the fact that they appear, on first reading at least, to have no general political or philosophical significance. They are more descriptions of men—and of women—than meditations on them, and the characters they portray seem, with one exception, to be much closer to the common run of humanity than the people described in Camus's other work. Meursault, Rieux, Tarrou, Clamence, Caligula and Martha are all beyond most people's ordinary experience, all to a greater or lesser extent incarnations of an idea or of a moral and philosophical attitude. The Janine of *La Femme Adultère*, however, like the school teacher Daru in *L'Hôte*, the workman Yvars in *Les Muets* and the engineer D'Arrast in *La Pierre qui Pousse*, is essentially a human being, and not the symbol of an attitude. This human warmth which one finds in the stories of *L'Exil et la Royaume* is particularly important when one considers that the three most moving stories are set in Algeria. The 'pèlerinage aux sources' which Camus described in *Retour à Tipasa* also showed him that the true source of his inspiration still lay in his native country. This inspiration, however, was no longer the revelation of happiness described in *L'Etranger* and *Le Mythe de Sisyphe*; it was the realisation that those whom he had described as happy barbarians in *L'Eté à Alger* were now ordinary human beings faced with the twin problems of growing old and of facing a terrible political situation. The different styles which Camus uses in *L'Exil et le Royaume*—descriptive, with a wealth of images in *La Femme Adultère* and *La Pierre qui Pousse*; stream-of-consciousness in *Le Renégat*; humorous and nostalgic in *L'Artiste au Travail*; simple and direct in *Les Muets* and *L'Hôte*—emphasise rather than hide the theme which runs through the whole of the collection: as men and women age, they find the problems of separation and loneliness more and more difficult to bear.

The first story *La Femme Adultère* (*The Woman taken in Adultery*) is the only one of Camus's works to have a woman as the chief character. Janine, the heroine, is accompanying her husband on a trip to the wilder regions of North Africa where he is trying to sell cloth directly to the Arab merchants. She is impressed and attracted by the primitive life of the nomad tribesmen, with its dignity and freedom, and looking out over the desert from the walls of the town, she sees the tents of these 'poverty-stricken but free lords of a strange kingdom'. Somehow she feels this kingdom to be her own, and Camus writes: 'Janine did not know why this idea filled her with so sweet and vast a sadness that it made her shut her eyes. She knew only that this kingdom had been from all time promised to her, and yet that it would never belong to her, never again except perhaps for that fleeting moment when she opened her eyes once again on the suddenly motionless sky and its waves of coagulated light, while the voices rising from the Arab town grew suddenly silent. It seemed to her that the world had stopped turning and that from now on-wards no one would die or grow old. At all places, henceforth, life was suspended, save there in her heart where, at that moment, someone was weeping with pain and wonderment.'

This nostalgia is mingled with the regret which she feels, as she grows heavy with approaching middle age, for the light-ness and purity of her youth. The desire of Clamence in *La Chute*, for 'the sun, beaches and islands in the path of the trade winds, youth whose memory drives me to despair',

7   185

parallels Janine's longing for her youth and the animal-like grace of the nomad tribesmen. But Janine escapes from her exile in the heavy body of her age, whereas Clamence cannot throw off his pride, guilt, and intellectual torment, and return to the happy islands of his guiltless youth (itself strangely reminiscent of Camus's own youth under the blinding sun of North Africa). At night, Janine steals out from her bedroom and climbs up again on to the terrace from which she had seen the tents of the nomads in the distance. There, like Meursault on the eve of his execution, she is 'opened to the tender indifference of the world', and attains an almost sexual union with the earth and stars, a union in which she escapes from the cold and loneliness which have gripped her all day.

'No breeze and no noise, except from time to time the muffled cracking of the stones which the cold was splitting up into sand, disturbed the silence and solitude which lay about her. After a moment, however, she felt that the sky was sweeping down in a heavy movement over her head. In the depths of the dry, cold night, millions of stars came ceaselessly into being, while glittering icicles, falling immediately from them, began to slide irresistibly towards the horizon. Janine could not tear herself away from the contemplation of these drifting fires. She turned with them, and the same motionless journey reunited her little by little with her deepest being, where cold was now struggling with desire. In front of her, the stars fell one by one and then died out among the stones of the desert, and each time Janine opened herself a little further to the night. She breathed deeply, forgot the cold, the heaviness of human beings, the hysteria or boredom of life, the long anguish of living and of dying. After so many years in which, running away from fear, she had fled madly with no goal before her, she had at last come to rest. At the same time, she seemed to find her roots again, and the sap rose into her no longer trembling body. Striving towards the morning sky, her whole stomach pressed against the parapet, she waited only for her still thumping heart to grow quiet in its turn and for silence to reign within her. The last stars of the constellations dropped their clusters of light a little lower on the desert horizon, and remained motionless. Then, with an unbearable gentleness, the waters of the night began to fill Janine, drowning the cold, moving little by little from the dark core of her being, until they overflowed in uninterrupted waves right up into her mouth filled with groans. The next moment, the whole sky stretched over her as she lay with her back against the cold earth.'

Her 'adultery' consummated, weeping with relief, she stammers out to her husband as she lies in bed on her return: 'It's nothing, dear, nothing at all.'

The most remarkable feature of this first story is Camus's ability to recreate the physical setting in which the apparently very ordinary events take place. The long journey in the bus through a blinding sandstorm in which 'a mineral-like dust' blocks out the whole landscape, the persistent cold which is such a surprising feature of the North African desert, the uncomfortable hotel with its blinding white walls and complete absence of furniture, are all brilliantly evoked by Camus's prose. The story is, of course, primarily about Janine's mystical 'adultery' with the forces of nature, but it also contains a well observed, critical but nevertheless basically sympathetic portrait of the *petite bourgeoisie* in French Algeria. Marcel completely misunderstands the Arabs and refuses to consider them his equals, but is nevertheless presented not as a 'colonial exploiter' but as a mediocre man whose helplessness in a new situation deserves pity rather than contempt. Although in no manner a 'plea for Algerian Europeans', *La Femme Adultère* is, like *L'Hôte* and *Les Muets*, one of the stories which does a good deal to explain and justify Camus's attitude on the Algerian question.

The second story in this collection, *Le Renégat*, was first published in review form in June 1956 under the title of *L'Esprit confus*. It is written in the stream-of-consciousness manner popularised in France principally by the novels of William Faulkner, and the confusion of mind implicit in this technique is exactly suited to the subject of the story. A rather stupid French missionary has gone out to what seems to be an extremely savage part of Africa—the actual place where the story is happening is not made clear—in order to try to convert a particularly barbarous tribe. The tribesmen have naturally refused to be converted, and have instead made the missionary a prisoner, cut out his tongue and castrated him. As a result of his privations, torture and imprisonment, the missionary has completely transformed the blind, unthinking allegiance which he had had for Christianity into an equally intolerant worship of the savages' idol. Determined now to serve this idol with the same absolute devotion that he had intended to serve Christ—but which had changed immediately into its opposite at his first real trial—the missionary has stolen an old rifle and escaped from his prison to wait in ambush for the priest who is coming to replace him. He shoots the priest, only to be killed himself by the tribesmen who have followed him to his ambush, and waited until he had done their work for them.

The story is told in a series of flashbacks, and the reader is obliged to piece the details together for himself. This is not, however, very difficult, as Camus's clarity of mind did not desert him in this experiment in a new medium. The story can be made to fit into the theme of exile in several ways. The missionary is, of course, in a savage country far from his homeland, but more important than this is the fact that he has always been a stranger to true Christianity. It is made clear that his religion has been only a mask for his pride and for his power worship—'In fact,' he says, 'I had only understood that one thing, in my mulish intelligent way I went right to extremes, demanded all penances, was impatient with ordinary things, yes, I wanted to be an example, I too, so that people could see me and on seeing me would pay homage to what had made me better, in me and through me salute the Saviour. . . . Powerful, yes, that was the word that I endlessly rolled around my tongue, I dreamed of absolute power, dreamed of being he who brings the others to their knees, forces the enemy to capitulate, finally converts him, and the more the enemy is blind, cruel, sure of himself, buried in his own certainty, the more his confession proclaims the regal power of him who has caused his defeat.'

It is his worship of power which has caused him so easily to deny Christianity and turn to the blind obedience of the savages' idol, Râ,[1] whom he now proclaims to be all-powerful. In a way, he illustrates one of the ideas expressed in *L'Homme révolté*—that he who rebels completely will be most easily tempted by complete conformity to a new set of absolute and intolerant values. It may be that the story is an allegory of the Christian intellectual who gives up Christianity for Communism because of the longing which he has for power and

[1] See notes.

because of his basic attitude of power-worship—an idea which recalls George Orwell's diagnosis of the attraction which Communism has for many intellectuals. But the point of the story does not lie in the possibility of any allegorical meaning which it might contain, but in the picture which it gives of a particular psychological case. It shows a perception of the true nature of intolerance as well as, indirectly, an understanding of the Christian virtue of humility. It stands out from the other stories in this volume by its extreme physical violence—once again a feature of all forms of intolerance.

Les Muets is in complete contrast to the first two stories, both in its subject matter and its style. It is written in a direct, realistic prose which differs from the impressionistic and poetic style of *La Femme Adultère* and from the interior monologue of *Le Renégat* (*The Betrayal*). It too is set in North Africa, and its central character, Yvars, is clearly an older and sadder version of the Vincent whom Camus had admired in *Noces* for his simple, instinctive love of life. Contrasting Vincent's straightforward sensuality with the complicated exploitation of the senses in Gide—whom Camus did not greatly admire in this respect—he wrote: 'My friend Vincent, who is a cooper and junior swimming champion, has a clearer view of things. He drinks when he is thirsty, if he wants a woman tries to go to bed with her, and would marry her if he were in love with her (this hasn't happened yet). Afterwards, he always says: "That's much better," which is a vigorous summing up of the apologia which one might write in defence of satisfaction.' Yvars is a cooper and, since he is lame in one leg, has always been fond of swimming. He might well be Camus's boyhood friend, now past his prime, and barely managing to make a living in an industry which is dying out. Camus had written in *Noces* that, in North Africa, a working man who was over thirty had already had all his fun from life, and had to resign himself to taking second place before the tempestuous young. He is now studying the same fact twenty years later, and from a necessarily more sober and pessimistic point of view. Yvars still likes to look at the sea, remembering 'the deep, clear water, the strong sun, the girls, the life of the body—there being no other happiness in this country, and this happiness disappeared with youth', but now prefers to look out over the sea only when it changes colour in the cool of the evening. In the morning, as he pedals to work on his bicycle, he prefers to look in the opposite direction.

Yvars and his friends have held a strike, but have been forced to go back without obtaining the increase they had asked for. In the workshop they refuse, partly through pride and partly through humiliation, to reply to the owner when he comes in and tries to talk to them. Then, in the afternoon of the same day, the owner's little daughter falls seriously ill and has to be taken away in an ambulance. As the men are preparing to go home, the owner comes into the workshop again, and this time it is shyness and not deliberate intention which prevents the men from replying. Some sort of contact has been re-established, but Yvars is made to feel how deeply each one of the acts which we perform involves us with the feelings of other people. That evening, as he looks out over the sea, he wishes he were young again and could sail away to the other side of the sea.

In *Les Muets*, Camus's technique is close to that of Joyce in *Dubliners*, with the selection of an isolated incident and its treatment in an apparently inconclusive way. It is only his refusal to treat his subject in detail which enables him to avoid the sentimentality inherent in such a theme. Here the exile is the inevitable conflict between men—which destroys the contact between the employees and the owner, whom they all quite like in the normal run of things—while the kingdom is the unity of all men in family affection, illness and suffering. The story is a melancholy one, not only in its theme of the failure to make contact, but also in its treatment of the loss of youth. Like *L'Hôte*, the story which follows it in the collection, it forms part of Camus's attempt to express himself on the Algerian problem through the medium of art rather than through that of political action. It is not that either *Les Muets* or *L'Hôte* is a work of *littérature engagée*. They are both descriptions of the kind of situation which Camus knew well —his uncle worked as a cooper—and it is only by implication that they can be said to have a political meaning. The quality which they both show most clearly is that of compassion— the sympathetic understanding of the human predicament that Camus had tried to express in his very first essays, and which runs through the whole of his literary work and political writing. The plot of *L'Hôte*, perhaps the most moving of all these stories, is the best expression which he gave to his attitude on the Algerian question, and the one which brings out most clearly the immense difficulties which he met in forming his opinions on Algeria towards the end of his life.

Daru, a French schoolmaster born in Algeria—'anywhere else, he felt himself in exile'—is alone in his school on a high plateau, almost cut off by a sudden fall of snow. The local gendarme, Balducci, comes to the school on horseback, bringing with him as a prisoner an Arab who, in a family quarrel, has killed one of his cousins with a hedging hook. Daru is told that he has to escort this Arab to the police station fifteen miles away, in order to avoid the trouble which is brewing up in the Arab's village. He is unwilling to do this, but is obliged to accept custody of the Arab, and does so with the intention of allowing him to escape. During the night which the Arab spends in the school, he feeds and looks after him, refuses to tie him up, and is disappointed that he does not escape during the night. The next morning, Daru takes him to a point from where he can walk either towards the town where the prison awaits him, or towards the desert where the nomad tribes will shelter him. He gives him food that will enable him to make the day's journey into the desert, and leaves him to choose. As he looks back, the Arab is marching towards the town.

On his return, through the strong sunlight which is drying up the snow, Daru finds that an uneducated hand has scrawled across the blackboard: 'You have handed over our brother. You will pay for it . . .'. The story closes with the sentence: 'In this enormous country which he had loved so much, he was alone.'

L'Hôte is a story of misunderstanding and of unhappy accident, and a much deeper study of the same theme than the play *Le Malentendu*. Daru wants to do good, and seems to symbolise the generous and civilising aspects of French administration. It is he, we are told, who has the task of distributing the corn sent by France to save the Arabs from famine when their crops fail through drought. He is horrified at the stupid crime which the Arab has committed, and refuses his invitation to leave the school and join the rebel bands. The Arab himself is hardly conscious of what is happening, is incapable of understanding that a European could offer him his freedom, and quite unable to live outside the narrow community which he has now had to leave. Daru's generosity is misinterpreted because the rebels judge only on appearances and refuse to see that Europeans can do any good except by joining the Arab rebel movements. If the story has any message, it is an appeal for understanding and for tolerance on all sides. Daru is tempted to hate men—'this man, all men, and their dirty wickedness, their untiring hatred, their mad thirst for blood'—but cannot bring himself to hand over a man for execution. His dilemma is that of the many French residents in Algeria who are unable to bear violence, unable to ally themselves with either side, but unable to live elsewhere than in the country where they were born and have made their home. It is the tragedy of exiles in a country which used to be their own which the 'minor incident' of *L'Hôte* expresses.

The order in which the short stories are presented was carefully thought out by Camus. Coming immediately after the two short, realistically described, rather sad stories of *Les Muets* and *L'Hôte*, the leisurely irony of *Jonas, ou l'Artiste au Travail* provides a slackening of tension before the final story gathers together the ideas of exile and of belonging, and expresses them in a final synthesis. In spite of its basically serious intention, *L'Artiste au Travail* is the most amusing story that Camus ever wrote. The humour is more subtle than in *Le Minotaure ou la Halte d'Oran* or in *L'Enigme*, and is free from the general unpleasantness which pervades the whole of *La Chute*. Jonas is a painter, and is in fact interested in nothing but painting. He has faith in his star, which he knows will being him good fortune, and he is not disappointed. But, as he becomes more and more famous, the small flat in which he lives—which is delightfully described—is invaded by a host of friends and of disciples, so that it becomes increasingly difficult for him to paint any more at all. He is presented with petitions and with foreign celebrities, invited to lunch and dinner, and constantly surrounded by disciples who 'explain to him at great length what he has painted and why'. Under their guidance, Jonas discovers in his work 'many intentions which surprised him a little, and a multitude of things which he had not put there', but he does not find their presence very helpful to his actual painting. The host of visitors, disciples and critics who add to the noise and confusion made by his wife and three children, and by the incessant ringing of the telephone, drive Jonas from one room to another in search of somewhere peaceful where he will be able to paint. Finally, he constructs a kind of attic in a high corner of his flat, and retreats there alone. After many days of quiet meditation, during which he sees only his friend Radeau, and eats practically nothing, he falls ill. On the one canvas on which he has been working is written, in tiny characters, a single word. His friend Radeau cannot make out whether this word is 'solidaire' or 'solitaire'.

While this story is primarily a humorous evocation, in an almost Paul Jennings style, of the difficulties of a man who has to work at home, and of the particular difficulties of an amiable artist in a critic-infested community, it has a serious theme: that of the relationship between the artist and the community. The idea which Camus expresses at the very end is that the artist or writer is most 'solidaire'—that is, in communion with his time—when he is most solitary. Or, in other words, it is impossible to tell an artist that he must try deliberately to come into contact with real life, and live surrounded by the same preoccupations as ordinary men. If he is a true artist, the contact will be made through his art, however lonely he may be—or appear to be—during the actual process of artistic creation. It is difficult to see the precise meaning of the title of the story, and especially of the quotation from Jonah, i. 12—'And he said unto them, Take me up and cast me forth into the sea . . . for I know that for my sake this great tempest is upon you'—which Camus places at the very beginning. One possible interpretation is that as Jonas is left less and less alone, he is less and less able to paint, and thus to gain the livelihood of those who are dependent upon him —an interpretation which underlines the need to provide the artist with a certain isolation if he and that part of society which depends upon him are to survive. In any case, these 'meanings' which can be read into it are incidental to the story itself, which is above all an ironic commentary—almost certainly drawn from personal experience—of the dangers surrounding a famous artist or writer in the modern world. It was also, at the time, a polite and amusing reminder to

Camus's critics, friends and imitators, as well as to those who had the great good fortune of having his own unfailingly generous comments on the book they had happened to write about him.

The first draft of *L'Artiste au Travail* appeared in the literary review *Simoun* in Algiers in March 1953, and the subject, like that of the other stories, had clearly been taking form in Camus's mind for some considerable time. The *Mimodrame en deux parties* entitled *La Vie d'Artiste*, was, moreover, very different in both its atmosphere and its final tableau from the completed story published in 1957. The artist begins poor and happy, as Jonas did, with his wife posing for him. After he has had his career ruined by all his disciples, he is completely without money and his wife falls ill. He continues to paint while she is dying, and finishes his picture at the very moment of her death. The rest of the action of the Mime is described by Camus in the following terms:

'The painter turns round, sees his dead wife, and comes down the ladder. He walks slowly towards her, and with a great silent cry falls down by her bedside. The neighbours come in, and, slowly filling up his studio, all move towards the bed. But suddenly all the spotlights are switched on, and light up the completed picture, the lights glisten in a river of music. Then, everyone suddenly turns towards the canvas, and are all obviously stricken with horror, while the artist, completely indifferent towards his work and towards their astonishment, weeps. Then he lifts his head, notices that the others are there, goes towards them and begins to usher them out. Then he goes and takes a new canvas from a corner of the studio, sets it up in front of the bed. His friend looks at him, hesitates a moment, and then goes out. The painter kisses his wife, looks at her again, goes back to his easel, looks at her again, and begins to paint her dead face while the curtain slowly falls.'

The happy ending of the short story, and the apparent resolution of the problem of the artist's relationship to society, may indicate that, by 1957, Camus had recovered from a temporary pessimism about his calling which is shown in his *Mimodrame*. The official speech of acceptance which he made in Stockholm in December 1957 after having received the

Nobel Prize, like the lecture *L'Artiste et son Temps* which he gave in Upsala, show that in 1957 he had no tendency to link the artist's destiny with the theme of egoism and the sacrifice of loved ones. Both the speech and the lecture contain an enthusiastic praise of art and a whole-hearted affirmation of the artist's right to freedom and independence. Much of what Camus said in 1957 often seems, to the non-French reader, something of an exaggeration, for it is surely not true to apply the following remark to either the England or the America of the mid-twentieth century: 'In 1957, Racine would apologise for having written *Bérénice* instead of fighting on behalf of the Edict of Nantes.' Indeed, even a French reader may feel that when Camus said this he was protesting against an imaginary rather than a real state of affairs, and that he had given too great an importance to the adverse criticism published on his work. Yet in spite of the tone of aggrieved self-righteousness which makes itself felt occasionally in Camus's lecture, his plea for the right of the artist to create without being required to fulfil any more specific political or social function is both moving and sensible. His repetition of the ideas on stylisation first expressed in *L'Homme révolté* is particularly interesting because of the refusal which it implies both of purely abstract art and 'socialist realism'. True art, in his view, lies between these two extremes, and he showed how he considered it both as a form of rebellion against the fleetingness of the world and as a means of improving its natural beauty when he wrote:

'The artist is always in this ambiguous position in which he cannot deny reality and yet is eternally obliged to fight against its eternally unfinished nature. To paint a still life, the painter and the apple must confront and mutually correct each other. And if forms are nothing without the light of the world, they in turn add to that light. The real universe which, by its radiance, calls forth bodies and statues, receives from them at the same time a second light which fixes for ever the light falling from heaven. Thus great style in art is midway between the artist and the subject which he treats.'

Since, as Sartre remarked, Camus's tragic early death must teach us to look upon an incomplete body of work as his final testimony, the last story in *L'Exil et le Royaume*, *La Pierre qui pousse*, reads almost like a symposium of his main themes. A French engineer, d'Arrast, has left Europe, where he could feel only 'shame and anger', in order to come to the small Brazilian town of Iguape and help in the building of a dam. This way of solving the problem of separation by service to man is not, however, immediately successful, since he cannot adapt himself to the primitive society around him. He finds an escape from loneliness only in a rather curious act of personal communion which has no practical usefulness at all. He has struck up a curious friendship with a ship's cook, who tells him of a vow that he has made to Christ if he should be saved from a shipwreck. He has promised that he will carry a heavy stone on his head all the way to the church on the local saint's day. Unfortunately, he is possessed by a fury for dancing at the more pagan ceremony which is held on the eve of the saint's day, and is too exhausted the next morning to be able to fulfil his promise. When he falls down under the weight of the stone, d'Arrast picks it up for him and carries it on his own head to the hut where the cook lives with the rest of his family. There, the family sit around and gaze at the stone which d'Arrast has placed in the centre of the floor. After a silence, d'Arrast is invited to sit down with them, and he does so, happy at having found a place where he once again belongs.

The book closes on this idea of separation and loneliness at least temporarily conquered, as d'Arrast finds his place by performing what is, for him, the absurd act of carrying a stone a long distance. He carries it not to a church but to his friend's home, for he can share religious feeling but not religious faith; he has saved his friend from humiliation, for the stone is there for him to carry again when he has recovered, and has temporarily ceased to be an outsider. He has been recognised and welcomed by a particular family as well as by a community, and has found his place among men. He cannot sacrifice his intelligence and join the natives of Iguape in the wild dancing through which they quite forget their own individuality, any more than he can live in his own country where 'the rulers are merchants or policemen'. Yet he can, by remaining 'solitaire' and 'solidaire', rejoin other men by sharing their struggles. The figure of Sisyphus has turned up again in a different form. In a grotto in the town of Iguape, there is a miraculous stone which grows a little more out of the rock each year. D'Arrast goes to see the pilgrims waiting to break off a piece of this miraculous rock, and feels that he has almost found what he has been waiting for during the whole of his long travels in Brazil. He does not, however, escape from his feeling of exile until he picks up the rock which his friend was carrying and places it on his own head. Service to man, Camus is saying, depends not upon the acceptance of miracles, but upon the assumption of tasks which may seem absurd but which are, in fact, full of significance.

It is not, however, a moral or intellectual message of any sort that gives its value to the short stories of *L'Exil et le Royaume*. Each is a perfectly finished work of art, yet the volume as a whole gives the impression of being above all else a preparation for some greater and more ambitious work. From 1955 onwards, Camus worked intermittently upon a novel with the provisional title of *Le Premier Homme*, the theme of which was to be the discovery of life by a man who had had no contact at all with civilisation and who did not even know how to read and write. He himself defined the truly creative writer as someone who 'doubtless always says the same thing, but unceasingly renews the form in which he says it', and the novel would doubtless have treated the themes that Camus had made peculiarly his own: separation, loneliness, the need for a man to find his home, the nature of compassion and rebellion, the fullness of joy in the physical life and the fleetingness of the world. It was the expression of these themes in prose of perfect clarity and elegance, in a style which exactly fitted and reinforced the ideas of each particular work, which made Camus into one of the finest writers of his day, a man whose triumph as an artist quite overshadows any criticisms that might be made of his philosophical ideas or political activity.

Chapter Eleven

THE POLITICS OF COMPASSION

NEITHER Camus's return to creative writing in *La Chute* and *L'Exil et le Royaume* nor his proclamation of the artist's right to independence in his Nobel Prize speeches in 1957 prevented him from writing about political questions during the nineteen-fifties. Apart from prefaces to books like Alfred Rosmer's *Moscou sous Lénine*—where he remarked that the task of our time was to 'witness the perversion of a revolution without losing faith in its necessity'—Camus's political activity from 1951 onwards can be divided into four main sections: his support for Pierre Mendès-France in 1955, his protests against the repression of the Hungarian revolt in 1956, his attack on the death penalty in 1957 and his numerous articles on Algeria. The guiding theme in everything he did and wrote is his intense concern for human suffering. His aims were non-political in the sense that he was only once associated with an actual political movement, and almost never wrote to support a specifically political line of action. His aims were essentially those which he had defined in *Ni Victimes ni Bourreaux* and in *La Peste*: to save 'precious human lives' and, in the midst of all calamities, to 'put himself on the side of the victims, to limit the damage'.

In October 1955 the weekly review *L'Express* became a daily paper in order to support the electoral campaign of Pierre Mendès-France and the *Front-Républicain*. Camus accepted to write twice a week in the paper between October and December 1955, and devoted most of his articles to the problems of Algeria. He had already, in May 1955, returned to journalism after a long silence and published two articles in *L'Express*, attacking the use of terrorism by both sides in Algeria and demanding that new elections be held immediately to give the Arabs the opportunity denied them in the faked election of 1948 of making their wishes known. It was in the articles published in the autumn of 1955 that he first made his famous appeal for a truce whereby both sides would undertake not to attack the civilian population, and proposed a round table conference to discuss Algeria's problems. He stated what considerations should be given most importance in settling the Algerian question when he wrote, on October 10th, 1955: 'Algeria is not French, as people will keep repeating with so superb a disregard for the facts. Yet it contains more than a million French people, a fact which is too easily forgotten.' Camus's views on Algeria will be discussed in more detail later in this chapter, but the frequency with which he discussed the problems of his native land in *L'Express* in 1955 shows how true his remark was that he had never really been interested in any other political problem.

The final article which he wrote in this series, on December 30th, 1955, also showed how seriously he had misrepresented his own political views in *L'Homme révolté*, for what he now appealed for was 'a vote for Mendès-France, for a French Labour party (un travaillisme français)'. His other articles show how, in the nineteen-fifties as in the nineteen-thirties, he sympathised with all those who suffered from the injustices of capitalist society. In December 1955 he introduced an investigation by Beatrice Beck into the condition of the working class in France and challenged anyone to 'read these pages without a feeling of shame and of revolt'. He continued: 'The sufferings of the working class are the dishonour of our civilisation. But bourgeois society has never been able to think of any remedy for family dishonour but silence.' Yet his attitude to the Communist party remained what it had been in 1952 when he wrote that 'None of the evils which totalitarianism claims to be fighting against is worse than totalitarianism itself'. When Mao-Tse-Tung proclaimed in November 1955 that China had nothing to fear from a nuclear war, Camus remarked that he hoped that such an attitude would not persist for very long. With a perspicacity rare in France, he argued that a certain salutary fear might yet be the beginning of wisdom and stated that the essential political fact of the mid-twentieth century was that 'the existence of nuclear arms announced the end of absolute ideologies'. As might be expected, Camus infinitely preferred the attitude of Gandhi, whom he described on November 22nd as 'the greatest man of our time' to that of any orthodox Communist or violent nationalist. It was Gandhi, he later said, who showed that 'it was possible to fight for one's people without ever losing the world's respect', and whose policy of passive resistance he would undoubtedly have liked to see applied by the Algerian nationalists.

There are two principal differences between these articles and those which Camus had published eleven years previously in *Combat*. In 1944 and 1945 he obviously had great hopes that a social and political revolution could give France the kind of government she needed. In 1955 his attitude was much more pessimistic, and he wrote on the eve of polling day that he had 'the feeling that our country is on the edge of an irretrievable disaster'. His pessimism was certainly justified by the actual results of the election which he had hoped would bring Mendès-France to power with a large majority. The people who profited most immediately were the supporters of Pierre Poujade, and Camus remarked after the results had been announced that the seven million electors who had voted either Communist or *Poujadiste* had voted 'whether intentionally or not' for the death of liberty. In yet another article pleading for a civilian truce, published in January 1956, Camus showed how seriously he took the Algerian problem and how gloomy he was becoming over its possible outcome:

'Let us at least recognise that we are fighting for mortal stakes. As for myself, I am living through it as through one of those crises which, like the Spanish civil war and the defeat of 1940, have transformed and changed the destiny of the men of my generation, forcing them to realise the decadence of the political formulae on which they were living. If, by an excess of misfortune, the unconscious alliance of these two equally blind attitudes (that of the French settlers and that of the FLN) were to bring about, in one way or another, the death of that Algeria which we had hoped to bring to life, we should then be forced, seeing how impotent we are to change the situation, to consider carrying out a complete revision of our commitments and of our doctrines in the midst of a history which, for us, would have changed its meaning.'

The second difference between these articles and those which Camus wrote in *Combat* just after the Liberation lies in the reasons for his political activity. In 1944, he was writing less as a man conscious of his rôle as an artist than as a revolutionary journalist. By 1948, however, during the period of political disillusionment which had begun in 1945, he was giving a different reason for joining in the political struggles of his time when he stated: 'It is not the combat which makes us into artists, but art which obliges us to become combatants.' Since he realised that freedom was a necessary condition for the serious practice of any art, Camus felt obliged, as an artist, to write in its defence. He showed how the phrase which ends short story *L'Artiste au Travail* could be interpreted as a statement of his own views when, explaining his reasons for supporting Mendès-France in 1955, he wrote: 'Liberty is neither a source of comfort nor an alibi; it is a wild cry followed by a long effort. And, as soon as we have defined it, we should cling to it with our whole being. That is why, at a time when, far from being acclaimed as a bride, liberty is being betrayed even within the camp that until to-day was most faithful to her, it is perhaps a good thing that a writer who is at one and the same time both *solitaire* and *solidaire* should proclaim outright his fixed decision and declare that, in these articles, he will fight for liberty before all else.' Camus's vision of the rôle of the artist in society was midway between that of Mallarmé and that of Sartre. He refused to accept the doctrine of art for art's sake because he wished neither to be cut off from his fellow men nor to have privileges that were unaccompanied by duties. At the same time, he rejected Sartre's idea that, because literature is inseparable from freedom, all good writing must necessarily have a political inspiration, for he realised how this could easily lead to the allocation of a purely secondary rôle to art itself.

He made his position clear in his speech of acceptance of the Nobel Prize in 1957 when he said: 'I cannot, as a person, live without my art. But I have never placed my art above everything else. If it is so necessary to me it is, on the contrary, because it separates me from no one else and enables me to live, such as I am, on the same level as everyone else. For me, art is not a solitary rejoicing. It is the means of touching the heart of the greatest number of men by offering them the privileged image of the suffering and joy which they have in common.' For Camus, art was nevertheless more than the means of expressing the fate of everyman. It was also the means whereby honour could be given to the persecuted and the oppressed. 'The silence of an unknown political prisoner' he wrote in the same speech 'given over to humiliation at the other end of the world, is enough to take the writer from his exile every time that he manages, amid the privileges of freedom, not to forget that silence but to make it re-echo by the means of art.' It was his compassion for human suffering which had, in the past, turned him from the exaltation of the solitary joys of swimming and contemplating nature, and which now made him say that the nobility of the artist's calling lay in 'the refusal to lie about what we know and in resistance to oppression'. Throughout his life, and especially in the later years, his views on art and on political activity were complementary, not contradictory. It was both his compassion for suffering and his burning awareness of the need for freedom that inspired his protests against the repression of the Hungarian revolt in 1956.

In an interview which he gave to the syndicalist weekly *Demain* in February 1957, Camus explained why he felt it his duty to make his position clear on the Hungarian question. The intellectual should not, he said, spend all the time talking, but must concentrate first and foremost on creating —'especially if his creation does not sidestep the problems of his time'. 'But in certain circumstances,' he continued '(Spanish war, Hitlerian persecutions and concentration camps, Stalinist trials and concentration camps, Hungarian revolution) he must leave no room for doubt as to the side he takes; he must be very careful not to let his choice be clouded by wily distinctions or discreet balancing tricks, and must leave no questions as to his personal determination to defend liberty.' These remarks make explicit the attitude which Camus had come to adopt towards political matters: the rôle of the artist and intellectual was not, for him, to take part in politics at the everyday level of argument, controversy, negotiation and compromise, but to tell the truth on those occasions when the threat to freedom existed beyond all possible doubt. It was clearly impossible for any intelligent person who could command an audience to refrain from making his views known on the Hungarian question, and Camus did make his own attitude abundantly clear. In doing so, he showed that the hatred of totalitarianism was still the most important feature of his political thought.

Both the value and the limitation of Camus's attitude to totalitarianism can be brought out by contrasting his articles on Hungary with the long analysis which Sartre published in January 1957. For Sartre, the suppression of the Hungarian revolt was a political act which had to be condemned not only because it was brutal and inhuman but also because it had been brought about by a political failure on the part of the Russian leaders. In Sartre's view, Stalinism had been a necessary evil which could now be discarded, and it was possible for Communism to emerge from its totalitarian stage and develop in the direction of increased personal and political freedom. All that was necessary was for its leaders to realise that the working class could now be trusted to defend socialism without the help either of the secret police or of the tanks of the Red Army. The decision to give or to withhold this trust was a political and not a moral one, and Russia's action in Hungary was inspired by a failure to follow a consistent policy of destalinisation.

For Camus, Sartre's attitude was completely wrong, because it implied that totalitarianism could be made to change its nature by specific political decisions which men were free to take. 'I regret having to play the rôle of Cassandra once again' he wrote in *Franc-Tireur* in February 1957, 'and having to disappoint the fresh hopes of certain ever-hopeful colleagues, but there is no possible evolution in a totalitarian society. Terror does not evolve except towards a worse terror, the scaffold grows no more liberal, the gallows are not tolerant. Nowhere in the world has there been a party or a man with absolute power that did not use it absolutely.' For Camus, there were only two possible ways in which the totalitarian states set up in Russia, China and Eastern Europe could evolve: they could either become progressively more and more tyrannical or they could, one day, be so weakened by the resistance of the oppressed people that totalitarianism 'collapsed everywhere in the East under the weight of its lies and contradictions'. Such pessimism is certainly less comforting than Sartre's idea that totalitarianism is not simply a manifestation of absolute evil but a form of society which can, like any other mode of political organisation, slowly change its nature. It is also very salutary in that it is not likely to raise false hopes and cause the West to neglect its defences, but one may doubt if so exclusively moral an approach to political problems is a very helpful one.

In Camus's own case, however, this intense hatred of Communism did enable him to appreciate the advantages of traditional democracy. It was in the articles which he published in the mid-nineteen-fifties that his defence of liberal humanism became more explicit than it had been in *L'Homme révolté* and his support for democracy more open. In October 1956 he delivered a speech in honour of Salvador de Madariaga in which he declared that both he and Madariaga belonged to the same political party: this was 'the party of the liberals', the men who were against dictatorship in both Spain and Hungary. It was thanks to the efforts of such men that Europe would be reborn and become once again 'the great teacher of liberty and order of which we have dreamed'. In 1957, paying homage to Eduardo Santo, formerly editor of the newspaper *Tiempo* but now exiled from Colombia, Camus showed how fully that he had now rejoined the tradition of classical humanism which he had at one time so violently rejected. He wrote that the liberty of each one of us is bounded by the liberty of his fellows, and argued that this liberty was defined by a body of law whose supremacy the state must recognise. The fact that this speech was published in *La Révolution Prolétarienne*, a 'revue syndicaliste révolutionnaire', showed how Camus still hoped to ally this liberalism with what he considered a genuinely revolutionary attitude. He clarified his reasons for trying to do this when he wrote in one of his articles on Hungary: 'The defects of the West are innumerable, its crimes and errors are very real. But in the end, let us not forget that we are the only ones to have the possibility of improvement and emancipation which lies in the free exercise of our minds.'

The paradox of Camus's later career as a writer 'determined to refuse nothing of the servitudes of our time' is that the more he came to recognise, at least in theory, the advantages of Western democracy, the less frequently did he try to use them to advance definite political suggestions. There were a number of reasons for this: first of all, Camus was growing more and more certain that he was best able to serve the interests of all free men by working alone as an artist; secondly, the ambiguous attitude adopted towards the Communist Party by some non-Communist left-wing thinkers—who three months after the suppression of the Hungarian revolt formed an electoral alliance with the Communists in a Paris by-election—convinced him that 'the so-called independent Left, in reality fascinated by the power of the Communist Party, has already given up its mission'; thirdly, the failure of the *Front Républicain* after February 1956 seemed to prove that, since a political solution to the Algerian problem was becoming impossible, the only action he could take was that of trying to 'limit the damage' by appealing for moderation on both sides. Yet his increasing reluctance to commit himself on any political problem, like the growing solitude which he felt as the only man in France to be really sincere in his attitude to the Algerian problem, were not only the result of the atmosphere in which he lived. They also reflected a side of his character which had come out in the more unfortunate phrases of *L'Homme révolté*, and which can perhaps be best described as high-minded impatience. Faced with an extremely difficult political situation, Camus tended to withdraw into a shell of abstract morality and to make statements that were so obviously and so completely true that they had very little practical value. Everybody agreed that tortures and atrocities were a deplorable feature of the Algerian war, but neither side trusted the other enough to observe a truce. What was needed was a political settlement which could only be achieved by practical but admittedly imperfect political compromises and alliances. Camus's impatience with compromise made him incapable of seeing that perhaps the best way of avoiding further suffering lay not in general appeals but in an alliance with the least objectionable political grouping that was trying to influence the situation. It may be unfortunate for his future reputation that his apparent withdrawal from politics coincided with a period in his life when he spoke frequently of himself as an artist but in fact added little to the considerable body of work he had already completed. *L'Artiste au Travail* is perhaps the expression of a disquiet which he felt in himself at the thought of how relatively unproductive the nineteen-fifties were when compared with the nineteen-forties. If he had lived to complete his projected novel *Le Premier Homme*, he and his critics would probably have had little cause to regret a silence which was essentially a period of repose and preparation. His plea for the abolition of the death penalty and his later articles on the Algerian problem show that, although he may not have been prepared to take part in politics on any other level than that of general moral ideas, his conception of the artist's calling had no place for the ivory tower.

Camus's *Réflexions sur la Guillotine* were first published in the June and July numbers of the *Nouvelle Revue Française* in 1957 and were reprinted in book form in the September of the same year, side by side with the French translation of Arthur Koestler's *Reflections on Hanging*. As has already been noted, Camus was quite open about the emotional origin of his opposition to the death penalty, and began his essay by relating the crucial incident of how his father, having seen an execution, returned home and was violently sick. The rest of the *Réflexions sur la Guillotine* consists, however, of a highly rational presentation of the case against capital punishment. Camus examines the various arguments put forward in favour of capital punishment. If it is intended to frighten potential murderers, why then does the execution take place in private, and why is it described—in France at any rate—in such euphemistic and neutral terms? If society really believed what it said, then executions, if not made public, would at least be fully described in the press. In fact, the last time that this happened in France—in 1939—*Paris-Soir* was reproved by the government for encouraging the sadistic tendencies of its readers. Camus gives, by quotations from medical witnesses, details of the act of execution by guillotine which are certainly enough to deter anyone likely to stop and think before killing. He opens his argument in the same way as does Tarrou in *La Peste*, who describes how a firing squad stands barely two yards away from the victim and how the bullets make a hole in his chest as big as a man's fist. Now, however, Camus does not limit himself to evoking the physical horror of execution.

Capital punishment does not, he continues, in fact deter, and he uses the examples and statistics taken from Koestler and the report of the British Royal Commission to show that an increase in the number of murders does not follow the abolition of the death penalty. It is uncertain, he argues, that capital punishment does deter would-be murderers—at least, it can never be *proved* that it does—whereas it is absolutely certain that it does kill men. Indeed, far from deterring murderers—which it *may* do—capital punishment exercises so powerful an influence upon certain minds that the number of applicants for the post of executioner by far exceeds the vacancies. It is likely, Camus points out, that unsuccessful candidates may satisfy their ambitions elsewhere.

Capital punishment, he continues, is merely the expression of vengeance by a society which does not believe sufficiently in their deterrent capacity to make executions public. But, for vengeance to be justified, the avenger must be innocent, and society is not innocent of the crimes which its members commit. This is particularly so in France, where bad housing and alcoholism—the first due to state inertia, the second, at least in part, to state subsidy—contribute to an estimated 60 per cent of crimes of violence. It cannot claim the absolute innocence which would alone give it the right to kill, and neither, at present, has the state the religious or metaphysical right to execute criminals. The Catholic Church justifies capital punishment by the argument that it is not a final and absolute judgment. The soul is immortal and God the final judge. Human justice is not regarded as definitive and its verdict is not final. In a society which fully accepted Christian theology, this idea—however contrary it may be, Camus remarks, to the teaching of Christ—could provide the justification for execution. But our own society no longer has this absolute religious belief. The judge who pronounces sentence may be an atheist or an agnostic who, believing only in the existence of this life, is thereby giving a definite and irredeemable verdict. He pronounces the criminal absolutely and irretrievably guilty, depriving him of any chance of improving or reforming himself, or attempting—however inadequately—to put right the wrong he has done. By the standards of a non-religious society—our own—capital punishment is definitive in an abstract moral sense. It is also definitive in a very practical way.

In Belgium, it was discovered that a man had been unjustly

executed, and as a result of that discovery, Belgium abolished the death penalty. In France, England and America there are cases where a similar irretrievable mistake is suspected. Society has no right to kill unless it is absolutely certain, first of all, that it has a religious or metaphysical right to do so, and secondly that there is no possible doubt in each particular case that there is no error of legal judgment. Neither of these two conditions, given the essentially limited nature of human knowledge—in both general, philosophical matters, and in the practical details of evidence—can ever be realised.

It is here that this essay on the death penalty most closely follows the ideas which Camus has expressed in his other works. Essential to his idea of revolt, and to the humanism which he draws from it, is the acceptance of limits and the recognition of human fallibility. Because we can never be certain that we are completely right, we can never be justified in performing actions as irretrievable and absolute as taking a man's life away from him. Our fallibility does not mean that we have no right to act or to punish—Camus suggests life imprisonment as an alternative to capital punishment—but it does imply that we should always hesitate before acting as if we were completely right. This attitude of consistent agnosticism is particularly applicable to state and political executions, where a change in the party line can easily make what may have seemed at the time a justifiable action into the useless destruction of an infinitely valuable human life. What is needed to-day, argues Camus, and needed urgently, is protection for the individual against the enormously increased danger that he may be one day executed by the state for political reasons. Camus's defence of the individual as the only possible source of value had already implied, in both his literary work and political activity, an attitude of extreme scepticism towards the ambitious claims of the modern state. Had he lived, he might perhaps have developed this aspect of his political thought even further, to the point where he revived the best tradition of what is known in France as 'Radicalism'. Alain's idea of *Le Citoyen contre les Pouvoirs* is one that is certainly in need of renewed and consistent support throughout the civilised world, and the extreme individualism of Camus's approach to political matters admirably fitted him to give it new vigour.

As it was, however, his appeal that in the United Europe of tomorrow the first article of any constitution should be the complete and solemn abolition of the death penalty was almost completely ignored by French public opinion. The Right has nowhere been interested in such questions, and both the Communist and non-Communist left preferred agitation over specific political issues to an organised campaign for the abolition of the death penalty. For English readers, it is one of the most surprising features of Camus's career that the two events which might be thought to have brought him most praise—the award of the Nobel Prize for Literature and the publication of *Réflexions sur la Guillotine*—in fact earned him more abuse than he had ever before received. As early as July 1957, François Mauriac wrote in his *Bloc-Notes* in *L'Express* that 'the discussion of the death penalty is, I am afraid, one of the means whereby the Noble Souls of our time avoid facing up to more urgent problems'. Mauriac was clearly referring to the campaign which the left-wing press, and particularly *L'Express* and *France-Observateur*, were conducting throughout 1957 against the use of torture by the French army in Algeria. Camus had refused to associate himself with this campaign, for reasons that he was later to explain, and it was his silence on this problem which led to many of the attacks which were made on him when he received the Nobel Prize.

The award was, of course, welcomed by large sections of the French press, from the conservative *Figaro*, through the independent *Le Monde*, to the syndicalist reviews *Demain* and *La Révolution Prolétarienne*. Camus's own modesty came out in the first remark which he made on hearing of the award: that, if the choice had been his, the prize would have gone to André Malraux. He was, however, not alone in sharing this view, and Roger Stéphane entitled his article in *France-Observateur, A défaut de Malraux.* . . . This article was a representative one because it combined the attack on Camus's 'conservatism' and 'conformity' which Jacques Laurent, the author of *Caroline Chérie*, had made in *Arts*, with the more reasonable reproach that Camus had completely withdrawn from normal political life. 'Are there' wrote Stéphane, 'acts of violence more worthy of condemnation than the tortures whose existence is no longer denied by anybody? I have not noticed Camus writing on behalf of Maurice Audin or demanding the publication of the report of the *Comité de Sauvegarde*. I know how much he dislikes collective manifestoes and how scrupulous he is in not prostituting his name. But for what more worthy cause is he keeping himself?'

However great one's emotional sympathy for Camus's attitude on the Algerian problem may be, it must be admitted that Monsieur Stéphane's point is a valid one. An outright condemnation of the use of torture by the French army in Algeria, at the very moment when the attention of the whole of the civilised world was focused on the latest winner of the Nobel Prize, could have made an immense contribution towards the disappearance of a practice which, Camus himself later recognised, did more harm to France's cause than a hundred armed enemy bands. It is no reply to say that Camus was 'an artist' who could not be expected to have any interest or responsibility in such matters. He had made innumerable political statements during his career as a writer, and it is ridiculous to start claiming benefit of clergy on his behalf at the very moment when he himself was emphasising the duties which the artist had towards his fellow men. It is, nevertheless, impossible to feel any emotional sympathy with critics like Stéphane, however much one may recognise the intellectual validity of their arguments. Constantly present in Camus's mind was the thought that his mother, his brother and his friends might be exposed to increased terrorism by words which he could utter without the slightest personal danger to himself. 'As for those who, knowing the situation in Algeria,' he wrote in 1958, 'continue to think that the brother should perish before our principles, I will content myself with admiring them from afar off. We are not of the same race.'

Were it not possible to correct it by constant reference to the facts, the impression given by many of the attacks made on Camus in 1957 and in the later years of his life is that he had never said or done anything at all about the Algerian situation. This impression is a completely false one. The articles which he wrote on Kabylia in 1939 have already been discussed, and he gave a detailed analysis of Algeria's problems when he was editor of *Combat* in 1945. In 1957, in the only full interview which he gave to a French newspaper after the award of the Nobel Prize, he appealed in *La Révolution Prolétarienne* for a halt in the killings that were decimating the ranks of the Arab trade-union leaders in Algeria. 'Are we,' he asked, 'going to allow the syndicalist militants in Algeria to be murdered by an organisation which seems to use murder in order to acquire a complete and totalitarian control over the whole Algerian movement? . . . This is a question which we must ask, and which we must ask as often and as loudly as we can, to prevent anti-colonialism from becoming the clear conscience which justifies everybody, beginning with murderers.' Camus's attitude to the Algerian problem never really changed during the twenty years in which he wrote about it. In 1939, he was not prepared to attribute the sufferings of Kabylia to the evils of colonialism as a system, and in 1955 and 1958 he saw no future for Algeria in a policy based upon the idea that its problems were essentially those of a colonial territory trying to achieve independence. In the praise which he gave Germaine Tillion's book *L'Algérie* 1957 he made it clear that, in his view, Algeria could solve her problems only with the technical and economic help which France alone was in a position to give. This did not mean that he wanted the colonial system, with all its faults and injustices, to remain unchanged, but that, as he said in one of his articles in 1955, he wanted to see 'an Algerian Algeria and not an Egyptian Algeria'. And, he never tired of repeating, the necessary pre-condition for any improvement was a readiness on both sides to declare a truce respecting the safety of the non-combatant civilian population.

In many ways Camus's attitude to his native land seems an object lesson in the inadequacy of good intentions. On January 22nd, 1956, he went to Algeria in order to make his appeal for a truce in person. Together with Father Huck, the Reverend Capieu, a Protestant pastor, and Doctor Khaldi, he spoke to 1,200 people at the *Cercle du Progrès* and asked for the following petition to be signed: 'That, without reference to any political position, and without implying any interpretation of the present situation, either in one way or another, we ask that an undertaking be made to ensure the protection of innocent civilians.' All those in the hall signed the petition, but European rioters belonging to the various

ex-servicemen's organisations and to the *Front Français de
l'Algérie* shouted abuse in the street outside and tried to get
in. Truce committees were set up in some parts of Algeria,
but never succeeded in exercising any significant control over
events. Although Camus refrained from making any direct
statement which laid the blame for this failure on either of
the two sides, his incidental remarks show that he was always
more critical of the FLN than of the European extremists who
had actually tried to break up his meeting. In his articles in
L'Express in 1955, he drew attention to the appeals broadcast
by Cairo radio—'Let not a single Frenchman escape', 'Death
to all Europeans'—and noted in 1958 that 'One must consider
the demand for Algerian national independence as being to a
certain extent one of the manifestations of this new Arab
imperialism which Egypt, overestimating her strength, wishes
to lead, and which Russia exploits for anti-Western strategic
aims. . . . One must in any case attribute to these nationalistic
and imperialistic demands the unacceptable aspects of the
Arab rebellion, and, in particular, the systematic and un-
discriminating murder of French and Arab civilians, simply
because they are French or friends of French people.' Although he stated that 'the long violence of the colonial system
explains the violence of the rebellion', he never made remarks about the French ultras in Algeria that were in any
way as critical as these comments on Algerian nationalism.
His appeals for a truce were certainly both necessary and
sincere, but it is easy to see why they failed. After so
many years of broken promises in Algeria, the FLN can
scarcely be blamed for considering any arguments in favour
of moderation as being simply an indirect defence of the
status quo.

In an article published in *La Nef* after Camus had been
awarded the Nobel Prize, the Algerian writer Albert Memmi
described him as *Le Colonisateur de bonne volonté* (*The well-
intentioned Coloniser*). After admiring the 'extraordinary
authenticity of his many lyrical descriptions of North Africa',
Memmi argued that Camus's silence on the Algerian problem
was a direct result of his having been born a French Algerian.
'That is to say,' he wrote, 'that he belongs to a minority which
is historically in the wrong. . . . It is by no means an intellectually or an emotionally comfortable position to have all

one's relatives on the side that one morally condemns.' Camus, he insisted, had spoken more frequently than many others, but his situation was such that he could never do anything but annoy both sides. In spite of its Marxist over-tones—or perhaps because of them—this judgment on Camus is an intellectually valid one. Although it is never his own fault, the privileged position which even the poorest European worker has in Algeria when compared to the average Arab is the result of an unjust and untenable situation. Yet Camus was peculiarly well placed to see how wrong it was to think that the one million, two hundred thousand French Algerians, eighty per cent of whom were poorer than their Metropolitan counterparts, could be sacrificed 'because they stood in the way of the movement of history'.

In 1958, Camus published *Actuelles III*, a representative selection of everything which he had written on Algeria since 1939. In his preface, he criticised the attitude which intellec-tually 'progressive' French thinkers often adopted towards the Algerian problem, using as he did so a phrase which indicated that he had not forgotten the possible political significance of *La Chute*: 'If some French people think that, because of her colonial enterprises, France is, alone among a host of saintly nations, in a state of historical sin, they have no right to point out the French Algerians as expiatory victims and say: "You can all die, for we have justly deserved it". They must, on the contrary, offer themselves in expiation. And it seems to me disgusting to proclaim one's sin by beating somebody else's breast, as our judge-penitents do, vain to condemn several centuries of European expansion and absurd to include Lyautey and Christopher Columbus under the same condemnation.' There was no doubt that Camus's defence of the interests of the French Algerians—and, it may be noted in passing, of the Algerian Jews—was both a neces-sary and a justified action. In many ways, it might have been better if he could have limited himself to this one point, concentrating at one and the same time on defending the economic interests of those among whom he was born, and on criticising the extreme form which all their political activity seemed to take. As it was, however, he remained on the plane of generalities, and revealed both the strength and weakness of his attitude in one of the articles which he published in 1956. ' "You must take sides", cry out those stuffed with hatred. Ah, but I have taken it. I have chosen my own country, the Algeria of the future where French and Arabs will associate freely together.' Unfortunately, the methods and abuses which Camus had for so long been condemning had created a situation where good intentions were no longer of any use. To call all those who argued in favour of a definite political choice 'men stuffed with hatred' (*les repus de la haine*) is no valid answer to the argument that when a political situation reaches a certain point, compassion can best achieve its effects by political action.

Actuelles III was already at the printers when the events of the 13th of May, 1958 began the movement which brought General de Gaulle back to power. Camus decided to allow the book to be published, but to offer it at the same time as his very last word on the Algerian problem. 'This,' he wrote, 'is my testimony, and to it I shall add nothing.' He joined none of his erstwhile colleagues in denouncing the danger of military dictatorship, and played no part in the Referendum campaign of September 1958. No one but a person as deeply involved in the Algerian situation as Camus himself has the right to criticise him either for this silence or for the note of finality given by the sentence just quoted. With complete consistency and great courage and honesty, Jean-Paul Sartre has declared that 'the cause of the Algerian rebels is the cause of all free men' and has thus accepted a specific political position, with all the risks, injustices and limitations that this involves. His action may make a greater appeal to the politic-ally-minded critic than Camus's withdrawal from the rough and tumble of political action, but Sartre himself recognised that Camus's deep personal involvement did make choices of this kind impossible for him. 'His very silence during these later years,' he wrote after Camus's death, 'had a positive aspect: this Cartesian of the absurd refused to leave the certain terrain of morality and embark upon the uncertain paths of practical action. We felt that we knew why and we felt that we knew what conflicts he was hiding. For, if we take morality and only morality, it both demands and condemns revolt.'

By a foreseeable chance, however, there is a criticism of Camus's attitude made by a man whose background and sympathies were very similar to his own and whose personal involvement was almost as great. Late in 1960, Camus's life-long friend Jules Roy—Camus had written of his novel *La Vallée heureuse* 'It is the book of a man. What more praise is possible?'—published *La Guerre d'Algérie*. Like Camus, Jules Roy is a French Algerian. He worked with Camus in Algeria in the nineteen-thirties, and then became a regular soldier, serving with distinction as a Free French bomber navigator in the RAF during the 1939–1945 war, and later in the Indo-Chinese war. Early in 1960, he went to Algeria and, on his return, dedicated to Camus's memory the book in which he made extensive criticisms of French policy and declared that his own sympathies were now very much with the Algerian nationalists. In his last chapter, he quoted Camus's refusal to associate himself with those who 'considered that the brother should perish rather than their principles' and made the following point: while the injustice and terror from which the Arab population was suffering throughout Algeria were immediate, present day realities, the injustice from which the French Algerians might suffer in the future was still only a possibility. 'I want to do justice to the Arabs without taking it from the Europeans,' he wrote. 'But I respect an order of priority based on urgency of need: I seek first to remedy the injustice which cries out in agony today, since, for the moment, the other is only a hypothesis.' Repeating what Camus had said when he declared: 'I love justice. But if I had to choose between justice and my mother, I would choose my mother,' he wrote: 'It is not a question of preferring one's mother to justice, but of loving justice as much as one loves one's mother.' Camus refused to give open support either to the Arabs or to the Europeans, because for him they were both equally innocent victims of a situation for which they were not responsible. Roy argued that it was possible to support the Arabs rather than the Europeans because their sufferings were greater. He was, himself, convinced that if Camus had lived he would have come to share his opinion.

On January 5th, 1960, however, Camus accepted an invitation to travel back to Paris from the South of France with his publisher and close personal friend Michel Gallimard. Just outside the little town of Petit-Villeblevin, the Facel-Vega in which they were travelling at high speed skidded and hit a tree. Camus was killed instantly and Michel Gallimard died in hospital a few days later. Camus was forty-six years old, and had said in 1959 that his career was only just beginning. His railway ticket to Paris was in his pocket.

BIBLIOGRAPHY

(*A*) WORKS PUBLISHED BY CAMUS IN BOOK FORM (*Dates of composition are given in brackets.*)

1. *Révolte dans les Asturies. Essai de création collective* (Play) (1935). Published in Algiers in 1936.

2. *L'Envers et l'Endroit* (Essays) (1935–36) *Charlot*, Algiers 1936. Republished, with a Preface, by *Gallimard* in 1958.

3. *Noces* (Essays) (1936–37) *Charlot*, Algiers (1938). Reprinted by *Gallimard* (1950).

4. *L'Etranger* (*Récit*) (1939–40) *Gallimard* (1942). Translated into English by Stuart Gilbert and prefaced by Cyril Connolly, *Hamish Hamilton* (1946). Schools' edition published by *Methuen* (1958), with a specially written *Avant-Propos* (dated 8th January 1955) by Camus. Introduction and notes by Germaine Brée and Carlos Lynes.

5. *Le Mythe de Sisyphe* (*Essai sur l'absurde*) (1940–41) *Gallimard* (1943). Translated by Justin O'Brien, *Hamish Hamilton* (1955). (The same volume contains a number of essays in translation, including *Summer in Algiers*, from *Noces*, *Le Minotaur* or *The Stop at Oran*, an essay written in 1940, *Helen's Exile* (1948), *Return to Tipasa* (1952) and *The Artist and His Time* (1953). This translation also has a short preface by Camus, written in 1955.)

6. *Lettres à un ami allemand* (Letters) (1942–44). First published in book form in 1945. Translated into English by Justin O'Brien in the collection *Resistance, Rebellion and Death*, *Hamish Hamilton* (1961).

7. *Le Malentendu* and *Caligula* (Plays). Written in 1942–43, and in 1938 respectively. Published together in book form in 1945. Republished in revised versions in 1958 by *Gallimard*. Translated by Stuart Gilbert, *Hamish Hamilton* (1947).

8. *La Peste* (*Chronique*) (1941–47) *Gallimard* (1947). Translated by Stuart Gilbert, *Hamish Hamilton* (1948). Schools' edition with an Introduction by W. J. Strachan, *Methuen* (1959).

9. *L'Etat de Siège* (Play) (1948) *Gallimard* (1948). Translated by Stuart Gilbert, *Knopf* (1958). (Translation not generally available in England.)

10. *Les Justes* (Play) (1948–49) *Gallimard* (1950). Translated by Stuart Gilbert, *Knopf* (1958). (Translation not generally available in England.) Schools' edition with an Introduction by Edward O. Marsh, *Harrap* (1960).

11. *Actuelles I, II* and *III* (Collections of political articles). Published in 1950, 1953 and 1958 respectively by *Gallimard*. A selection of these articles appeared in translation in the volume *Resistance, Rebellion and Death, Hamish Hamilton* (1961).

12. *L'Homme révolté* (Essay) (1945–51) *Gallimard* (1951). Translated by Anthony Bower, with a preface by Sir Herbert Read, *Hamish Hamilton* (1953).

13. *L'Eté* (Essays) *Gallimard* (1954). The various essays were written between 1939 and 1953.

14. *La Chute* (*Récit*) (1955–56) *Gallimard* (1956). Translated by Justin O'Brien, *Hamish Hamilton* (1957).

15. *L'Exil et le Royaume* (Stories written between 1953–57) *Gallimard* (1957). Translated by Justin O'Brien, *Hamish Hamilton* (1957).

16. *Réflexions sur la Guillotine* (1957) *Calmann-Lévy* (1957). Translated in *Resistance, Rebellion and Death* (1961).

17. *Discours de Suède* (Speeches made in Stockholm on the occasion of the award of the Nobel Prize for Literature 1957) *Gallimard* (1958). Translated in *Resistance, Rebellion and Death* (1961).

(B) ADAPTATIONS AND TRANSLATIONS

1. James Thurber. *The Last Flower* (*La Dernière Fleur*). Translated by Camus, *Gallimard* (1952).

2. Calderón de la Barca. *La Devoción de la Cruz* (*La Dévotion à la Croix*). Texte français d'Albert Camus. Short preface by Camus, *Gallimard* (1953).

3. Pierre de Larivey. *Les Esprits*. Short Preface by Camus, *Gallimard* (1953).

4. Dino Buzzati. *Un caso clinico* (*Un cas intéressant*). Adaptation d'Albert Camus. L'Avant-Scène (1955).

5. William Faulkner. *Requiem for a Nun* (*Requiem pour une nonne*). Adaptation d'Albert Camus, *Gallimard* (1956).

6. Lope de Vega. *El Caballero de Olmedo* (*Le Chevalier d'Olmedo*). Texte français d'Albert Camus. Short *Avant-Propos* by Camus.

7. Dostoievski. *Les Possédés*. Pièce en trois parties adaptée du roman de Dostoievski par Albert Camus, *Gallimard* (1959). Stage adaptation translated into English by Justin O'Brien, *Hamish Hamilton* (1960).

(C) LITERARY AND PHILOSOPHICAL ARTICLES PUBLISHED IN REVIEW FORM AND NOT YET REPRINTED.

1. *Un Nouveau Verlaine*, Sud, Algiers (March 1932), p. 90.
   Jehan Rictus, Sud, Algiers (May 1932), pp. 90–91.
   Essai sur la Musique, Sud, Algiers (June 1932), pp. 125–130.
   La Philosophie du Siècle, Sud, Algiers (June 1932), p. 90.

2. Book reviews in *Alger-Républicain* between October 1938 and July 1939. Articles on Remarque, Sartre, Blanche Balain, Jean Hytier, René Janon, Paul Nizan, Edmond Bruca, Giono, Renaud de Jouvenel, Montherlant, Pascal Pia, Jorge Amado, Simenon, Silone, André Chamson, Berdiaeff, Bernanos, Albert Ollivier.

3. *Barrès ou la querelle des héritiers*, La Lumière (5.4.40).
   Giraudoux ou Byzance au théâtre, La Lumière (10.5.40).

4. *Portrait d'un élu*, Les Cahiers du Sud (April 1944), pp. 306–311.

5. *Sur une Philosophie de l'Expression*, Poésie (1944), pp. 15–23.

6. *L'Intelligence et l'Echafaud*, Article on the French novel in *Problèmes du Roman. Confluences* (July–August 1943). Reprinted in Brussels, (1945), *Editions Prévost*.

7. *L'Exhortation au Médecins de la Peste*, Archives de la Peste. Cahiers de la Pléiade, Gallimard (1947).

8. *Réflexions sur le Christianisme*, Vie Intellectuelle (April 1949), pp. 336–351. (With commentary by L. Roynet. Both Brée and Brisville, op. cit., give the date for this as December 1946, but with no page references.)

9. *Recontres avec André Gide*, NRF (1951), pp. 223–228.

10. *Une macumba au Brésil*, Biblio (November 1951), pp. 5–7.

11. *Herman Melville*, in Les écrivains célèbres, III, Mazeroud (1953).

12. *Le Vie d'artiste : mimodrame en deux parties*, Simoun (March 1953), pp. 14–20.

13. Walt Disney. *Désert vivant. Société française du livre* (1954).

14. *Lettre à Roland Barthes*, Club (January 1955), pp. 7–9.

15. *Lettre à Francis Ponge*, NNRF (1956), pp. 386–392.

(D) POLITICAL ARTICLES NOT REPRINTED.

Most of Camus's more important political articles can, of course, be found in the three volumes of *Actuelles*. Details of some of the articles not at present available in book form are given in the notes to Chapter 1 (*Alger-Républicain* (1938–39), notes to page 8); Chapter 5 (*Combat* (1944–45), notes to page 89); Chapter 11 (*L'Express* (1955–56), notes to page 199).

Other political articles not reprinted include:

1. *A Quoi sert L'O.N.U.? Combat* (9.12.48).

2. *Réponse à l'Incrédule. Combat* (26.12.48).

3. Letter protesting against the killing of seven Tunisians by the French police on (14.7.53). *Le Monde* (19.7.53).

4. *Hommage à Salvador de Madariaga. Monde Nouveau* (April 1956), pp. 1–9.

5. *Hommage à un journaliste exilé. La Révolution Prolétarienne*, (November 1957).

(E) PREFACES NOT YET REPRINTED IN BOOK FORM.

1. Présentation of *Rivages: Revue de culture méditerranéenne*, Charlot, Algiers (1939).

2. Chamfort. *Maximes et Anecdotes. Dac*, Monaco (1944).

3. André Salvet. *Le Combat silencieux. Le Portulan* (1945).

4. René Leynaud. *Poésies posthumes. Gallimard* (1947).

5. Jacques Méry. *Laissez-Passer mon peuple. Editions du Seuil* (1947).

6. Jeanne Héon-Canonne. *Devant la Mort*. Paris (1951).

7. Daniel Mauriac. *Contre-Amour. Editions de Minuit* (1952).

8. Louis Guilloux. *La Maison du Peuple. Grasset* (1953).

9. Oscar Wilde. *La Ballade de la Géôle de Reading. Falaize* (1952).

10. K. F. Bieber. *L'Allemagne vue par les écrivains de la Résistance française*. Lille (1954).

11. C. Targuebayre. *Cordes-en-Albigeois. Privat*, Toulouse (1954).

12. Roger Martin du Gard. *Oeuvres Complètes. Bibliothèque de la Pléiade* (1956).

13. William Faulkner. *Requiem pour une nonne. Gallimard* (1957).

14. *La Vérité sur l'Affaire Nagy. Plon* (1958). English translation published by *Secker and Warburg* for the Congress for Cultural Freedom (1959).

15. Jean Grenier. *Les Iles. Gallimard* (1959).

(*F*) INTERVIEWS.

Camus gave a large number of interviews during his literary career. Some of these are reprinted in the different volumes of *Actuelles*. Those not reprinted include:

1. *Opéra.* 12.9.45 and 10.10.45.
2. *Les Nouvelles Littéraires.* 15.11.45.
3. *Terre des Hommes.* 26.1.46.
4. *Le Littéraire.* 18.8.46.
5. *Combat.* 17.1.47.
6. *Paru.* no. 47 1948, pp. 7–13.
7. *Les Nouvelles Littéraires.* 10.5.51.
8. *La Gazette de Lausanne.* 28.3.54.
9. *Le Monde.* 31.5.56.
10. *Demain.* 24.10.57.

. . . . . .

The following full length studies have been published on Camus:

1. Léon Thoorens. *A la rencontre d'Albert Camus.* Brussels (1946).
2. Robert de Luppé. *Albert Camus. Presses Universitaires* (1951).
3. Albert Maquet. *Albert Camus ou l'invincible été. Debresse* (1955).
4. Roger Quilliot. *La Mer et les Prisons. Essai sur Albert Camus. Gallimard* (1956).
5. Thomas Hanna. *The Thought and Art of Albert Camus. Henry Regnery Company,* Chicago (1958).
6. John Cruickshank. *Albert Camus and the Literature of Revolt. Oxford University Press* (1959).
7. Germaine Brée. *Camus. Rutgers* (1959).
8. Henry Bonnier. *Albert Camus ou la force d'être. E. Vitte* (1959).
9. Jean-Claude Brisville. *Camus. La Bibliothèque Idéale. Gallimard* (1959).

All these studies, with the exception of that by Bonnier, contain lists of the very large number of articles that have been published on Camus. Books and articles found particularly useful in the preparation of this study include:

1. Robert Champigny. *Sur un héros païen. Gallimard, Les Essais* (1959).
2. Stephen Ullmann. *The Image in the French Novel. C.U.P.* (1960).

3. A. J. Ayer. *Novelist-Philosophers. Horizon*, (March 1946).

4. Rayner Heppenstall. *Albert Camus and the Romantic Protest. Penguin New Writing* (1948).

5. W. M. Frohock. *Camus: Image, Influence and Sensibility. Yale French Studies* (1949).

6. *Symposium*. Syracuse, USA. Vol. XII, Spring–Fall 1958. Articles by a number of scholars, including Germaine Brée and Carl A. Viggiani. This number also contains some previously unpublished *Pages de Carnet* by Camus himself.

7. Carl A. Viggiani. *Camus's first publication. Modern Language Notes*, November 1960, pp. 589–96.

A number of other articles found useful are mentioned in the course of the notes.

Acknowledgments

A grant from the Sir Ernest Cassel Educational Trust enabled me to go to Paris and collect material for this book in August 1960. Madame Caldaguès, Directrice de la Phonothèque de la Radio-Télévision française, was most helpful in enabling me to hear recordings made by Camus. Claude Bourdet, Robert Champigny, John Cruickshank, Thomas Hanna, Roger Quilliot and Jules Roy sent very helpful replies to letters in which I asked them for information and advice.

NOTES AND REFERENCES

CHAPTER ONE

In order to avoid encumbering the text with footnotes that are of only incidental interest to the general reader, I have decided to put all the notes at the back of the book. When a fairly important point is discussed in the notes, the reader's attention is drawn to it by a sign in the text. Should any reader wish for information not provided in the notes, I should be very pleased to try to satisfy the curiosity of anyone who cares to write to me.

The following abbreviations are used in the notes.

EE.—*L'Envers et l'Endroit.*
N.—*Noces.*
Et.—*L'Etranger.*
MS.—*Le Mythe de Sisyphe.*
RR.—*La Remarque sur la Révolte.*
C.—*Caligula.*
M.—*Le Malentendu.*
L.—*Lettres à un ami allemand.*
ES.—*L'Etat de Siège.*
J.—*Les Justes.*
HR.—*L'Homme révolté.*
P.—*La Peste.*
AI, AII, AIII.—*Actuelles I, II and III.*

All page references are to the standard Gallimard edition of Camus's works.

p. 1. I am indebted to Germaine Brée's and Roger Quilliot's studies for most of the biographical information in this book. I have also made use of the special number of the *Figaro Littéraire* devoted to Camus on 26.10.57, and of the special numbers of *La Table Ronde* (February 1960), and *La Nouvelle Nouvelle Revue Française* (March 1960). Various other sources are acknowledged in the course of the notes, but this book has no pretensions to being a complete biographical study. Camus's letters and private papers have not yet been made generally available to critics. Miss Germaine Brée was allowed to consult

Camus's private notebooks while he was still alive, and this gives her book an especial biographical value. A study by Jean-Claude Brisville in *Gallimard's Bibliothèque Idéale* (1959) contains some very interesting photographs of Camus.

In an interview on the French radio on 5.12.57 Jules Roy, a close personal friend of Camus, said that both his mother's and father's family had been living in Algeria since before 1840. This would seem to indicate that Camus's father did not come from one of the families of French settlers who chose to come and live in Algeria after Alsace and Lorraine were ceded to Germany after 1870.

EE. pp. 63–66. All quotations from this work are taken from the 1958 edition.

p. 3. *Réflexions sur la peine capitale*, Calmann-Lévy (1957), p. 125. It is perhaps interesting to note, in view of the unenthusiastic reception given to Camus's plea for the abolition of the death penalty (cf. later Chapter 11, p. 209) that it was published in a series entitled *Liberté de l'Esprit* which contained a fairly high proportion of anti-Communist books. This may have put some French left-wing readers and critics off.

This photograph can be found in Brisville, op cit.

p. 4. Preface to 1958 edition of EE. p. 13.
AI. p. 189.

p. 5. Cf. Brée, p. 17.
Cf. Pierre de Boisdeffre. *Métamorphoses de la Littérature*, Paris (1951), p. 272.
Cf. *Hommage à André Gide. NRF* (1951), pp. 223–228.

p. 6. An excellent study of this *diplôme* can be found in *Symposium*, Spring–Fall 1958, Syracuse University, in an article by Professor Carl A. Viggiani entitled *Camus in 1936: the Beginnings of a Career*, pp. 7–18, especially pp. 12–18. Professor Viggiani, who has had access to the unpublished typescript, makes the following points: the *diplôme* is a solid piece of research, objectively presented in rather a dry manner, and not throwing very much light on Camus's own ideas. Camus, he remarks, had had no religious education (but cf. later p. 20), yet, 'his own obsession with death and natural and moral evil, engendered by a near fatal illness and his sensitivity to injustice, created in him a natural affinity for the Christian religion' (p. 17). However, a quotation which Professor Viggiani makes from the thesis itself would seem to show that in 1936 Camus was already more attracted to pagan Greek thought than to Christianity.

Professor Viggiani's article also contains a detailed study of *Révolte dans les Asturies*.
Cf. *Caliban*, August 1951.

p. 7. The numbers of *Alger-Républicain* can be consulted at the Bibliothèque Nationale in Paris. They are at the annexe at Versailles, so that a wait of a few days is necessary. Camus's review of *La Nausée* was published on 20.10.38, and his review of *Le Mur* on 5.3.39.

p. 8. His defence of the International Brigade appeared on 19.12.38 in an article entitled *Au Pays du Mufle*. This was a reply to a very hostile article published by the conservative *Dépêche Algérienne*. The attack on Daladier was entitled *Dialogue entre un président du conseil et un employé à 1.200 francs par mois*, published on 3.12.38. His remark about the Versailles peace treaty was part of a review which he wrote on 25.4.39 of a lecture given by M. R. E. Charlier.

Other subjects which attracted Camus's attention in *L'Alger-Républicain* were the activities of a right-wing municipal administrator, Monsieur Rozis, who tried to dismiss a group of employees for taking part in a strike; a series of articles on the conditions of North Africans working in France, published in May 1939; a series of articles dealing with the arrest and torture of a number of Arabs suspected of incendiarism, published in July 1939; and a defence of the *Parti Populaire Algérien*, published on 18.8.39, and which contained the phrase: 'La seule façon d'enrayer le nationalisme algérien, c'est de supprimer l'injustice dont il est né.'

p. 10. Justice and judges—cf. *Alger-Républicain*, 5.3.39.

Most of the articles on Kabylia were reprinted in *Actuelles III* in 1958.

Critics who consider Camus to have not really been interested in politics: cf. *Symposium*, Spring 1960, C. G. Christophides, pp. 62–64; also Brée op. cit. passim.

The letter quoted was sent to me in August 1956, after Camus had read through the original version of this study and made comments upon it.

p. 11. Quotations from the articles on Kabylia are from *Alger-Républicain*, 5.6.39 and 14.6.39.

p. 12. *Alger-Républicain*, 15.6.39.

Brice Parain in *NNRF* special number, p. 408.

p. 15. Camus's articles in *La Lumière* included a long study of Barrès published on 5.4.40 and an article on Giraudoux on 10.5.40. In Camus's view, it was futile to try to resurrect Barrès since he had 'rien à faire avec nous . . . à sa façon, qui fut émouvante parfois, Barrès a été un esthète du patriotisme comme il le fut de l'individualisme'. Camus was not a very great admirer of Giraudoux, and he wrote that his art consisted solely of replacing 'les grands thèmes de la fatalité par les acrobaties de l'intelligence'.

CHAPTER TWO

p. 16. Cf. Preface to *Les Iles, Gallimard* (1959, re-edition), pp. 9–16.

p. 17. Lay ill—was told that he was going to die—cf. *Noces*, p. 38.

p. 18. Cf. Preface to *Les Iles*, p. 12.
EE. p. 39. An obvious reference to Pascal's 'la misère de l'homme sans Dieu'.

p. 19. Pascal—cf. *Poésie* 44, pp. 15–23. Review of Brice Parain's *Sur une Philosophie de l'Expression*, p. 21.
EE. p. 124.

p. 20. EE. pp. 76–77.
'total abrutissement du soleil'—cf. *Les Temps Modernes*, August 1952, p. 325.

p. 21. The photograph of Camus dressed in the conventional suit of the little boy about to take his First Communion is in the special number published by *Paris-Match* on 16.1.60 just after his death. This is not, of course, necessarily a guarantee of its authenticity, and the authors of the article have chosen not to reply to the letter sent to them asking for details about this photograph, which has not yet been published elsewhere. Jean Grenier, who as Camus's teacher might perhaps have been expected to know whether or not Camus did receive a religious education, has informed me in a short letter that he is quite ignorant on the subject. Professor Viggiani (loc. cit.) repeats Camus's own statement that he was brought up outside all conventional religions, and José Orlandis, in *La Table Ronde*, (February 1960), p. 71 says that Camus 'est le produit d'une société radicalement laïcisée; comme beaucoup d'autres hommes de sa génération, il est né dans une terre lointaine, pays de mission où l'on n'a pas prêché l'Evangile'. It seems improbable, however, even if the *Paris-Match* photograph is not of Camus, that he should have been able to avoid *all* religious instruction. In his review of *L'Etranger*, Etiemble, writing in *France Libre* 15.11.45, begins by contrasting Camus with Rimbaud 'encore esclave de son baptême', but then argues, from the violence of Meursault's rejection of the consolation offered by the priest, that Camus is really less 'spontaneously' a pagan than at first appears. It is an interesting question, but one that cannot at the moment be answered. What is certain, however, is that Camus soon rejected any religious faith that might have been offered to him, and remained consistently outside Christianity for the rest of his life. As will be argued in the rest of this study, it is very dangerous to confuse Camus's concern with questions of morality and of religious belief with any supposed 'Christian cast of thought' on his part. As Thomas Hanna observes in his excellent

article on *Camus and the Christian Faith* (*The Journal of Religion*, Vol. XXXVI, no. 4, October 1956, p. 230): 'It is a curious thing about the thought of Albert Camus that he has not estranged himself from Christian readers. This may possibly be because Christian thinkers have not as yet realised the full import of what he has said about the Christian faith.'
MS. p. 167. EE. pp. 112–113. N. p. 61.

p. 22. Roblès—cf. *NNRF*, March 1960, p. 412. N. pp. 18, 23–24.

p. 23. N. pp. 32 and 34.

p. 24. N. pp. 45 and 63.

p. 25. Cruickshank—op. cit. p. 37.

p. 27. The review of Guitton's book about Father Pouget was published in *Les Cahiers du Sud*, February 1943, pp. 225–228. In an article in *La Table Ronde* in February 1960, Monsieur Guitton quotes Camus as having said to him 'Ah, si la religion catholique avait été celle de votre Monsieur Pouget . . .', and adds that, in his view, Camus was poorly acquainted with Catholicism, having come to it through a study of Saint Augustine (p. 173).
Cf. *Combat* 24.11.44 and *L'Eté* p. 149. *Retour à Tipasa*, text written in 1952.

p. 28. N. p. 55. *Eté* p. 147.

CHAPTER THREE

p. 30. Cf. Interview with Gaeton Picon, *Le Littéraire*, 10.8.46.

p. 31. Et. p. 89.

p. 32. Et. p. 94.

p. 33. Et. p. 110.
'A man without apparent consciousness'—cf. Camus's reply to an inquiry made by *Combat* in 1947 into the extent of the influence of the American novel in France. On January 17th 1947 Camus remarked that he had borrowed Hemingway's technique of narration because it suited his particular purpose, but that he preferred the American novelists of the nineteenth century, and particularly Hawthorne and Melville, to Hemingway or Steinbeck. For further discussion of this point, see Professor Harry R. Garvin's article *Camus and the American Novel* (Comparative Literature VII, 1956, pp. 194–204) and my own article in the same journal in Summer 1957, pp. 243–249, *A Note on Camus and the American Novel*.

ALBERT CAMUS, 1913-1960

p. 34. Cf. Frohock, *Yale French Studies*, II.2. pp. 91-99.

Brée, op. cit. p. 114. Since Miss Brée knew Camus well and certainly discussed her book with him, he may perhaps also have endorsed this interpretation. A problem here arises, however, which results from Camus's own very agreeable nature. He was reluctant to displease any of his academic critics, with the result that he often seems to have endorsed different and contradictory interpretations of his work. For example, he said that he agreed with Robert de Luppé's study of *L'Etranger* which saw Meursault as a rather dim and unsatisfactory character, but also agreed with Robert Champigny's view of him as an exemplary pagan hero.

p. 35. The schools' edition was published in England by *Methuen and Co. Ltd.*, in 1958, edited by Germaine Brée and Carlos Lynes.

Cf. Luppé, op. cit. p. 67, and Wyndham Lewis's *The Writer and the Absolute, Methuen* (1952), p. 87: 'A moron is not the same as a dumb ox, but they are of the same family.'

Interview—cf. Brisville, op. cit. p. 258. Camus's other two favourite characters from his own work are Maria (from *Le Malentendu*) and Dora (from *Les Justes*).

p. 36. Sundays—cf. N. p. 56.

Et. p. 148.

Cf. Préface to *Poésies Posthumes*, of René Leynaud, *Gallimard* (1947).

p. 37. EE. p. 100. MS. p. 96.

p. 38. Et. p. 64 and pp. 169-170.

p. 39. MS. p. 30. N. pp. 80-81.

Cf. Champigny's *Sur un héros paien*, Gallimard, Les Essais 1959. This is an excellent study of *L'Etranger* and cannot be too highly recommended. I should like to thank Monsieur Champigny for explaining his point of view on the problem of Meursault's consciousness in more detail in a personal letter.

p. 40. Preface to schools' edition p. 2.

p. 41. Et. p. 99.

p. 42. Et. p. 147.

p. 45. HR. p. 322.

p. 46. Et. p. 32 and p. 171. MS. p. 167. ' "Je juge que tout est bien", dit Oedipe, et cette parle est sacrée. Elle enseigne que tout n'est pas, n'a pas été épuisé. . . . Elle fait du destin une affaire d'homme, qui doit être réglée entre les hommes.'

p. 47. Cf. Brée, op. cit. pp. 64-67. It is rather disappointing that Miss Brée did not, in view of her enthusiasm for Camus as an artist, include a consideration of this question in her book.

p. 48. Cf. AII. p. 64. Interview in *La Gazette des Lettres* (1952).

CHAPTER FOUR

p. 49. Et. p. 160. MS. p. 30 and p. 87.

p. 50. Camus declared that MS was directed against 'les penseurs existentialistes' in an interview in *Les Nouvelles Littéraires* on 15.11.45. Although he did not formally make the distinction, he was rejecting both what he considered to be the moral nihilism of Sartre's atheistic existentialism and the intellectually unjustified 'leap into faith' which, in his view, is the main characteristic of Christian existentialism.
MS. p. 27.

p. 51. MS. p. 37.

p. 52. MS. p. 55 and p. 76.

p. 53. MS. p. 158.

p. 54. MS. pp. 165–166, p. 168.

p. 55. Claude Mauriac made this remark in the course of his rather unfavourable review of HR in *La Table Ronde* (December 1951), pp. 98–109.
Roger Stéphane in *La France Libre*, January 1947, p. 243.
Daniel-Rops—*La Nef*, June–July 1951, p. 200.
Claude-Edmonde Magny—*France Libre*, 15.2.45, p. 107.
Professor Ayer—*Horizon*, March 1946, pp. 165–168.

p. 56. Cruickshank, op. cit. p. 72.

p. 57. Hanna, op. cit. p. 19. In a private letter, Professor Hanna has expanded the meaning of this sentence, pointing out that MS could be a great use in warning Christian apologists to be very wary of using the methods of Existentialism in formulating any defence of Christian belief. Cf. above, notes to p. 21, and especially Professor Hanna's article.

p. 58. Pascal—cf. *Poésie* 44, *Sur une Philosophie de l'Expression*, pp. 15–23, especially p. 19.
MS. p. 184. Cf. Ronald Gray's *Kafka's Castle*, C.U.P. (1956), passim, but especially p. 40.

p. 59. MS. p. 120.
Cf. Maurice Cranston, *The London Magazine*, April 1958, p. 63.

p. 60. Montherlant—cf. *Carrefour* 20.12.49.
Angus Wilson—cf. *NNRF* Special Number, p. 547.
Cf. *L'Enigme*, an essay written in 1950. *Eté* 1954, p. 133.

CHAPTER FIVE

p. 63. Et. p. 114.

Cf. later, in notes to p. 66 for details of these remarks about *Le Malentendu*.

M. p. 29. All quotations are from the 1958 edition.

p. 64. M. p. 94.

p. 65. M. p. 95.

A very convenient way of studying the critical reception of plays in France is provided by the *Fonds Rondel* at the Bibliothèque de l'Arsenal. Students of Camus's work are particularly well served, since there is a special dossier of articles on Camus.

p. 66. In *Panorama*, on 25.5.44, Camus warned spectators against interpreting his play in too pessimistic a light, and repeated the same ideas in more detail in *Le Figaro Littéraire*, 15.10.44. The essence of his remarks on both *Le Malentendu* and *Caligula* is repeated in the preface to the collected edition of his plays in the American translation published by *Knopf* (Borzoi books) in 1958.

p. 67. Date of composition of *Caligula*. There is a very good article on this subject by Germaine Brée in *Symposium*, Vol. XII, Spring–Fall, 1958, pp. 43–51. Miss Brée traces the first idea of a play about Caligula from Camus's notebooks for the years immediately following 1935, through the first, unpublished 1938 version, to the different editions of 1945 and 1958. She quotes a letter from Camus to Jean Paulhan which shows that Camus never intended *Caligula* to have any immediate political significance (cf. later, note to p. 75), and shows how Camus tightened up the 1938 version both as far as the dramatic construction and the dialogue are concerned. She does not, however, give any indication as to whether or not the scenes with Cherea were added between 1938 and 1945. In her analysis of the difference between the 1945 and 1958 versions, she insists upon the greater importance given to Helicon and on the insertion into the text of 'dubiously jocular remarks and aphorisms' and also of remarks which reflect 'a rather facile and direct attack against certain aspects of the contemporary scene which he dislikes'. It seems indeed at times as if Camus did allow the 'Clamence' aspect of his personality to run away with him when he was writing the 1958 version of *Caligula*. (Cf. later, Chapter 10, pp. 177–179.)

p. 68. Interview given on the French radio 8.2.58.

p. 69. C. 1958 edition, pp. 111 and 112.

Cf. Anthony Curtis, *New Developments in the French Theatre*, London, *The Curtain Press* (1948), p. 31.

p. 70. C. pp. 203 and 216.

p. 71. C. p. 188.
Jules Roy in radio interview 5.12.57. See above, notes to p. 67.

p. 72. C. pp. 176 and 125.

p. 73. C. p. 120.
Camus's remark about wanting to draw Caligula as objectively as he said Molière drew Alceste was made in a radio interview on 12.2.58.

p. 74. This programme note can be consulted in the *Fonds Rondel*.

p. 75. Foreshadowing accidental—cf. *France-Libre* 22.9.45, in which Camus said: 'Je tiens à signaler que mon dessein n'a pas été de faire un drame politique.' See also notes to p. 67 above, for indication that Camus's aim in this play was to show the moral and personal but not the political results of an 'absurdist' philosophy of life.

p. 76. Sartre in *Les Temps Modernes*, August 1952, p. 345.

p. 77. This letter to Francis Ponge was written in 1943 and published in the special number which the *NNRF* devoted to Ponge in 1956, pp. 386–392. Camus also remarked in this letter: 'Je veux me ménager la possibilité d'être tout à fait personnel, c'est-à-dire de penser en marge de ce nihilisme moderne dont *Le Mythe* est très exactement un essai de définition passionnée.'

CHAPTER SIX

p. 79. Cf. Quilliot, op. cit. p. 14.
Extract from *La Peste* in *Domaine Français*, Geneva (1943), pp. 37–47. The relatively few changes that Camus had to make when this passage was incorporated into the standard edition of the novel, pp. 81–91, is an indication of how well he had worked out the allegorical aspect of his work.

p. 80. Cf. *Le Figaro Littéraire* 26.10.57.
L. p. 19.

p. 81. L. p. 42 and p. 78.

p. 82. L. p. 26.

p. 83. Sections of Camus's notebooks have been published in *Symposium*, Spring–Fall 1958, pp. 1–7. They deal particularly with the different ideas which he had when writing *La Peste*.

p. 84. Cf. MS. p. 77.

p. 86. *La Remarque sur la Révolte* was published in the collection *Existence*, edited in 1945 by Jean Grenier, published by *Gallimard*. All page references are to this edition.

p. 87. RR. pp. 13, 22, 18–19.

p. 87. RR. p. 17. *Combat* 23.11.44.

p. 88. RR. p. 14 and HR. p. 34. RR. pp. 15–16.

p. 89. A number of the articles replying to Mauriac are reprinted in *Actuelles I*. Camus later admitted (1948) that Mauriac had been right and he himself wrong, AI. p. 213.

Other articles published in *Combat* but not reprinted in *Actuelles* include:

21.8.44. *De la Résistance à la Révolution.* 'La France sera désormais ce que sera sa classe ouvrière.'

22.8.44. *Le Temps de la Justice.* (Punish Vichy politicians responsible for the sufferings of France and the death of children.)

4.9.44. *Morale et Politique.* 'Nous sommes décidés à supprimer la politique pour la remplacer par la morale. C'est ce que nous appelons une révolution.'

6.9.44. *La Fin d'un monde.* (i.e. of the rule of the bourgeoisie, whose support for the Vichy government was an attempt at revenge for the Popular Front).

11.9.44. *Ce que nous attendons du gouvernement.* 'Le pays n'a pas besoin de Talleyrand ou de Bergery. Il a besoin de Saint-Just.'

12.9.44. *Sur le discours du Général de Gaulle.* 'Là, nous retrouvons le destin de la France, celui qui a conféré à la Révolution de 1789 sa puissante expansion, celui que mettait en évidence Saint-Just quand il déclarait à la tribune de la Convention: "Le bonheur est une idée neuve en Europe".'

23.9.44. On England—'Ce peuple supérieur a oublié de se plaindre.'

26.9.44, 27.9.44, 28.9.44.—approving the arrest of Louis Renault.

13.10.44. On North Africa—'Il serait stupide, en effet, de laisser ignorer au pays que la plus grande partie de cette population (i.e. French settlers in North Africa) était acquise à la politique de Vichy.'

8.11.44. *Sur l'Assemblée consultative.* Quotes Saint-Just: 'Tout le monde veut bien de la République. Personne ne veut de le pauvreté ou de la vertu.'

10.11.44. *Sur le parti socialiste.* 'Les socialistes ont un peu confondu la réalisation de leurs doctrines et l'obtention d'une majorité à l'Assemblée.'

16.11.44. On Renault again.

10.11.44 and 11.11.44. Attack on British policy in Greece.

3.4.45. 'Nous n'avons pas la nostalgie des révolutions, mais nous savons que nous avons vécu le plus pur dans les journées d'août 1944, et qu'il est désormais un désintéressement que nous ne connaîtrons plus.'

p. 91. *Ni Victimes ni Bourreaux* were published between the 19th and the 30th November, 1946 in *Combat*. It is rather curious that Camus should give their date in *Actuelles I* as 1948.

p. 92. Cf. *France-Observateur* 7.1.60. *Camus ou les mains propres.*
Cf. *Symposium*, Spring–Fall 1958. *Pages de Carnets*, pp. 1–6.

CHAPTER SEVEN

p. 94. RR. p. 18.

p. 96. Grand the true hero. Cf. P. p. 156.

p. 97. P. p. 241. RR. p. 19 and p. 17 (footnote).

p. 98. P. p. 248.

p. 99. Confirmed the values which inspired *La Peste*—cf. *Combat* 8.10.44. 'Par une révolte du coeur, elle (la Résistance) a consolidé quelques vérités de l'intelligence.'

p. 100. P. p. 82. AI. p. 92 (*Combat* 22.12.44). P. p. 336.

p. 101. P. p. 336. Cf. Brée, op. cit. p. 115. TLS. 2.8.47, p. 389.
Letter to Roland Barthes, *Club*, January 1955, pp. 7–9.

p. 102. Pouillon in *Les Temps Modernes* no. 26, pp. 911–920, and Etiemble, idem, pp. 911–920.
Bertrand d'Astorg. *Esprit*, November 1947, pp. 615–621.

p. 103. Cf. Cruickshank, op. cit. p. 176.
Letter to Roland Barthes—cf. above.

p. 104. Tarrou's confession goes from p. 269 to p. 278.

p. 105. Interview with Claudine Chonez—cf. *Paru* no. 47, 1948, pp. 7–13.
Hegelian theory of history—cf. *Terre des Hommes* 26.1.46.

p. 106. P. p. 150.

p. 107. P. p. 330 and p. 278.
Roger Stéphane—cf. *Revue Internationale* no. 16, 1947, pp. 464–468.
Radio interview on 13.9.55 with Jean Magin.

p. 108. P. pp. 18, 82, 192.

p. 109. P. p. 200.

p. 110. P. p. 90.

p. 111. P. pp. 43, 129, 131, 161, 187, 188, 323.

p. 112. P. p. 88. N. p. 32. Et. p. 88 and p. 169. P. pp. 52, 114, 118–119, 187, 209.

p. 113. P. p. 236 and p. 315.

p. 114. The *Discours de la Peste à ses administrés* was published together with the *Exhortation aux Médecins de la Peste* in the *Cahiers de la Pléiade, Gallimard* (1947).
Cf. letter to Roland Barthes, quoted above.

p. 115. Cf. Claude Bourdet, loc cit.

CHAPTER EIGHT

p. 117. ES. pp. 92, 189.

p. 118. ES. pp. 178, 211.

p. 119. ES. p. 220. P. p. 266.

p. 120. ES. p. 233.

p. 121. Simiot—cf. *Hommes et Mondes*, December 1948, pp. 712–716.

p. 122. Cf. AI. pp. 239–250.

p. 123. Cf. Gabriel Marcel. *Nouvelles Littéraires*, 22.12.49.
Article in *La Table Ronde* no. 1, 1948, reproduced in HR. pp. 206–216.

p. 124. Cf. Savinkov. *Souvenirs d'un terroriste*, tr. Bernard Taft, *Payot* (1931).
J. p. 77 and p. 74.

p. 125. J. p. 161—cf. Savinkov, p. 152. J. p. 169 and p. 149.

p. 126. J. p. 149.
Rolland, in *Action* 28.12.49.

p. 127. *Le Malentendu* and tragedy—cf. *Panorama* 25.5.44 and Camus's preface to American edition of collected plays, *Knopf* (1958), p. vii: 'The language shocked too. I knew this. But if I had dressed my characters in peplums, everyone might have applauded. Putting the language of tragedy into the mouths of contemporary characters was, however, my intention.'

p. 128. Cruickshank, op. cit. p. 220.

p. 129. Claude Roy—cf. *France-Observateur* 7.1.60.

CHAPTER NINE

p. 131. The figures for the number of copies of HR sold were given to me by Camus himself, who rather modestly added that he found the popularity of his book difficult to understand.
Claude Bourdet. *L'Observateur* 13.12.51.
André Rousseaux. *Le Figaro Littéraire* 17.11.51.

p. 132. Frank—*The New Republic* 18.1.54.
Rolo—*The Atlantic*. March 1954, pp. 85–86.
Toynbee—*The Observer* 1.11.53.

p. 134. HR. p. 122. RR. p. 18.

p. 136. HR. p. 301 and p. 45.

p. 137. HR. p. 53.

p. 138. HR. p. 378.

p. 139. HR. p. 233. Attempt to understand my time cf. HR. p. 14.
Richard Wollheim—cf. Cambridge Journal, October 1953. *The Political Philosophy of Existentialism*, pp. 3–19.

p. 140. *New Statesman* 16.1.54.
HR. pp. 208, 215–216, 269, 307.

p. 141. HR. pp. 288, 376, 371.
Cf. *Caliban*, November 1946, and AII. p. 166.

p. 142. Cf. *Arts* 19.10.51.
Cf. Brée, op. cit. p. 192. HR. p. 138.

p. 143. HR. p. 232.
Analysis in HR not new: It must, of course, be said in Camus's favour that he made little attempt to hide his debt to other thinkers, and especially to Jean Grenier. The book was dedicated to Grenier, and Camus stated in an interview in the *Nouvelles Littéraires* on 10.5.51 that 'Grenier fut mon maître et il l'est resté'. His principal debt to him in *L'Homme révolté* lies in the importance given to the influence of the Hegelian dialectic on the development of Communism, and on the remedy which Camus recommends of a return to the tradition of

moderation represented by Greek thought. In *Le Choix* (*Gallimard* 1941), Grenier speaks on p. 34 of the Hegelian dialectic as 'Hybris qu'ont connue et condamnée les Grecs' and himself condemns 'cette monstrueuse dialectique qui sépare les hommes qu'elle prétend unir'. In an earlier work, *Essai sur l'esprit d'orthodoxie* (*Gallimard* 1938), Grenier announces one of the main themes of Camus's criticism of Marx in HR pp. 240–260 when he writes, commenting on a Marxist text about the dialectic in biology, 'Nous sommes ici en plein messianisme, un messianisme qui justifie à l'avance tous les massacres, car qu'est-ce que la vie de quelques milliers ou quelques millions d'hommes à côté d'un paradis terrestre dont on est sûr ?' (p. 35).

This is not to say that Camus's criticism of Marxism, and especially his enumeration in HR. pp. 262–263 of the various facts which nowadays show how inaccurate the Marxist prediction of the future was, does not show a personal reading of Marx. The point is that his criticism of Marx for the 'messianistic' aspect of his thought is not original and is not therefore sufficient to compensate for his neglect of the actual circumstances in which revolutionaries have taken and retained power. His insistence on the importance of the nihilist tradition in forming the spirit of twentieth-century Communism also seems to be literary as well as personal in inspiration.

The main argument in favour of looking at HR as a highly idiosyncratic and therefore highly valuable personal evaluation of Communism is this: Camus, having lived through nihilism and its temptations himself, is warning others of dangers which he has himself experienced. This would be a good argument were it not that the linking up of nihilism and Communism is already the main theme of one of the books that he himself mentions in a footnote on p. 194. Wladimir Weidlé's *La Russie absente et présente* (*Gallimard* 1949) puts forward the theory that the revolution of 1917 interrupted a great cultural renaissance—the 'silver age' of Russia—and that Russian industrial progress in the twentieth century could have been more easily and effectively accomplished with no revolution at all. He also stated, in terms which anticipate Camus's argument on the relationship between Communism and nihilism, that 'La révolution fut faite par des hommes qui se croyaient marxistes, mais qui étaient les héritiers directs du nihilisme révolutionnaire de 1860' (p. 132). Elsewhere, Weidlé writes that 'ce qui importe, c'est le positivisme niais, l'utilitarisme barbare que les communistes russes ont hérité de leurs ancêtres, les nihilistes, qu'ils ont imposé à leur monde, et qu'ils essaient d'imposer au nôtre' (p. 197). Such close parallels give some force to Sartre's remark on p. 344 of the August 1952 number of *Les Temps Modernes* that Camus had read neither Hegel nor *L'Etre et le Néant* and that he had a 'mania' for not using first-hand sources. This was also brought out by Gaston Leval, the editor of *Le Libertaire, Organe de la fédération anarchiste* when he pointed out in a series of articles, published on 4.1.52, 7.3.52, 4.4.52, 11.4.52 and 18.4.52, that Camus had not actually read any original texts by Bakounine, and had made a number of apparently elementary mistakes in what he said about him. Although it is perhaps unwise to take everything Monsieur Leval says quite seriously—he stated at one point that the fifty pages of Bakounine's *Revolutionary Catechism* contained the sum total of human wisdom—the evidence of Camus's frequent use of secondary sources must be taken into account when the argument is put forward that HR 'has the unity and value of a personal experience' (TLS 27.12.57, p. 783). It would undoubtedly have been a better book had this been so, but it contains too many second-hand and sometimes inaccurate statements.

Camus's debt to the general climate of right-wing thought in France is even more marked when HR is compared to Father Delubac's *Le Drame de l'Humanisme Athée, Spès* (1944). The general argument of Father Delubac's book is that 'construire un humanisme contre Dieu, c'est le construire contre l'homme', and he studies very much the same people as Camus—Nietzsche, Feuerbach, Marx, Comte, Chigalev—to arrive at very much the same conclusions. Both books speak of a 'tentative de divinisation de l'homme' (HR. p. 232 and Delubac p. 8), and both thinkers emphasise nihilism and consider that Dostoievski provided, in *Crime and Punishment* and *The Possessed*, the key to an understanding of last half century of Russian history. Both quote the remark by Chigalev, 'Parti de la liberté illimitée, j'arrive au despotisme illimité' (HR. p. 218, Delubac p. 66), and both argue that Comtian positivism leads to spiritual despotism (HR. p. 243 and Delubac pp. 256–257). Camus may not actually have read Delubac, but the coincidences are remarkable. What both they and a number of other ideas in HR show is that even if Camus did originally set out to write a 'personal' confession (cf. his remark to Gaston Berger AII p. 63), he did not finally write a very original book.

p. 145. HR. p. 377.

p. 146. Cruickshank, op. cit. p. 116.

p. 147. Hervé's article appeared in *La Nouvelle Critique* in April 1952, pp. 66–76. Camus's letter was published in *L'Observateur* on 5.6.52. It is reprinted in *Actuelles II*.

The correspondence between Sartre, Camus and Jeanson appeared in *Les Temps Modernes* in August 1952. Camus's letter is reprinted in AII.

p. 146. *Temps Modernes*, loc. cit. pp. 333, 335. HR. pp. 231 and 378.

p. 149. Cf. AII, for Camus's letter asking for the release of Henri Martin, first published in *Franc-Tireur*, December 1952. He recognises that the condemnation of Henri Martin is purely political (AII. p. 129), but refuses at the same time to have anything to do with the campaign organised in his favour by *Les Temps Modernes*, since to do so would 'compromise the cause of liberty'. He condemned the Indo-Chinese war in general terms (p. 128) saying that it was both expensive and unjust, but, unlike Sartre, was not prepared to pursue a specific policy that might have ended it more quickly.

It is notoriously difficult to prove sins of omission, and Germaine Brée (op. cit. p. 51) says that Camus did write about Korea. She does not, however, give any date or reference for any article published by Camus on this subject. To judge by a remark that Camus made on the radio on 21.1.58 about 'l'exemplaire Israel' and the attempts to destroy it in the name of anti-colonialism, he may even have supported the attack against Egypt in 1956.

p. 150. *Les Temps Modernes*, loc. cit. p. 327. When Camus read through the typescript of the first version of this study in August 1956, he noted by the side of this quotation about the influence of the *Phenomenology of the Mind* on Communism, 'Oui, cela est, et cela continue d'être, la question'.

Temps Modernes, loc. cit. pp. 352 and 362.

p. 151. Ibid. p. 378.

Leon Roth, in *Philosophy*, October 1955, pp. 291–303, writes that HR is 'a sustained and reasoned apology for liberalism'.

p. 152. Cf. AII. p. 55. RR. p. 23. MS. p. 130.

p. 153. MS. p. 134. HR. pp. 316 and 330.

p. 154. Cf. Viggiani, *Modern Language Notes*, November 1960, pp. 589–596.

Professor Viggiani also insists upon Camus's 'anti-rational approach', and quotes him as saying that 'L'Art ne souffre pas la Raison'. He also shows how Camus looked upon philosophy in the early nineteen-thirties when he quotes him as saying of Bergson that 'Sa philosophie me paraissait la plus belle de toutes, car elle était une des rares, avec celle de Nietzsche, qui refusa tout à la raison'. It is clear from this article that any assertions made about Camus's early ideas at this stage are very likely to need considerable revision when more material comes to light in a few years time. The article *L'Intelligence et L'Echafaud* was first published in *Confluences* in July 1943 and reprinted in 1945. HR. p. 324.

p. 155. HR. a confessional work—cf. AII. p. 63.
Armand Hoog—cf. *Carrefour* 21.2.46.

Claude-Edmonde Magny. *Poésie* 46, no. 31, pp. 62–78.

On Sade and Saint-Just—cf. my own articles in *The Twentieth Century*, July 1957, pp. 41–53, and *History Today*, June 1958, pp. 404–412, respectively. The quotation by Maurice Nadeau is from his introduction to a collection of selected texts by Sade. *Editions du Seuil* (1947).

p. 156. Gaucheron—cf. his introduction to an edition of *Le Gouvernement Révolutionnaire jusqu'à la paix. Editions Raison d'être* (1946).

HR. pp. 323, 330 and 334.

p. 157. HR. pp. 115 and 119.

p. 158. This controversy took place in *Arts* on 19.10.51, 16.11.51, and 23.11.51. Camus's letters are reprinted in *Actuelles II*.

Cf. AII. p. 83.

p. 159. Cf. *Arts* 23.11.51. and Bataille, *Critique*, December 1951, p. 1019.

p. 160. Cf. Brisville, p. 258.

p. 161. N. p. 13.

Decision to write HR taken alone—cf. *Demain* 24.10.57.

CHAPTER TEN

p. 163. *Le Monde* 16.6.53.

p. 164. Interview in *Le Monde* 31.8.56.

p. 165. The preface to the translation of *The Ballad of Reading Gaol* was translated in *Encounter* in 1953.

p. 166. Humour the most neglected quality—cf. Brisville p. 259.

p. 168. *Eté*, pp. 29, 19, 21, 34–35.

p. 167. *Eté*, pp. 127–128.

p. 170. *Eté*, pp. 71–72.

p. 171. *Eté*, pp. 155 and 160.

p. 172. Cf. Donnat O'Donnell. Talk on the BBC Third Programme 6.12.56.

Objective writer—cf. *Eté*, p. 132.

Chute, pp. 23 and 24.

p. 173. Idem, pp. 66–67, 162.

p. 174. Idem, p. 153.

Gazette de Lausanne 28.3.54.

p. 175. Kanters—cf. *L'Express* 1.6.56.
Le Monde 31.8.56.

p. 176. Sartre—in *France-Observateur* 7.1.60.
Chute, pp. 102–103. Camus a good dancer—cf. *Le Figaro Littéraire* 26.10.57. Article by Brisville.

p. 177. *Eté*, p. 160. *Chute*, p. 35.
Chute, p. 60. *Eté*, p. 167.
Chute, pp. 45–55, 121.

p. 178. *Chute*, p. 116. AIII, p. 24.
Chute, p. 11. *Preface to Ballad of Reading Gaol, Falaize* (1952), p. 22.
Cf. *La Révolution Prolétarienne*, November 1957, *Hommage à un journaliste exilé.*

p. 179. AII. 23.
Discours de Suède, p. 58.
Preface—*Bibliothèque de la Pléiade*, p. xxix.
Radio interview 21.1.58.
Hanna, op. cit., p. 165.

p. 180. Preface to René Char—cf. Radio interview 6.3.49. This preface has not yet to my knowledge been published in French in book form. There is, however, a version of it, reprinted in *René Char's poetry. Editions de Luca* (1956). (Cf. Brée, op. cit. p. 255.)

p. 181. *Chute*, pp. 161–162.

p. 182. Idem, pp. 28, 57, 33.

p. 183. This remark is quoted by Boisdeffre, op. cit. p. 275.

p. 185. ER. p. 32. *Chute*, p. 166.

p. 186. ER. p. 39.

p. 187. ER. p. 48.

p. 188. Râ—doubt has been expressed (cf. *The Personalist*, USA, 1959, pp. 433–434) as to whether this does indicate the savages' idol or whether it is simply a device whereby Camus gives an additional rhythm to his prose. However, in his excellent *The Image in the Modern French Novel* (C.U.P. 1960) Professor Ullmann writes: 'The very name of the fetish, Râ, is symbolical: it was the name of the sun god in ancient Egypt' (p. 293).
N. p. 47. ER. p. 76.

p. 191. ER. p. 123.

p. 192. ER. p. 109.
ER. p. 146.

p. 194. Cf. *Simoun*, no. 8, March 1953. Oran, pp. 14–20.

p. 195. *Discours de Suède, Gallimard* (1958), p. 29. This remark, with 1954 in place of 1957, was originally made in an essay entitled *L'Artiste et son temps, Quaderni Aci*, Turin (1955), pp. 5–24. This essay does, in fact, contain many of the ideas of the Nobel Prize speech, and many longish passages are identical in both texts.
Idem. p. 55.

p. 196. ER. p. 202.

CHAPTER ELEVEN

p. 198. Rosmer—cf. AII. p. 150.
P. p. 278.
L'Express 14.5.55, 9.7.55 and 23.7.55. Camus did not reproduce all these articles in AIII. They are often more critical of French policy than some which are included in AIII, e.g. 9.7.55. 'La grande propriété algérienne n'a pas la mauvaise conscience de la bourgeoisie française. Elle sait, clairement et fortement, ce qu'elle ne veut pas, et ne reculera devant rien pour assurer sa victoire.'

p. 199. Other articles published in *L'Express* during this electoral campaign included:

8.11.55. *La Princesse et le couvreur*—contrasts the amount of space devoted by the French press to the possibility of a marriage between Princess Margaret and Group-Captain Townshend with the neglect of social question. Remarks of the English: 'Leur manière de ne pas se vanter ou de ne pas souffrir est tonitruante.'

29.11.55. *La Loi du Mépris*—protests against the racial intolerance shown towards Algerians by the French police.

6.12.55. *L'enfant grec*—against the execution of Michel Karaolis. Argues that Britain should leave Cyprus.

20.12.55. *La Vie d'artiste*—protests against the refusal of French nationality to the composer Tibor Harsanyi on the grounds that he 'exerce une profession socialement inutile'.
Nothing worse than totalitarianism—cf. AII. p. 56.
Comments on Mao-Tse-Tung—*L'Express* 11.11.55.

p. 200. *L'Express* 30.12.55.
AIII. pp. 165–166.

p. 201. AI. p. 264.
L'Express 8.10.55.
Discours de Suède, p. 14.

p. 202. The interview with *Demain* is translated in *Resistance, Rebellion and Death*, pp. 119–123.

p. 203. The interview in *Franc-Tireur* is also in *Resistance, Rebellion and Death*, pp. 113–118.

p. 204. *Monde Nouveau*, April 1956.
La Révolution Prolétarienne, November 1957. Reprinted in *Resistance, Rebellion and Death*, pp. 72–79.

p. 209. Cf. *L'Express* 12.7.57.
France-Observateur 24.10.57.
Arts devoted a whole section of its issue of 24.10.57 to insulting Camus. Jacques Laurent wrote: 'En décernant son prix à Camus, le Nobel couronne une oeuvre terminée.'

p. 210. AIII. p. 14.

p. 211. *L'Express* 17.1.56.
Cf. AIII. pp. 167–184 and *Le Monde* 23.1.56.

p. 212. AIII. p. 203.
La Nef, November 1957, p. 95.

p. 213. AIII. pp. 23–24.

p. 214. AIII. pp. 158–159.
Sartre, loc. cit. 7.1.60.

p. 215. Jules Roy, *La Guerre d'Algérie, Julliard* (1960), pp. 207 and 215.